ECOSYSTEMS AND TECHNOLOGY

Idea Generation and
Content Model Processing

Innovation Management and Computing

ECOSYSTEMS AND TECHNOLOGY

Idea Generation and
Content Model Processing

Edited by

Cyrus F. Nourani, PhD

Research Professor, Simon Fraser University,
British Columbia, Canada

Academic R&D at Berlin, Sankt Augustin-Bonn and
Munich, Germany

APPLE
ACADEMIC
PRESS

Apple Academic Press Inc.	Apple Academic Press Inc.
3333 Mistwell Crescent	9 Spinnaker Way
Oakville, ON L6L 0A2	Waretown, NJ 08758
Canada	USA

©2017 by Apple Academic Press, Inc.

First issued in paperback 2021

Exclusive worldwide distribution by CRC Press, a member of Taylor & Francis Group
No claim to original U.S. Government works

ISBN 13: 978-1-77-463681-7 (pbk)
ISBN 13: 978-1-77-188507-2 (hbk)

Library and Archives Canada Cataloguing in Publication

Ecosystems and technology : idea generation and content model processing / edited by Cyrus F. Nourani, PhD, Research Professor, Simon Fraser University, British Columbia, Canada, Academic R&D at Berlin, Sankt Augustin-Bonn and, Munich, Germany.

(Innovation management and computing)
Includes bibliographical references and index.
Issued in print and electronic formats.
ISBN 978-1-77188-507-2 (hardcover).--ISBN 978-1-77188-508-9 (PDF)

1. Technology--Social aspects. 2. Computer networks--Social aspects. 3. Technological innovations--Data processing. 4. Telematics. I. Nourani, Cyrus F., author, editor II. Series: Innovation management and computing

T14.5.E36 2016	303.48'3	C2016-907185-5	C2016-907186-3

Library of Congress Cataloging-in-Publication Data

Names: Nourani, Cyrus F., editor.
Title: Ecosystems and technology : idea generation and content model processing / editor, Cyrus F. Nourani, PhD.
Description: Toronto ; [Hackensack?] New Jersey : Apple Academic Press, 2017.
| Includes bibliographical references and index.
Identifiers: LCCN 2016049823 (print) | LCCN 2016051014 (ebook) | ISBN 9781771885072 (hardcover : alk. paper) | ISBN 9781315365664 (CRC Press/Taylor & Francis eBook) | ISBN 9781771885089 (AAP eBook)
Subjects: LCSH: Technology--Social aspects. | Computer networks--Social apects. | Technological innovations--Data processing. | Telematics.
Classification: LCC T14.5 .E36 2017 (print) | LCC T14.5 (ebook) | DDC 303.48/3--dc23
LC record available at https://lccn.loc.gov/2016049823

Apple Academic Press also publishes its books in a variety of electronic formats. Some content that appears in print may not be available in electronic format. For information about Apple Academic Press products, visit our website at **www.appleacademicpress.com** and the CRC Press website at **www.crcpress.com**

BOOK SERIES: INNOVATION MANAGEMENT AND COMPUTING

Innovation is the generation and application of new ideas and skills to produce new products, processes, and services that improve economic and social prosperity. This new book series aims to cover important issues in the burgeoning field of innovation management and computing, from an overview of the field to its current and future contributions. The volumes will be of value and interest to computer and cognitive scientists, economists, engineers, managers, mathematicians, programmers, and engineers.

Current books in the series:
- Ecosystems and Technology: Idea Generation and Content Model Processing

Tentative forthcoming volumes in the series:
- Computing Predictive Analytics, Business Intelligence, and Economics Models
- Haptic Computing Logic, Emotional Intelligence, Neurocognitive and Genetic Computing
- Innovations on Agent Cooperation and Coordination
- Newer Developments on Computability, Languages, Sets, and Model Theory
- Economic Game Models and Predictive Analytics
- Epistemic Computing, Model Checking, Spatial Computing and Ontology Languages
- Content Processing, Intelligent Multimedia Databases, and Web Interfaces
- Agent Software Engineering, Heterogeneous Computing, and Model Transformations

CONTENTS

LIST OF CONTRIBUTORS

Maria Carmela Annosi
Ericsson AB—Research, Färögatan 6, SE-164 80 Stockholm, Sweden; IPD, School of Industrial Engineering and Management—KTH Royal Institute of Technology, Brinellvägen 8, 114 28 Stockholm, Sweden

Federica Brunetta
Department of Business and Management—LUISS Guido Carli University, Viale Romania, 32, 00197 Roma, Italy

Selem Charfi
HD Technology, Europarc du Chêne, 8 rue Pascal-BP90, 69672 BRON Lyon, France, E-mail: Selem. Charfi@hdtechnology.fr

Jagdish Chaturvedi
Director Clinical Innovations, InnAccel, 5th Floor, Aanand Towers, Municipal No. 4, Rajaram Mohan Roy Road, Ward No. 77, Sampangiramanagar, Bangalore–560025, India

Patrik Eklund
Umeå University, Department of Computing Science, SE-90187 Umeå, Sweden

Michel Floyd
Founder of "cloak.ly," Board Member of VLAB, the MIT Enterprise Forum of the Bay Area, 767 Upland Rd, Redwood City, CA 94062, USA, Mobile: +1-650-814-3961

Christine G. Kapp
DataPsy, Inc., 1503 Ross Ave, Kissimmee, Florida 34744, USA, E-mail: ckapp@DataPsy.com

Mats Magnusson
IPD, School of Industrial Engineering and Management—KTH Royal Institute of Technology, Brinellvägen 8, 114 28 Stockholm, Sweden

Eunika Mercier-Laurent
University Jean Moulin Lyon 3, France, E-mail: eunika.mercier-laurent@univ-lyon3.fr

Cyrus F. Nourani
Research Professor, Simon Fraser University, British Columbia, Canada

Ramakrishna Pappu
Business Associate, InnAccel, 5th Floor, Aanand Towers, Municipal No. 4, Rajaram Mohan Roy Road, Ward No. 77, Sampangiramanagar, Bangalore–560025, India

Dace Ratniece
Distance Education Study Centre, Riga Technical University, Kronvalda Boulevard 1, Riga, LV 1010, Latvia; Faculty of Sciences and Engineering, Liepaja University, Liela Str.14, Liepaja, LV-3401, Latvia

LIST OF ABBREVIATIONS

AHA	active and healthy ageing
AI	artificial intelligence
AII	abstract intelligent implementation
AIIMS	All India Institute of Medical Sciences
AU	action units
BI	business intelligence
BIOME	Bio Innovations and Opportunities in Medicine and Engineering
CRDM	cardiac rhythm disease management
EBM	evidence-based medicine
EDB	Economic Development Board
ERP	Enterprise Resource Planning
FACS	Facial Action Coding System
IIC	Industrial Internet Consortium
IPMP	innovation process management process
ITESM	Monterrey Institute of Technology and Higher Education
IUSSTF	Indo-US Science and Technology Forum
JFMDA	Japan Federation of Medical Devices Associations
JMSUICE	JurInfoR-MSU Institute for Contemporary Education
KM	knowledge management
KPI	Key Performance Indicators
LBM	logic-based medicine
MVP	minimum viable product
NEET	not in employment, education or training
OISPG	Open Innovation Strategy and Policy Group
OM	organizational memory
PLM	product lifecycle management
RDF	Resource Description Framework
RMNCH	Reproductive, Maternal, Newborn, and Child Health
SDC	System Development Corporation
SIB	Stanford India Biodesign
SMS	Short Message Service
SSB	Singapore-Stanford Biodesign

ABOUT THE EDITOR

Cyrus F. Nourani, PhD
Research Professor, Simon Fraser University, British Columbia, Canada;
Academic R&D at Berlin, IMK Bonn and Munich, Germany

Dr. Cyrus F. Nourani has a national and international reputation in computer science, artificial intelligence, mathematics, virtual haptic computation, information technology, and management. He has many years of experience in the design and implementation of computing systems. Dr. Nourani's academic experience includes faculty positions at the University of Michigan-Ann Arbor, the University of Pennsylvania, the University of Southern California, UCLA, MIT, and the University of California, Santa Barbara. He was also a Research Professor at Simon Frasier University in Burnaby, British Columbia, Canada. He was a Visiting Professor at Edith Cowan University, Perth, Australia, and a Lecturer of Management Science and IT at the University of Auckland, New Zealand.

Dr. Nourani commenced his university degrees at MIT where he became interested in algebraic semantics. That was pursued with a category theorist at the University of California. Dr. Nourani's dissertation on computing models and categories proved to have intuitionist-forcing developments that were published from his postdoctoral times on at ASL. He has taught AI to the Los Angeles aerospace industry and has worked in many R&D and commercial ventures. He has written and coauthored several books. He has over 350 publications in mathematics and computer science and has written on additional topics, such as pure mathematics, AI, EC, and IT management science, decision trees, predictive economics game modeling. In 1987, he founded Ventures for computing R&D. He began independent consulting with clients such as System Development Corporation (SDC), the US Air Force Space Division, and GE Aerospace. Dr. Nourani has designed and developed AI robot planning and reasoning systems at Northrop Research and Technology Center, Palos Verdes, California. He also has comparable AI, software, and computing foundations and R&D experience at GTE Research Labs.

PREFACE

Innovation is the generation and application of new ideas and skills to produce new products, processes, and services that improve economic and social prosperity. This includes management and design policy decisions and encompasses innovation research, analysis, and best practice in enterprise, public, and private sector service organizations, government, regional societie,s and economies. This volume presents important new innovations in the area of management and computing, particularly venture planning for innovations and competitive business modeling.

Ecosystems and context-driven innovation modeling systems assist in the generation of better ideas faster; in measuring relevant data on ECO systems; in creating idea streams, innovation platforms, and virtual interfaces; in enhancing business intelligence and content processing; and in analyzing haptic expression and emotion recognition innovations, with applications to neurocognitive medical sciences.

This volume starts with a glimpse on technology selection for startups. Startups face tremendous challenges across many fronts, from fundraising to attracting talent to getting their first customers. In the early days of a technology startup, the focus is on creating a minimum viable product (MVP). Chapter 1 explores the early technology choices made by startups and how they can impact future success with real-world examples. Facing today's challenges and competition involves continuous innovation, which is considered as ecosystems generating impact. Balancing these ecosystems for sustainable success requires connecting and combining multidisciplinary knowledge, know-how, and intelligence. Focusing on an ecosystem model of innovation, a condition for balance, and the role of technology in making it effective are explored in chapter 2. Agile methods are explored in a following chapter. Intensified competition putspressure on organizations to outperform their competitors by addressing customer needs in a timely, cost-effective, and superior manner. Newer trends with decentralized structures, abandoning hierarchical organizational forms in favor of flattened hierarchies and a massive use of self-managing teams, are explored.

Agile software development paradigm is conceived of being about feedback and change. However, there is a lack of clear or detailed recommendations about how to successfully drive autonomous teams towards high innovation performances. Additional areas treated are Swedish Medical Apps Management.

Innovations in education systems are considered in chapter 4. Young people, who are the fundamental asset of our economies and societies across the world, face real and increasing difficulties in finding decent jobs more and more often. The aim of this study is to find the optimal ratio of e-learning and conventional learning for first-year students to increase motivation. Research methods on "Entrepreneurship (Distance Learning e-Course)" are reviewed. The students were tested by (i) a survey about the course on "Entrepreneurship (Distance Learning e-Course)" assessment; (ii) psychologist M. Lusher's color test, which is based on the method of projection individual's emotional state of the diagnosis; (iii) the degree of risk appetite according to Schubert's method of success; (iv) motivation after T. Elersamethods, failure avoidance motivation in correlation with T. Elersa method; and (v) a survey about optimal proportion between traditional and e-learning studies.

The healthcare domain area examples are presented in several chapters (chapters 5 and 8) that provide an overview of the various methods used today for identifying unmet needs and developing products. The healthcare domain is chosen as the medium for the description. The biodesign process as developed at Stanford University is described, along with multiple alternate adaptations of the process. Chapter 5 analyzes other processes examining the critical factors that lead to the success of these programs. It also analyzes through examples of medical devices and medical technology developments, where a lack of a structured process has led to 'failures,' the key learning from these case studies.

Building a successful innovation platform for affordable medical technology is important to address. This chapter 5 emphasizes the need for an innovation platform for successful accomplishments. It takes the example of healthcare innovations and explores the different facets that need to be brought together to create an innovation platform in the medical technology space and its use today to enable affordable medical technology in low-resource settings. The authors use various case studies of innovation platforms accessible to healthcare innovators and highlight the thought process behind developing such platforms (Stanford Biodesign, John's Hopkins' innovation platform, CAMtech'd innovation platform, InnAccel's acceleration program, government-run incubation programs, etc.). The chapter details a stage-wise process that begins with the identification of gaps in the ecosystem through feasibility studies to setting up a physical medical technology innovation platform. Further, the authors highlight the need for the incorporation of structured processes for needs identification and product development embedded within innovation platforms. An overview of how this is being used today in different settings is described.

In chapter 9, logic-based medicine versus evidence-based medicine for modeling qualified self-health kits is examined. In this chapter formal logic is applied to bridge the gap between information management in qualified self apps and information classification and structures residing within health and healthcare ontology. Mathematical innovative techniques are briefly described to enable a well-founded logical and ontology representation. Modeling uses these theoretical notions in order to extend the logical structure of classifications of health. The author focuses on active and healthy aging, including aspects of assessment and classification so that individuals and patients can manage their own data, in particular for self-monitoring purposes. There is the need to shift from society owning all individual health data to individuals themselves owning their data. Another aspect is that the quantified-self movement is still rooted mostly in wellness and even fitness, and as having various apps at their disposal.

Chapter 6 begins by describing the art of innovation as an analogy that shows the exponential level of complexity when scaling innovation management processes from personal innovation to visionary and led innovation, and finally to enterprise/ecosystem innovation. Soft factors to the innovation process are explained at each level, with the emphasis being on enterprise and level factors with suggestions for overcoming them. We have the perception that process models, idea generation platforms, and cognitive products are all necessary to improve an organizational innovation management process. However, many soft factors provide the real key to innovation success. There is an inhibitive factor when the role has been designed to be 95% reactive. This chapter describes some of the factors inherent in people and organizations that can inhibit innovation.

The new IoT areas are considered in a chapter that presents the impact of the IoT concept on the manufacturing systems and the challenges that R&D actors face in order to anticipate future evolution. The author first presents the general concepts related to IoT and M.E.S. Then the announced benefits from this exposition are presented. These benefits present new challenges.

The newer realistic challenges are previewed in chapter 10 on virtual mobile or cloud interfaces, business intelligence, and analytics content processing. Intelligent business interfaces are designed with intelligent multi-tiers and interfaces applying agents and intelligent business objects with applications to intelligent WWW. Basic content management with multi-tier designs for interfaces are presented. The field of automated learning and discovery has obvious financial and organizational memory applications. A computing model based on a novel competitive learning with database warehousing, model discovery, and customizing interface design is discussed. Intelligent visual computing paradigms are applied to define the multimedia computing paradigm and active databases. The intelligent multimedia paradigms can be applied to databases and query processing applications to stock trading. A view-model-controller design prototype for mobile business platforms with content processing specifics is presented. Web content is an important interface to preview.

The volume concludes with innovations on haptic and neurocognitive computing for visual facial expression emotion recognition. The chapter presents novel modeling techniques for facial and visual expression computation and recognition. Based on the functions on the haptic computing logic, we can state expression-spanning schemas—hereon called Eigen Schemas—that on tuples are morphed to characterize facial expressions. The Eigen schemas allow us to express or detect human emotions expressed on facials. The haptic logic encompasses a predictive Bayesian confidence on the characterizations.

CHAPTER 1

TECHNOLOGY SELECTION FOR SOFTWARE STARTUPS

MICHEL FLOYD

Founder of "cloak.ly," Board Member of VLAB, The MIT Enterprise Forum of the Bay Area, 767 Upland Rd, Redwood City, CA 94062, USA, Mobile: +1-650-814-3961

CONTENTS

ABSTRACT

Many, perhaps most, software startups start with just an "idea."
- It should be easier to get a ride to go where I need to go now;
- I want to sell my beanie babies online;
- It should be easier to find information.

If the inventor is a software engineer they might just start writing software-using tools that they already know. Some might think a little harder and learn a new tool that seems particularly well suited to the job. The founder of Instagram famously taught himself to code while creating the app. In every case, a decision will be made and a minimum viable product will be built using some set of tools. In this chapter we will lay out how this choice—made during a software startup's birth—can affect a startup's culture and eventual success.

1.1   TOOLS

When a carpenter shows up at a construction site he or she can be recognized instantly by the tools on their belt: the hammer, a tape measure, a pencil, some screwdrivers or a power drill, and a few others. That the carpenter has these tools doesn't guarantee they are skilled, it just means they are equipped and ready to work.

Meanwhile a software developer shows up at their office with nothing more than a laptop and a pair of headphones. While the laptop, like the hammer, is itself a tool, the developer's real tools are the invisible pieces of software inside, on servers, and in the cloud. The laptop is just a means to gain access to the real tools. In a way the laptop can be thought of as a tool belt in the carpenter metaphor.

The hammer is a tool, which is over 2.6 million years old. PCs have been around for about 40 years, laptops for around 30. The oldest software tool on that laptop might be the text editor or a C compiler, both just slightly older than the PC itself. The *tools of the trade* in software are incredibly young by comparison to most of the carpenter's tools. The very oldest software tools in current use are barely older than the developers using them. The very newest tools on the other hand, may only be years or even months old. Software tools are being invented and refined at an incredible rate, which brings us to our first observation.

Software tools and technology are changing all the time. Many of the ones you choose for your new company will soon be out of date.

Knowing this, it can be hard, especially for a nontechnical founder, to understand how software engineers can be so incredibly opinionated about the choice of tools used to build a system in a new company!

1.2   WHY TOOLS MATTER?

If the carpenter with his tool belt is asked to frame a two-story house he or she is probably going to be able to do it if they have any basic skills. A more skilled carpenter will do it faster, several skilled carpenters will do it faster, and if the team has worked together before and built many similar houses they will be faster yet. This I learned building tract homes for a summer.

On the other hand if you ask even a great team of carpenters to build a 12-story building they will fail. Buildings that tall need steel and concrete structures and a completely different set of workers (e.g., welders, concrete pourers) with different tools and materials.

Similarly in software, different kinds of applications need different developer skills and tools. Developing for smartphones can be pretty different than developing for web browsers which is very different than developing for embedded devices like the computerized engine controller in your car. The problem domain itself, for example, deep learning or e-commerce, or search, also influences much of the expertise required. Some top-tier developers can migrate from one such domain to another relatively quickly but many cannot. In any case, many of the tools they use can be quite different.

1.2.1   SKILLS MATTER MORE

When Mark Zuckerberg started building the Facebook he used what he knew: the LAMP stack. LAMP stands for "Linux, Apache, MySQL and PHP/Perl/Python." These acronyms formed the basis for most new web applications being developed in the early 2000s. Mr. Zuckerberg specifically chose PHP as the language with which to build his project. PHP is widely derided by computer science "purists" as a hack that has evolved over time. It's original author, Rasmus Lerdorf was quoted as saying "I don't know how to stop it, there was never any intent to write a programming language [...] I have absolutely no idea how to write a programming language, I just kept adding the next logical step on the way."

My favorite observation about PHP came from a Stanford professor who derided Facebook's early efforts with the comment "PHP won't scale." One and a half billion users later that comment sticks with me as being one of the most dramatically wrong assessments of a startup I've ever heard. Technically, he was correct. PHP is not the ideal choice for a massive website project, especially one involving thousands of engineers. Facebook compensated for their initial non-ideal tools by hiring the best developers on the planet and applying relentless effort to the problem. Along the way Facebook altered many of the basic premises of PHP, for example by creating a compiler for it. This leads us to our second observation:

"Great developers using mediocre tools will almost always outperform poor developers with great tools."

It is not the case however that *any tool will do,* even given the world's best talent. Non-technical managers who have a passing knowledge of software are prone to suggesting tools that are completely inappropriate to the job at hand. If such a leader said "Let's use PHP for our self-driving car project" their developers would view them with the kind of disdain that Dilbert normally reserves for his pointy haired manager.

1.2.2   MOST INTERESTING SOFTWARE SYSTEMS ARE BEING BUILT FOR THE FIRST TIME

A carpenter only frames a house for the first time once. Each additional house is a near repetition of their first. Even if the size and floor plan change the basic tools and techniques are very similar. Carpenters learn on the job fast and quickly reach a point where every new build seems fairly routine. With repetition comes predictability and usually increasing quality.

Some classes of software projects can seem very similar, for example e-commerce sites, corporate websites, or blogs. Developers who do many of these also build up their skills over time and become able to build them repeatedly and predictably.

However, many interesting software projects are being built for the very first time using new tools and a team that has never worked together before to address brand new requirements. The large number of unknowns can be overwhelming. Figuring out how to best approach the problem can take several rounds of trial and error. Furthermore as the first prototypes are created the problem to be addressed is also continuously being redefined. During this process it's important to get to "good enough" quickly. Is the *immediate* problem solvable with the team you have using the tools you already know or have just learned during experimentation? If so you want to get going.

Had Facebook's early team been required to consider scaling Facebook to 1.5 billion users they would have quickly concluded that would be impossible for their young team using *any* existing set of tools and then given up. Instead they got going, their success gave them the wherewithal to improve their team and tools and even invent many brand new tools along the way.

1.3   LEADING EDGE OR MERE SURVIVAL

In the selection of the toolset there will be a tension between *being on the bleeding edge* and *staying with the tried and true.* A fairly big part of the developer population wants to be on the bleeding edge in terms of tools. Why? Several important reasons:

- They get to learn more. Developers love to learn new things. This is just how their brains are wired. Learning is fun.
- It gives them a chance to be an expert in a new thing. If you want to become a world-renowned expert on UNIX or SQL, good luck. There are already many experts in such tools, people who've been working on them for 30 years, have written books on them, given many talks at well established conferences, gurus basically. When a new technology arises the people who start using it first get to become the first experts. They might get to write the first book, their talks are packed, people read their blogs, and companies start recruiting them because they have unique skills. Fundamentally, their *market value* increases.
- It makes them *indispensable.* This is a kind of employee lock-in. If your team are the world's only experts on a new technology that

you're betting your company on, they are almost impossible to replace. Throw them out and you're going to be stuck starting over.

How can you tell if you're picking a bleeding edge technology? Are there several books on the topic, or has the first book yet to be published? Look up the term on *Google trends* (https://www.google.com/trends) and see how recently it started gaining attention. Is it on its way up or stuck on a plateau? Another great place to look is *Stack Overflow* (https://stackoverflow.com/), the leading question-and-answer site for software developers. Once enough questions have been asked about a technology it will gain it's own *keyword*. For example if you search for *[meteor]* (https://meteor.com) (the square brackets denote a keyword.) then you can see that, today, over 19,000 questions have been raised about it. If you looked for *[mariadb]* (https://mariadb.com), you would only find 1,441 questions which makes it considerably newer and, perhaps in some people's minds, riskier. By way of comparison, a very mature technology such as *java* has over 1 million questions on Stack Overflow.

If you plan to scale and grow your development team quickly, dependence on a niche or bleeding edge technology can become a major constraint.

You will be hiring among a small pool of talent, your outsourcing/offshoring options will be limited, there will be fewer resources with which to train new talent (books, blogs, conferences). Your developers may be highly productive but you can easily find yourself boxed in with a mounting development backlog and no easy way to add resources.

Sometimes a technology can be mature yet have never gotten past the niche phase. Take *erlang* [5], for example. Originally invented in 1986, this language has fierce proponents but never became truly mainstream. For some types of applications it is the best possible solution but finding people that know it well may be difficult.

From a founder's point of view, if your engineers are *primarily* concerned with becoming experts on a new technology or in making themselves indispensable then they are the wrong people. Find someone who is interested in learning how to build a great company, being an expert in making your product great, and who is eager to (eventually) help bring on new talent. You can attract new talent with the lure of working with the latest and greatest tools but that can't be the only thing.

There is plenty of risk on the *nearly dead* end of the spectrum as well. Picking long-in-the-tooth technology will make it very hard to attract new talent and you'll find it correspondingly hard to scale. Interoperability with other systems will be difficult or even impossible. You won't be as *agile* as your competitors. If this sounds a bit like the temperature of the porridge needs to be *just right*, rest assured that it's really only the extremes that should concern you. There's a broad middle of up-and-coming to tried-and-true technology that is likely to be applicable to your problem.

1.4   TOOLS AND CULTURE

In much the same way that human language and culture are intertwined, the set of development tools (including programming *languages*) used within an organization and its culture are intertwined. Two areas where these differences manifest themselves most distinctively are in *open source* vs. *closed source* and in *on-premise* vs. *cloud* (or SaaS).

Closed source developers are comfortable paying large software companies for software that (nominally) *works*, is documented, is going to be supported for many years, interoperates well with other tools and applications from the same supplier or related suppliers, is kept up-to-date with changes to operational hardware, and for which expert consultants are readily available. The managers of these developers also like having a big company to *blame* for their problems. Closed-source developers tend to be more secretive about their work; they are less likely to contribute to open-source projects or reuse them. They can also be less likely to share information with others outside their own companies. Lack of visibility into the tools they are using begets lack of transparency into what they are themselves creating.

Open source developers, on the other hand, viscerally *hate* paying for software. Commercial, closed-source software is often seen as bloated, inefficient, dated, and ridiculously overpriced. Taking hard-won startup capital and forking it over to Microsoft, Oracle, or IBM is seen by such developers as profligate spending. Better to put that money into a ping-pong table or bigger monitors! Open source developers are by their very nature *integrators:* they pull together various open source components to build a complete system. They are also tinkerers. If a package doesn't work and there's no ready alternative, then they will go try to fix the problem themselves and even contribute the fix back to the community so that everyone else (even their competitors!) benefits. Starting or contributing to open source projects can help build a developer's reputation in what end up being global communities. Top open source developers are referred to by single names just like pop stars! Open source developers take quite a bit of pleasure in helping others, which may be a big factor in your own organization developing strong teamwork.

On the *on-premise* vs. *cloud* axis, developers who run their applications in their own data centers (on-premise) tend to be much more well versed in hardware and optimization. They strive to get maximum performance from their systems (hardware + software) and need total *control* in order to do so. They also love to tinker and try new hardware combinations (more memory, faster disks, using GPUs instead of CPUs). Cloud developers on the other hand, have gradually become almost disinterested in any hardware beyond their own laptop. *If the cloud is too slow, just spin-up more instances!* This saves time in terms of tinkering but can lead to a rude shock when you open your Amazon Cloud Services bill! It can also lead to poorly performing applications because the developers have lost their optimization and performance tuning skills.

Is your innovation highly performance-sensitive? For example, are you building a high-frequency trading application? If so, you're going to want some of those optimization-focused *on-premise* developers to get you there. Are you looking to grow your company globally and quickly? The cloud people are going to get you there faster and cheaper, with a lot less capital equipment!

KEYWORDS

- agile
- choices
- CTO
- innovation
- startups
- technology

REFERENCES

http://languagemagazine.com/?page_id=2103, Blurring the Lines Between Language and Culture.

https://mariadb.com, an open source relational database based on MySQL.

https://meteor.com, Meteor, as of this writing, is a fairly new JavaScript framework for developing web applications.

CHAPTER 2

INNOVATION ECOSYSTEMS AND TECHNOLOGY

EUNIKA MERCIER-LAURENT

University Jean Moulin Lyon 3, France,
E-mail: eunika.mercier-laurent@univ-lyon3.fr

CONTENTS

ABSTRACT

Today facing challenges and competition involves continuous innovation. It became an integrated part of organizational and business activities. Technology has a potential to empower the both interrelated steps of the innovation dynamics.

While many focus on research and development, innovation should be considered as ecosystems generating also 7D impacts to manage.

Balancing these ecosystems to ensure sustainable success requires connecting and combining multidisciplinary knowledge, know-how and intelligence.

After a short presentation of related work, this chapter focuses on ecosystem model of innovation, conditions for balance and the role of technology in making it effective and successful.

2.1   INTRODUCTION

Innovation has always been associated with research centers, R&D departments of large companies and start-up challenged to grow. The recent economic crisis in developed countries has increased the interest for innovation—politics hope that innovation will generate economic growth and create jobs. The word "innovation" is in the headlines of reports, articles and business media, and is also the subject of events, projects, think-tanks, clubs and blogs. Numerous forums on social networks are devoted to various forms of innovation. This is a global phenomenon. Now, it is no longer a confidential matter: we innovate in politics, organization, management, business models, in managing of intellectual capital and other intangibles, in training, services, gastronomy and even DIY and gardening.

Many, including European Union, consider mainly technological innovation issue from research, but it is changing—now open and social innovation are leveraged in aim to involve more people.

The innovation process nourishes by multidisciplinary knowledge and needs "soft sciences" such as management, marketing, intellectual capital to succeed. The organization and management of related knowledge influence the speed of innovation and its efficiency. Technology and in particular artificial intelligence approaches and techniques have a great role to play in accelerating the innovation dynamics, balancing related ecosystems and leading innovation to sustainable success.

After presenting some research work in concerned areas, this chapter focuses on the innovation context, ecoinnovation process and the role of technology in making it successful.

2.2   RELATED WORK

Innovation is a very large topic covering all domains of activity. Scientific publications on innovation are numerous and address mostly technological innovation, product design, medical equipments including surgery robots, augmented human, biotechnologies, nanotechnologies, chemistry and environmental concern such as intelligent building, energy and water consumption, but also organizational, social and economic innovation. Smart home, smart city and smarter planet, ambient intelligence, connected objects, biomimicry, entertainment and others are technology-based.

We can still notice confusion between research and development (R&D) and innovation. Most of persons in charge of R&D renamed recently their position to "Chief Innovation Officer." But what innovation really is?

2.2.1   SOME DEFINITIONS

The amplified interest for innovation and extension of its spectrum into multidisciplinary dimensions enriched traditional definitions "from idea to products and to market" (Dubuis, 2007). However, those of Schumpeter (1912), remain still among the most complete. In his theory of economic evolution Schumpeter specifies that "innovation meets five main criteria: the manufacture of a new good, introduction of a new production method or of new means of transportation, implementation of a new organization, opening a new market and the conquest of a new source of raw materials."

According to OECD references such as Oslo Manual and Frascati Manual "innovation is the implementation of a new or significantly improved product (good or service), or process, a new marketing method, or a new organizational method in business practices, workplace organization or external relations."

They consider innovation as a "complex, diversified activity with many interacting components. Successful innovation requires involvement of scientific, technological, organizational, financial and commercial actors" (Oslo Manual, 1996; Frascati Manual, 2002). This definition fits well to industrial era, but what is an appropriate definition for transition era we are living and for Knowledge Era?

There are as much as definitions as fields concerned by innovation. According to *The Webster's New World Dictionary* (Second College Edition, 1982),

Invention is the power of inventing or being invented; ingenuity or creativity; something originating in an experiment; and

Innovation is the act or process of innovating; something newly introduced, new method, custom, device, etc.; change in the way of doing things; renew, alter.

More definitions can be found in Entovation International (1998). All these definitions express the various points of view.

Finally, innovation can be seen as trajectory from idea to product, from idea to market or from idea to success (Amidon, 1997) and sustainable success (Mercier-Laurent, 2011).

Amidon's (1997) definition embodies a holistic vision of it influence on world welfare:

"Creation, evolution, exchange and application of new ideas into marketable goods and services for:
- the success of an enterprise;
- the vitality of a nation's economy;
- the advancement of society."

Overall image of innovation needs to be seen from different perspectives.

2.2.2 MULTIPLE FORMS OF INNOVATION

Technological innovation is the most popular and there is a plethora of publications on it, such as Technology and Innovation, Journal of the National Academy of Inventors, International Journal of Innovation Management, Journal of Innovation Economics and Management, European Journal of Innovation Management, Journal of Innovation Management, Journal of Innovation and Entrepreneurship, International Journal of Innovation Science and many others representing respective points of view. Many related papers are available on http://researchgate.net and on http://academia.edu.

The European Database Cordis (http://cordis.europa.eu/) is a real treasure and resource for innovation. It contains all publications on European Research Programs and results since its beginning by the Spirit 1 program in 1984.

As innovation is often associated with industry, design is an innovation field per se; many publications focus on product, technology related to design and product lifecycle management (PLM) (Stark, 2004). Industrial tools for design as, for example, CATIA provides 3D library of forms, knowledge about materials and product related constraints checking facilities. However, in many fields and in SMEs basic technology is only used to support innovation activities, if innovation is managed.

Newly, ecodesign ambitions in integrating environmental principles into design activities of all involved professionals. The Convergence project is among examples of such integration with strong focus on what is required by norms and environmental aspects (Ecodesign Your Future, 2012; Zhang et al., 2013).

Biomimicry, or nature inspired design is a step to conceive more respectful products if their ecosystems are considered. Nature is full of ingenious solutions, people have to observe and learn more from environment instead of destroying it (Mercier-Laurent, 2015).

Because technological innovation did not brought expected results in Europe in term of growth and job creation, the other forms of innovation are now encouraged and experimented such as ecoinnovation (Ecoinnovation, 2015) and social innovation (This is European Social Innovation, 2010).

Ecoinnovation focuses mainly on generating business from planet protection—intelligent management of energy and water, smart transportation, recycling and ecodesign. Any form of innovation leading to the improvement of environment protection is considered, such as new production processes, new products and services, new management methods, as well as all uses or implementations able to prevent and reduce environmental risks: pollution and other negative impacts due to the use of resources in the lifecycle of human activities. Priorities are transportation, recycling, use of sustainable building techniques and materials, cleaner production and packaging techniques for food and drinks and the recognition of environmental criteria for purchases, and adoption of a rational use of resources by companies.

The social innovation powered by technological platforms facilitates communication and "trade of ideas"; social networks connect people and play sometimes a role of brainstorming support. Many topics are addresses such as fixing Greek economy, solving migrants' problems, distributing goods, connecting people offering services with those who need them. The hidden objective of social innovation is to involve PhD from "soft sciences" to the innovation process.

Economists, influenced by environmental concern and those involved in Corporate Social Responsibility push "product-service" (Buclet, 2015) and circular economy. Product–service economy interest in generating revenue not from sales of products, but from sales of services that product can offer; for example, Michelin sales the function of bearing instead of tires.

The objective of circular economy is a continuous development cycle that preserves and enhances natural capital, optimizes resource yields, and minimizes system risks by managing finite stocks and renewable flows.

"All material are recycled indefinitely, all energy is derived from renewable, human activities support ecosystems and the rebuilding of natural capital, resources are used to generate values, human activities support human health and happiness, and healthy and cohesive society and culture (Webster, 2015)."

Circular economy prefers repairing instead of recycling. But the main problem with recycling is that spare parts and repairing cost today more than buying a new product.

Knowledge Economy—related to Knowledge Management—is about generation of values from knowledge, which is also embedded in products and services, for ex design and reparation requires knowledge and know-how (Amidon et al., 2005). For instance we are used to estimate the ROI in financial term, but accounting of intangible appears now in some reports (Pablos and Edvinsson, 2015). According to the World Bank (www.worldbank.org/kam), knowledge economies are defined by four pillars: institutional structures that provide incentives for entrepreneurship and the use of knowledge, skilled labor availability and good education systems, ICT infrastructure and access, and, a vibrant innovation landscape that includes academia, the private sector and civil society.

The emergence of innovation as a mean to impulse growth and job creation made it trendy but the performances are not measured and the right indicators are still missing. Only short-term economic impact is evaluated. Some institutions measure number of start-up created but not their "death rate," neither the reason of fail. Innovation is not really managed in most of companies and institutions.

Innovation in management methods and organizational innovation follow the trends, but Collaborative innovation involving selected users is at its beginning.

There are few publications on innovation metrics, mainly limited to statistics (Frascati Manual, 2002, 2015), only few publications are related to technology and intelligent technology (Mercier-Laurent, 2005, 2011; Mercier-Laurent and Pachet, 2013) supporting the overall innovation process. Recently European Union introduced evaluation of the innovative potential of selected funded research projects.

The innovation facets are shown in Figure 2.1.

European Union has invested in education and research. Many interesting prototypes with high potential of innovation were developed in the framework of successive programs Esprit 1, Esprit 2, 6th Framework Program, 7th Framework Program and recent Horizon 2020 (Horizon, 2020).

Open Innovation Strategy and Policy Group was created to promote open innovation integrating researchers, companies and territories (Curley and Salmelin, 2013). The research results should be now transformed into commercial products and services—"Succeed in getting research results to market" is among three challenges expressed by Carlos Moedas, Commissioner for Research, Science and Innovation last July (Moedas, 2015).

FIGURE 2.1   Innovation spectrum.

The Frascati Manual 2015 as well European Union distinguishes two activities: research and innovation. Implementation is considered as "innovation process" (Frascati Manual, 2015).

2.2.3   INNOVATION PROCESS

According to Frascati Manual (2015), "innovation activities also include the acquisition of existing knowledge, machinery, equipment and other capital goods, training, marketing, design and software development. These innovation activities may be carried out in-house or procured from third parties."

They consider that "design plays a key role in the development and implementation of innovations. Design can be described as a potential multifaceted innovation activity aimed at planning and designing procedures, technical specifications and other user and functional characteristics for new products and processes. Among these activities are initial preparations for the planning of new products or processes, and work on their design and implementation, including adjustments and further changes (Frascati Manual, 2015)."

Linear process model, technology push model or market push models are mainly considered (Khurana, 2013).

The environmental aspects of innovation enter to industrial design; the involved professionals have to respect the related norms (Zhang et al., 2013; AFNOR ISO 26000). It may be a very heavy task for SMEs.

Only few companies include customers into their innovation process.

2.2.4   THINKING

The ability of thinking and of problem solving is the most important to innovate quickly and effectively. According to Tony Buzan everybody can be creative (Buzan, *How to Improve Your Creative Thinking?*). Edward de Bono, the inventor of six hats method, claims that the worst tread of current generation is poor thinking (De Bono, 1999, 2000). Finding a simple solution requires imagination, capacity of thinking without barriers between fields and art of combination of multidisciplinary knowledge (Mercier-Laurent, 2011).

Artificial intelligence has been brought a significant contribution in term of thinking methods and reasoning models (Russel and Norvig, 2010). Over hundred reasoning models are available for adaptation and reuse (Open KADS, 1990).

An example of different thinking in designing computers is those of Apple. Lisa, the first Apple personal workstation, inspired probably by Star of Xerox, did not brought expected success on the market for several reasons: price, to early ("time to market") and new way of using computers—personal instead of server. On the advice of Regis McKenna, Apple designed McIntosh for publishers, offering intuitive interface.

TRIZ method and related tools improve a capacity of thinking without the borders between domains—when all possible solutions in a given area were already explored, this method offer solutions from the other areas that apply in a given case (Altshuller et al., 1997).

Finally the most important is the ability of mental flexibility.

2.2.5 KNOWLEDGE MANAGEMENT AND INNOVATION

The success of innovation depends on how the related internal and external knowledge is organized and managed. An optimized knowledge flow containing an idea generator amplifying human imagination, simulators, past experiences, knowledge models supporting design, constraints propagation engine will enhance all involved capacities (Mercier-Laurent, 2011; The Institute for Knowledge and Innovation).

Actually, Knowledge Management was introduced as management method in the 1990s (Drucker, 1992). In its beginning the focus was on organizing people knowledge to be more effective. Artificial Intelligence interest have emerged in the same period, from experiences of transferring knowledge into computers and organizing it to help human in his work (Mercier-Laurent and Boulanger, 2014).

One of the first that made a connection between knowledge and innovation was Amidon (Amidon, 1997). She introduced "Knowledge Innovation" and put emphasis on importance of involving clients and others stakeholders, that she calls "Extended Business Network," into the innovation process. Since, others have been added the word innovation to Knowledge Management (The Institute for Knowledge and Innovation).

Stakeholders are now considered in Corporate Social Responsibility approach (Corporate Social Responsibility, 2015).

While many agree that technology helps sharing knowledge, those who use the right technology are few. Among technology supporting usually separate Knowledge Management blocs the commonly used is Intranet, groupware software, and social networks (Moing, 2014).

Considering knowledge related to innovation involves architecturing of an appropriate Knowledge Flow including several techniques that apply in a given situation.

A Knowledge Flow can be defined as: "creation, collection, processing and sharing of information and knowledge in an organized and optimized way, taking into account the different activities of the extended enterprise as well as the needs, individual and collective motivations of all the participants" (Mercier-Laurent, 1997, 2011).

The success of innovation depends on how knowledge is organized and managed, on a comprehension of innovation dynamics and respecting balance conditions of innovation ecosystems.

2.3   MODEL OF INNOVATION ECOSYSTEMS

Many, including the European Union, consider that the innovation comes mainly from research—researchers invents things, create start-ups (or sell to Google). Only few start-ups are able to grow quickly and become a big company.

The US government strategy is to help developing start-ups by creating a bridge over "death valley" (Gray, 2011). This bridge is composed of four elements: funds, regulation, mentoring and taxes. Technology that may improve these actions is not mentioned.

The European Union allocates funds for research programs, but is up to each partner to transform the project results into marketable products and services.

The strategy of the European Union is expressed in the recent talk of Carlos Moedas: "we must focus on opening up our research and innovation systems and succeed in getting research results to market (Moedas, 2015)."

An innovation ecosystem is presented in Figure 2.2. Researchers invent things and create their start-up or push the results to large companies that need them or able to explore these results commercially.

But the other way is a little explored. Companies and organizations have to face today challenges and solve specific problems related to their activity. These topics are challenging for research, but often require connecting interdisciplinary knowledge and "out of the box" thinking.

Politics set strategy, rules and incentives for innovation. For example French government invested to contests, incubators, clusters and special programs allocating funds for research but the funds for making grow start-ups are confidential, difficult to got, and low (Contest of French Ministry of Research, 1999; Houel and Daunis, 2009; Report on Incubators France, 2009). The feedback from field will allow them adapting their policy to the real needs, but they are not open. It is the same for EU policy.

In France, technology transfer departments were created inside of universities to encourage students and especially PhD students to start their company. But entrepreneurship is not integrated into education programs.

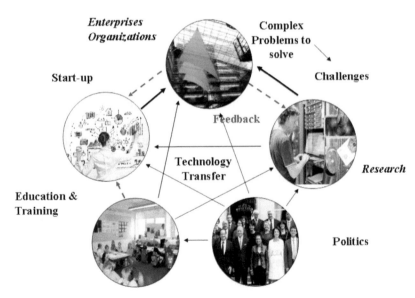

FIGURE 2.2   Innovation Ecosystems (Mercier-Laurent, 2011).

By consequence the start-ups do not have skills for successful management of a company. The educational programs are set by the Ministry of Education and it is impossible to suggest evolving them.

Each component interacts with the others. This ecosystem balance depends on the integration of feedback from experimentation, on the right use of technology and on mastering of all 6D impacts of the innovation activity. Environmental impact is one of them.

2.4   ECOINNOVATION PROCESS—CONDITIONS FOR BALANCE

After heavy industrialization, the awakening about planet condition is growing– we have to reduce our footprint—control energy and water consumption, CO_2 emissions, optimize and green transportation, design and others human activities, reduce garbage and recycle.

All this tasks need to be supported by right technology. The paradox with technology is that it is supposed to helps us, make our lives more comfortable, but it also generates waste (Mercier-Laurent, 2015). The overall balance depends also on how far we are able to change our attitudes form having more to knowing more and to share.

2.4.1   ECOINNOVATION

Main principles of ecoinnovation are shown in Figure 2.3. It takes roots in past and today knowledge and experience and creates new knowledge continuously. It is about never-ending collaborative process involving intelligences and technology, generating tangibles and intangible values and multiple impacts to manage. It requires and influences education systems.

2.4.2   ECOINNOVATION PROCESS

The innovation process has been evolved from closed to open, global and collaborative (Mercier-Laurent, 2015).

It is composed of two interlinked stages—creativity and transformation, shown in Figure 2.4.

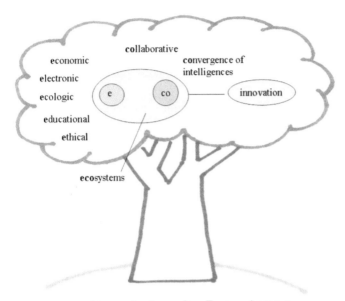

FIGURE 2.3   Ecoinnovation (Mercier-Laurent, 2011).

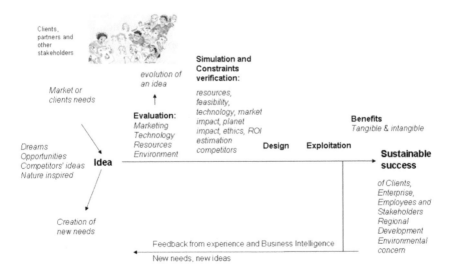

FIGURE 2.4   Ecoinnovation process (Mercier-Laurent, 2011).

The first aims in producing ideas that will be evaluated and the most valuables will be transformed into products or services.

An idea can be born from observation of individuals or group, from trends, detected opportunity (collaborative "business intelligence"). New ideas may also come from dreams.

An idea can address existing needs or create new needs, as for example Apple did with smartphone, connected pocket computer and camera. Opening to the world, imagination and cognitive flexibility is required here.

Stakeholders such as clients, distributors, and partners should be also involved. They know both products and competitors offer. At the university or in school parents, professors, providers of internship and of equipments are concerned.

Generated ideas are evaluated by a committee composed at least of three professionals in charge of technology, marketing and human resources. The first checks the feasibility, the second verifies if the addressed market is big enough and third plans the resources needed for successful transformation of idea into commercial product or service.

Before transformation it is vital to verify all constraints, such as, technological feasibility, competitors' offers, availability of resources, market impact, return on investment in term of tangible and intangible values, environmental impact and ethics.

Knowledge of competitors is an important element—if we have some, it should be decided how to improve our initial strategy—modify our product or work in synergy with them. For example when Michelin invented PAX system (Mercier-Laurent, 2003) they associated with Pirelli and Goodyear to take a bigger part of market.

The others constraints that must be also verified before transformation are the price and availability of raw materials, recyclability of our future product and social impact (use of local resources) as well. Simulators may be of considerable help in this task.

After these verifications decisions can be taken on future development and scheduled.

The next steps are the design and exploitation. Design is in fact about ecodesign, because we integrate the environmental principles, verify the impacts, optimize the use of raw material, shape, recyclability and ergonomics. The exploitation phase has to generate values, as well tangible as intangible to share among the participants of the innovation process. The objective is sustainable success of all actors mentioned in Figure 2.4, including clients. The integration of feedback and continuous capturing of opportunities all along these activities helps improving existing and generating new ideas.

Connecting, combining and managing related knowledge, know-how, intelligences and experiences is among conditions of sustainable success of innovation.

2.5   IMPORTANCE OF MANAGING KNOWLEDGE

The impact of innovation depends on how quickly we capture opportunities and to the speed of ambient information and knowledge exploitation.

According to three laws of Knowledge Dynamics (Amidon et al., 2005) "knowledge is a multiplier to be managed and leveraged; innovation is a process that convert knowledge into action, through Knowledge Innovation, a collaborative, open process."

The innovation dynamics able to ensure a sustainable development of the companies, regions and countries rely on both current and past knowledge and on tools able to amplify the innovation capacity of humans and machines involved in knowledge flow. Such an organization will enable disruptive innovation and will facilitate managing risks related to innovation.

The concept of knowledge management (KM) was born in the 1980s, as a new managerial method. Since organizations have been implemented various approaches on top and middle-management levels.

Three ways of introducing this method in organizations have been experimented: KM as corporate strategy, tool oriented and users oriented (Mercier-Laurent, 2011).

Some of the collaborative work tools may work to start ecoinnovation. Main difficulty to face is the education of the ability to work in collaboration instead of competition. Social networks are certainly helpful in finding the right resources. We should add to this, specific tools for creativity, design, customer relationship management, e-learning, e-commerce and others. However, to enhance the efficiency of the innovation process all related knowledge should be organized and optimized.

Considering the participants needs is probably the best way of introducing the useful help. Using this approach allows building incrementally, thinking global doing small, an appropriate knowledge flow exploring at best the abilities of both humans and computers.

Since 1956 Artificial Intelligence (AI) researchers and practitioners have invented methods and techniques to process knowledge by computers. Most of them have been experimented and successfully used in robots and in decision support systems, in order to learn, predict, plan, simulate, innovate and play.

AI techniques are useful all along the knowledge lifecycle: creation-transfer—processing-sharing.

The challenge for intelligent technology is particularly important in the current context, where the information overload and a lot of nontargeted push make us loose time, which has become a valuable asset. It would be extremely useful to eliminate unsolicited mail at the source before it arrives in our email box, or influence other ethics. Computers in all forms powered by AI help storing a large amount of information, simultaneously taking into account a large number of parameters; researching solutions respecting the given constraints set by exploitation, in a huge space of possibilities; searching for relevant information within an immense quantity of data and information; and knowledge discovery in databases, texts and images. They are able to check the coherence of information from multiple sources, "read" documents and make a summary of them as a function of the current user interests, to report information, articles, events or books that are of interest. Able to learn by discovery, analogy, observation, computers can help in complex system diagnosis, translate simple and well-structured texts, help to capitalize knowledge, to design documents, products or to gather know-how in a given field.

The human-machine synergy, or even symbiosis, strongly depends on the last architecture, interfaces and on programming, which is preferably user-centered.

Artificial Intelligence provides methods and techniques supporting the knowledge innovation that help succeed innovation by
- knowledge modeling allow building a blocs for future reuse;
- gathering and organizing knowledge related to the given problem solving;

- providing techniques for problem solving, knowledge processing, simulation, decision support and constraints verification.

Technology can play several roles in the innovation process: that of a facilitator of the collective intelligence; a generator of ideas, able to check if a new idea has already been carried out somewhere in the world; a business intelligence specialist; a consistency and constraint controller; a simulator "to see before doing"; a design assistant; an adviser and a box of ideas. Equipped with artificial intelligence techniques, computers can "think," solve problems, become experts, and accumulate a collective experience, under the condition that we transfer to them the relative knowledge and the necessary reasoning and learning techniques.

Solving complex problems begins with understanding the problem in context, the discovery of real needs, analysis of the nature of knowledge to be exploited and the decision making mechanisms. The choice of a technique will be made as a function of all these elements. Very often, several techniques are necessary.

Among them, we can mention:

- the expert system, where the reasoning is based on rules. In reality, there are few situations where the rules are used to solve a given problem. This technique is effective in the areas where the rules are well-defined and there are few exceptions, such as the allocation of taxes at customs, equipment configuration, process control or in administration;
- the cause to effect graph is useful for finding a cause of an observable symptom by exploring the branches. This technique is used for diagnosis and to model the correct operation state. Building a graph for a complex system is time and energy consuming;
- the decision tree or static induction, used for diagnosis and in data mining. A tree is automatically generated from examples (Quinlan and Michalski, 1983);
- analogy (Bergmann et al., 2003) is very useful to learn and get inspiration from already known solutions, to build a collective experience and for any matching of the supply and demand, such as job-, travel- or house-hunting. This technique can be used to build an idea generator;
- dynamic induction (Auriol, 1995; Manago and Mercier-Laurent, 1994) including the advantages of induction and analogy. The

decision tree is built while the user is answering the questions asked by the system. The processing of unknown values is taken into account by the analogy engine, which proposes the best choice among the possibilities;

- constraint programming (Dingbas et al., 1988) integrating a constraint propagation engine and algorithms of optimization and generation of solutions, which respect the given constraints. This enables us to solve combinatory problems, such as scheduling, planning, resource allocation and management, optimization and routes or frequency allocation;

- natural language processing techniques, based on semantic networks, conceptual graphs, ontologies and grammatical analysis are helpful to communicate with computers, for database queries, web searching, for knowledge discovery in texts, confirmation or discovery of experts from texts they have written, as well as for automated translation;

- multiagent systems (Russel and Norvig, 2010) are programmed to perform various distributed and collaborative tasks. Their organization copies that of humans—there are agents, tasks managers using different forms of reasoning. There are even agents preventing the others from working, what enables the simulation of dynamic constraints. They can organize themselves to "create" a collective intelligence, inspired from insects (Quinqueton, 2006);

- neural networks are generally applied to form recognition in image processing, in data mining in association with other techniques, or in design. They are equipped with automated learning "ability" (Cardon, 2000).

The Figure 2.5 presents a variety of AI techniques.

The current trends and works of the researchers are mainly focused on ontologies and multiagent systems (Open KADS 1990).

The usefulness of "knowledge thinking" and of the aforementioned techniques in creativity and in the innovation process lifecycle is undeniable (Mercier-Laurent, 2013). However, their choice should be made as a function of the problem to be solved, the objectives and processing to consider (constraint verification, simulation, and computation), the way of working with stakeholders and the expected results. Involving computers,

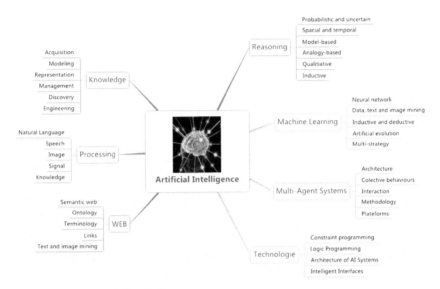

FIGURE 2.5   Map of AI techniques.

in all their forms, and using suitable approaches and techniques, can boost the innovative capacity of individuals and groups. The organization and management of knowledge increases the chances of successful innovation.

2.5.1 AMPLIFYING CAPACITY TO INNOVATE— COLLABORATIVE HUMAN-MACHINE INTELLIGENCE

Technology has a potential to empower the two interrelated components of the innovation process—creativity and transformation. It is never-ending process, because organizations, should innovate permanently for sustainable success.

The first step of the innovation process—creativity can be amplified by an analogy based generator of ideas and/or TRIZ based finder of solutions in addition to opportunity "hunting" by all participants.

The creativity sessions may be powered by generator of ideas, shown in Figure 2.6.

The ideas of employees and stakeholders are stored in the electronic "box of ideas."

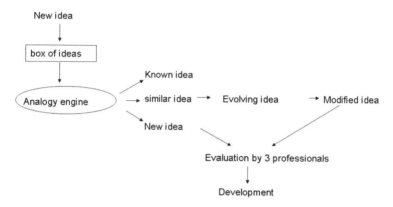

FIGURE 2.6   Generator of ideas based on analogy engine (Mercier-Laurent, 2011).

Such a generator is available according to corporate strategy for every-body in a given organization and may be shared with stakeholders. A small base of cases (ideas) should be available to initiate the system. The HMI allow entering new idea to electronic "box of ideas" using knowledge model of case to be process automatically by analogy engine.

When someone enters a new idea, the analogy engine compares with what is "known" and display one of three possibilities:

- new idea—submit for evaluation;
- similar idea—someone already enter something similar—person that enter new idea is the invited to contact this person and enrich idea together;
- known idea—this idea was already explored.

New idea is then evaluated by at least three professionals to estimate the market, technological feasibility and skills available for working on new project.

The similar idea can be modified and than evaluated or "frozen" for future exploration.

The next step of the innovation process is a transformation that begins by evaluation of impacts before doing can be also empowered by technology. It involves often the virtual connection of multidisciplinary knowledge.

At this stage the various simulators help verifying availability, con-straints and impacts.

2.6 MULTIPLE IMPACTS OF INNOVATION

As mentioned before, the innovation generates multiple impacts that should be minimized or enhanced in aim of preserving the ecosystems balance.

The main impacts are shown in Figure 2.7

Each impact may influence each other. All impacts have to be evaluated all along of the innovation process.

Technological innovation impact is often evaluated only in economic terms—generated revenue. Unfortunately many investors as well public as private evaluate short-term revenues and not at all the innovative capacity of a given company vital to sustain in the future.

Sustainable development put emphasis on only economic, societal and environmental impact, technological is not considered. Many companies employed Chief Sustainability Officer. Most of these persons organize actions aiming in enhancing the company image as respectful of environment, forgetting often the importance of balancing economic impact as well.

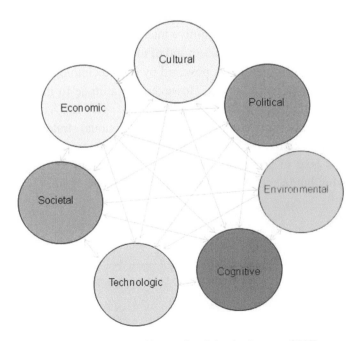

FIGURE 2.7 7D impacts of innovation (Mercier-Laurent, 2013).

Quick development of technology and accelerated push of many technological objects and solutions influence our cognitive capacity. The automated processing of emails or FAQ based only on key words, automated help desk, tracking the users navigation without understanding purpose and context, connected objects that reasons and take decisions for the users, prevent us of using our brain that we disconnect at the point of losing the ability to think. We have also added the impact of ubiquitous electromagnetic field on our health, navigation on several screens for our eyes and influence of war games on our behaviors.

The sustainability of ecoinnovation process depends on how company manages all these impacts. On the long run, preserving our heath and planet should be also considered better than immediate revenues.

2.7   CONCLUSIONS AND PERSPECTIVES

Technology has an extraordinary capacity of enhancing the ecoinnovation process, amplifying our creativity and help as taking right decisions by organizing knowledge and verifying all related constraints. Their design and programming should consider not only intuitive interface, but also facilitation of a synergy between them and their users and of mutual learning.

Collaborative innovation systems powered by right technology enable us to innovate real time and globally. However, the attitude to innovate with stakeholders including clients is to cultivate.

Innovation should become companies and organizational strategy.

Ecoinnovation for human and planet purpose in harmony with nature has an ambitious goal to preserve and reuse the best of our knowledge without destroying human conditions and replacing humans by machines.

KEYWORDS

artificial intelligence
creativity
ecoinnovation
innovation

knowledge management
multiple impact
technology
thinking

REFERENCES

AFNOR ISO 26000, http://www.iso.org/iso/home/standards/iso26000.htm.

Altshuller, G., Shulyak, L., Rodman, S. *40 Principles TRIZ keys to Technical Innovation*, http://www.triz40.com/aff_Principles.htm, 1997.

Amidon, D. M. *The Innovation Strategy for the Knowledge Economy*, Butterworth Heinemann, Boston, 1997.

Amidon, D., Formica, P., Mercier-Laurent, E. *Knowledge Economics: Principles, Practices and Policies*, Tartu University Press, Estonia, 2005.

Association Française pour Intelligence Artificielle.

Auriol, E., *Intégration d'approches symboliques pour le raisonnement à partir d'exemples*, PhD thesis, Paris IX, 1995.

Bergmann, R., Althoff, K. D., Breen, S., Göker, M., Manago, M., Traphöner, R., Wess, S., *Developing Industrial Case-Based Reasoning Applications the INRECA Methodology*, Lecture Notes in Artificial Intelligence, 2nd edition, vol. 1612, Buchreihe, Springer Verlag, Berlin, 2003.

Buclet, N. *Concevoir une nouvelle relation a la consommation: l'économie de fonctionnalité.* Série des Annales des Mines: Responsabilité et environment, 2005, pp. 57–67.

Buzan, T. *How to Improve Your Creative Thinking?* https://www.youtube.com/watch?v=zO2LdDpx-Tc.

Cardon, A. *Conscience artificielle et systèmes auto-adaptatifs*, Eyrolles, Paris, 2000.

CATIA—http://www.3ds.com/products-services/catia/capabilities/design/

Contest of French Ministry of Research, 1999. http://www.enseignementsup-recherche.gouv.fr/cid22991/concours-national-aide-creation-entrepriseentreprises-technologies-innovantes-2009.html.

Corporate Social Responsibility, 2015, http://ec.europa.eu/growth/industry/corporate-social-responsibility/index_en.htm.

Curley, M., Salmelin, B.: *Open Innovation 2.0: A New Paradigm*, European Union, Open Innovation Strategy and Policy Group (OISPG), 2013. See also Yearbook 2014 and 2015.

De Bono, E. Re-thinking the Future, Creative Innovation 2010, Melbourne, https://www.youtube.com/watch?v=e20lpMyXFj4.

De Bono, E. *Six Thinking Hats*, Little, Brown & Co., London, 1999.

Dingbas, M., Van Hentenryck, P., Simonis, H., Aggoun, A., Herold, A., *The CHIP System: Constraint Handling, in the Prolog*, CADE (International Conference on automatic Deduction), Argone (IL), United States of America, 1988.

Drucker, P. F. *The New Society of Organizations*, Harvard Business Review, September–October 1992.

Dubuis, B. *J'innove. Comment gérer son innovation: de l'idée au marché*, Les Clefs du Savoir, Suisse, 2007.

Ecodesign Your Future. How Ecodesign Can Help the Environment by Making Products Smarter, European Union, 2012.

Ecoinnovation: When Business Meets the Environment, 2015, http://ec.europa.eu/environment/eco-innovation/.

Entovation International, *Ten Definitions of Innovation*, 1998, http://www.entovation.com/innovation/10definitions.htm.

Frascati Manual, Guidelines for Collecting and Reporting Data on Research and Experimental Development, OECD, October 8, 2015.

Frascati Manual. Proposed Standard Practice for Surveys on Research and Experimental Development, Chapter 2, OECD, 11 December 2002.

Gray, T. *Tell the White House How to Power Startups*, http://www.fastcompany.com/1740238/tell-white-house-how-power-startup, 2011.

Horizon, 2020. European Union Program, http://ec.europa.eu/programmes/horizon2020/en/what-horizon-2020.

Houel, M., Daunis, M., *Les pôles de compétitivité: bilan et perspectives d'une politique industrielle et d'aménagement du territoire*, Rapport du Sénat, no. 40, 14 October 2009.

Khurana, V. K. *Innovation Process*, http://fr.slideshare.net/VijayKrKhurana/innovation-process-models, 2013.

Le Moing, B. *Gestion de connaissances au cœur du program d'entreprise*, Qualitique No 256, November 2014, pp. 46–48.

Manago, M., Mercier-Laurent, E., *INRECA+Integrating Induction and Case Based Reasoning for Diagnostic Problems with Focus on Medical Domains*, Project INTAS, 1994.

Mercier-Laurent, E. Artificial Intelligence Supporting Innovation Ecosystems, AAIA, Fedcsis 2015, September 14, Lodz, Poland.

Mercier-Laurent, E. *Innovating Corporate Management: Introducing Environmental Aspects to Design Activities*, ICICKM, Washington, September 2013, pp. 267–271.

Mercier-Laurent, E. *Innovation Ecosystems*, Wiley, 2011.

Mercier-Laurent, E. *Innovation globale à partir des connaissances*, Technologies Internationales, No. 94, 2003, pp. 41–44.

Mercier-Laurent, E. The Innovation Biosphere—Planet and Brains in Digital Era, Wiley, 2015.

Mercier-Laurent, E., Boulanger, D. Artificial Intelligence for Knowledge Management, Springer, IFIP AICT 422, 2014.

Mercier-Laurent, E., *Global Knowledge Management Beginning from Website– How to Organize the Flow of Knowledge in An International Company—Theories and Practice*, ISMICK 97, Compiègne, France, 1997.

Mercier-Laurent, E., Pachet, F. *Créativité et innovation*, Bulletin AFIA N° 78, 2013.

Moedas, C. *A New Start for Europe: Opening up to an ERA of Innovation*, Brussels 22 June 2015, http://ec.europa.eu/research/conferences/2015/era-of-innovation/index.cfm.

Open KADS, http://cordis.europa.eu/project/rcn/8773_en.html, 1990.

Ordonez de Pablos, P., Edvinsson, L. Intellectual Capital in Organizations. Nonfinancial Reports and Accounts, Routledge, Taylor & Francis Group, New York, 2015.

Oslo Manual, European Commission, Eurostat, 2nd edition, 1996, p.31, http://www.oecd.org/sti/inno/2367580.pdf.

Quinlan, J. R., Michalski, R. S., *Machine Learning—An Artificial Intelligence Approach*, p. 463–482, Tioga, Palo Alto, 1983.

Quinqueton, J. *Aspects socioorganizationnels dans les systèmes multiagents. Intelligence artificielle en essaim*, RIC 2006, Nîmes, France, 2006.

Report on Incubators France. *Recherche et Développement. Innovation et Partenariats*, DGRI, September 2009.

Russel, S., Norvig, P. *Artificial Intelligence: A Modern Approach*, Pearson, 2010, http://aima.cs.berkeley.edu/.

Schumpeter, J. *Theorie der wirtschaftlichen Entwicklung*, Dunken & Humblot, Berlin, 1912.

Stark, John. *Product Lifecycle Management: Paradigm for Twenty-First Century Product Realization*, Springer-Verlag, 2004. ISBN 1852338105.

Technology and Innovation, Harvard Business School, 2015, http://www.hbs.edu/faculty/topics/Pages/technology-and-innovation.aspx.

The Institute for Knowledge and Innovation, http://phdkim.bu.ac.th/.

This is European Social Innovation, European Union, Belgium, 2010, ISBN 978-92-79-17075-1.

Webster, K. *The Circular Economy—A Wealth of Flows*, Product Life Institute, Geneva, 2015.

Zhang, F., Rio, M., Allais, R., Zwolinski, P., Reyes Carrillo, T., Roucoules, L., Mercier-Laurent, E., Buclet, N., Toward a Systemic Navigation Framework to Integrate Sustainable Development into a Company, *Journal of Cleaner Production*, Volume 54, 1 September 2013, pp. 199–214.

CHAPTER 3

SELF-ORGANIZING COORDINATION AND CONTROL APPROACHES: THE IMPACT OF SOCIAL NORMS ON SELF-REGULATED INNOVATION ACTIVITIES IN SELF-MANAGING TEAMS

MARIA CARMELA ANNOSI,[1,2] FEDERICA BRUNETTA,[3] and MATS MAGNUSSON[2]

[1]Ericsson AB—Research, Färögatan 6, SE-164 80 Stockholm, Sweden

[2]IPD, School of Industrial Engineering and Management—KTH Royal Institute of Technology, Brinellvägen 8, 114 28 Stockholm, Sweden

[3]Department of Business and Management—LUISS Guido Carli University, Viale Romania, 32, 00197 Roma, Italy

CONTENTS

ABSTRACT

The development of social norms, as well as how and under which conditions social norms impact behavior, are determined by the social influence process. By leveraging the influence process we can create and handle change in self-managing teams in order to foster growth and steer team members in a positive direction, away from negative habits. At the same time, if poorly managed the developed social norms can inhibit change, and in the worst case result in conflict and resentment within the team.

If team members feel part of a group and consider that group membership is relevant for them, they will adapt their behavior to align to the group's norms and standards, which in turn will dictate context-specific attitudes and behaviors that are appropriate for the team.

This chapter focuses on teams' social norms, distinguishing between descriptive (what most others do) and injunctive (what most others approve or disapprove of) norms, investigating important moderators in the relationships between descriptive norms and behaviors, discussing the role of the social environment on the changes to and inculcation of injunctive social norms, and describing how individual team members' attributes refine the susceptibility of individuals to normative influences.

3.1   INTRODUCTION

Intensified competition puts pressure on organizations to outperform their competitors by addressing customer needs in superior ways. To increase their ability to fulfill customer demands, firms are becoming more and more aware of the need for overarching change, converting to decentralized structures and abandoning hierarchical organizational forms in favor of flattened hierarchies and massive use of self-managing teams. This has resulted in several organizations moving from traditional, planning-intensive and linear development approaches to more iterative and self-organized approaches inspired by Agile methodologies (e.g., Martin, 2003).

The popularity of Agile methods has grown, especially in relation to technology projects, which are designed to address high volatility in the market environment (Lindvall et al., 2002). They are able to cope with the different types of changes that occur in projects, in relation to: (i) goals; (ii) materials, resources, tools, and techniques; and (iii) relationships with other projects, services, or products (Collyer et al., 2010). Consistent with this, Williams and Cockburn (2003, p. 39) define Agile software development as being "about feedback and change," and argue that Agile methodologies have been conceived to "embrace, rather than reject, higher rates of change."

Despite the increased adoption of Agile by companies, clear and detailed recommendations about how to drive autonomous teams towards successful high innovative performance are lacking. The attention in research on Agile methodologies focuses on the introduction and adoption phases of Agile (Dybå & Dingsøyr, 2008), rather than on the long-term effects of Agile implementation and the impact on innovation (Abrahamsson et al., 2009).

Agile methods are appropriate to foster innovation and creativity and to explore new fields (Highsmith, 2002). The autonomy and self-organization among team members provides conditions conducive to the development of learning capabilities and solving problems through creativity (Imai et al., 1984), and renders team members more open to novel ideas (Lyytinen and Rose, 2006). In addition, creativity and innovation are favored by the fact that Agile creates a balanced but not fully structured context (Highsmith, 2002).

However, in such a context, the social aspect is fundamental. Agile software development methods emphasize teamwork (Nerur and Balijepally, 2007) in contrast to the plan-driven development approach which foresees individual role assignment (Nerur et al., 2005).

Integrating individual knowledge is not sufficient to generate innovative ideas if the team environment does not provide the proper conditions to allow team members to develop the ability and motivation to use their potential (Aalbers et al., 2013; Shin et al., 2012). The generation of team-level knowledge is derived from the joint effect of members' individual personal characteristics and their belonging to a social context (Shalley et al., 2004). In order to create and act on teams' internal knowledge and individual innovative ideas, team members need to share their thoughts with their peers, and to sense and seize other members' insights to create proper associations which potentially could result in the creation of workable solutions (Baer et al., 2010; Harrison and Rouse, 2014). Consequently, we argue that a relevant part of a team's self-regulated innovation activities stems from established social interaction processes and norms which act as source of influence that guides the behavior of team members.

A team's social behavior is influenced heavily by the team norms to the extent that team members adopt a relevant group identity (Cialdini and Trost, 1998). Team identification is responsible for the development of injunctive characteristics based on the perceived sanctions associated with conformity to or violation of these norms (Cialdini and Trost, 1998). Specifically, using the theoretical lens of self theories (Dweck, 2000; Dweck and Molden, 2005), it is seen that injunctive norms constitute self-standards that identify whom people ideally would like to be or whom they ought to be (Higgins, 1987; Moretti and Higgins, 1999; Schwartz, 1977; Schwartz and Fleishman, 1978). However, in contrast to the explicit sanctions imposed by injunctive norms, descriptive norms provide insights into the group's typical conduct: they provide information on what team members are really doing allowing identification of group adaptive behaviors (Cialdini et al., 1991). Descriptive norms may not reflect the favored identity, with the result that the process guiding the impact of descriptive norms may differ from that guiding the team's injunctive norms. Consequently, both types of norms are salient for identifying the group's behavior and predicting any kind of committed team action.

Based on this reasoning, this chapter analyzes the roles of two types of norms, descriptive and injunctive, to predict team innovation activity. It examines the nature of the stimuli likely to lead to the formation and activation of these norms, and determining the conditions in which a unique effect of Agile work routines and managerial practices will emerge. This chapter also emphasizes the influence of the source of these norms—whether they are promoted in-group (i.e., the group to which the individual belongs) or out-group (i.e., in another group than that to which the individual belongs but which forms part of the surrounding social environment such as team stakeholders and manager). This differentiation might explain why individuals might respond differently to injunctive and descriptive norms as a function of whether the norms are in-group or out-group. This also highlights the roles of the team's executives and leaders, and allow us to propose a new approach to managerial organizational controls as crucial determinants of the functioning of organizational units and firm performance (Loughry and Tosi, 2008; De Jong et al., 2014), which can replace the close monitoring and supervision imposed by social-ideological modes of control.

Additionally, the chapter analyzes the relationships between descriptive and injunctive norms, underlining their interactive effect on team behavior, demonstrating the importance of injunctive norms, and identifying the environmental conditions that make injunctive norms more important in an Agile context.

The chapter builds on the results of a four-year study of hundreds of teams in several organizational units dealing with product development. Initially, we ran a pilot study in a small research and development (R&D) organization; we then conducted 17 group interviews and an exploratory survey, plus three follow up meetings in three bigger R&D organizations to discuss the relevant findings. This allowed us to scale up the analysis to involve an entire product development unit comprising four large R&D departments and a total of 1,700 employees. We interviewed 44 individuals selected from different hierarchical levels and functions. Finally, we launched a global, multilevel and multisource survey involving participation of 20 different R&D organizations in 11 countries, including the members of 97 teams and their team managers, plus their higher-level managers in the related organizations. Our main research methods used grounded theory, cross-case analysis, triangulation, and linear and hierarchical linear regression models. We collected organizational documentation from each organization involved which constituted a valid source of secondary data.

The remainder of this chapter is structured as follows. We outline the general concept of team innovation, and accompanying team norms and peer pressure (sections Teams and innovation and Team norms). We discuss complementarity among control mechanisms, and describe Agile methodologies to provide the research setting for this research (section Agile Software Development). We integrate and apply the theoretical logics of social identity and stakeholder theory with control mechanisms to explain how combinations of controls operate to affect a team's self-regulated learning process. On this basis, we develop a conceptual model that captures how combinations of norms and peer pressure affect team's self-regulated learning strategies, and ultimately, team innovation performance (sections Team descriptive norms' influence over individual social conduct for innovation and Influence of Team injunctive norms on individual social conduct for innovation).

3.2   TEAMS AND INNOVATION

By innovation we mean "the intentional introduction and application within a job, work team or organization of ideas, processes, products or procedures which are new to that job, work team or organization and which are designed to benefit the job, the work team or the organization" (West and Farr, 1990, p. 9). There is an important differentiation in this field of research between creativity and innovation. Innovation involves two stages: the production of new ideas, and their implementation (Amabile, 1996; West and Farr, 1990; Woodman et al., 1993). Creativity is involved in the first stage of the innovation process—idea generation—which can be considered as a subprocess of innovation. The study in this chapter investigates the antecedents to idea generation in a self-managing team context. Idea generation is seen as an outcome of the team's development of a novel and useful solution to a problem encountered in the pursuit of a work goal (Drucker, 1985; Hirst et al., 2009). In what follows, we use the term innovation to also include creativity.

Despite the relevance of creative ideas at the fuzzy front end of product innovation, studies of creativity at team level are limited (Amabile, 1983, 1988). Anderson and West (1998, p. 239) argue that, "comparatively few studies have focused at the level-of-analysis of the work group. This is a notable shortcoming because it is often the case that an innovation is originated and subsequently developed by a team into routinized practice within organizations." Investigations of how groups within organization can promote or constrain innovation are scarce (e.g., Burningham and West, 1995; Drach-Zahavy and Somech, 2001).

Although there is some research indicating that both individual qualities and environmental factors affect the level of creativity in teams (e.g., Amabile, 1988; Hargadon and Sutton, 1997; Oldham and Cummings, 1996) there is little evidence showing how team-level factors influence creativity in teams. Some studies show that team processes are key components of the development of innovation (Taggar, 2002), and meta-analysis of the team level antecedents to creativity and innovation in the workplace (Hulsheger et al., 2009) shows that team input variables (e.g., team composition, team structure) have a weaker effect than team process variables (vision, participative safety, support for innovation, and task orientation). However, these findings are inconsistent, suggesting unknown moderating effects in addition to simple direct effects (Hülsheger et al., 2009).

Among team processes, team learning plays a dominant role and the empirical evidence suggests that organizational and collective learning form the basis for the development and adoption of organizational innovation (Argyris, 1993). Specifically, the learning function describes the extent to which team members put their effort to reflect on the team's objectives and strategies aimed at creating a team-level intellectual product which triggers change (Larson and Christensen, 1993; Swieringa and Wierdsma, 1992; West, 1996). Additionally, although not connected directly to innovation, research shows that team learning leads to improved problem recognition (Hirokawa, 1990), better scanning of the environment (Ancona and Caldwell, 1992), and generation of creative solutions (Maier and Solem, 1962), all of which could be relevant to team innovation. However, by limiting the analysis to the cognitive representation of knowledge and interpretation of information, important dimensions explaining the team's psychosocial functioning based on motivational and personal factors and the related social contextual influences (Bandura, 1986) are neglected.

The creation of new knowledge at team level relies on individual characteristics and social interaction (Shalley et al., 2004): team members need to share knowledge within their group, and to identify and capture other members' solutions and ideas in order to combine them into workable solutions (Baer et al., 2010; Harrison and Rouse, 2014). A willingness to interact is essential for team members to secure a creative outcome within a proper team environment where the individual is motivated to exploit his or her full potential (Aalbers et al., 2013; Shin et al., 2012).

In this light, researchers have analyzed more in depth the cognitive motivating processes that foster innovation, as recommended by Locke and Latham's (1990) goal-setting theory.

In the case of self-managing teams, investigation of the organizational learning processes requires greater attention to the motivational and social dimensions of teams. In contrast to traditionally managed teams in which team members had little autonomy and restricted decision making authority, self-managing teams can make their own decisions about work processes and regulate their own behavior. For instance, self-managing teams usually have the authority to establish their own work plans, define budgets, manage production orders, and monitor product quality (Barker, 1993; Stewart et al., 1999).

On the other hand, shared responsibility for the assigned team task, a smaller number of team members, and delegation of authority over the team's work processes promotes collective thinking and a collective intention (Searle, 1990) by enabling the emergence of naturally occurring team interactions which however, eventually constrain individual activity in ways that often are difficult to perceive and understand (Barker, 1993). Along these lines, Tuomela (1995, p. 2) proposes a we-intention as the "commitment of an individual to participate in joint action, and involves an implicit or explicit agreement between the participants to engage in that joint action." Accordingly, we-intentions rely on individual commitment, and commitment to offering mutual support meaning that a member is "not only committed to performing the preassigned part but he is also committed to furthering" (Tuomela, 1995, p. 129) the joint action (such as supporting others in running their parts, when needed). Thus, unlike the traditional personal intention which points to an action that a person can perform by her- or himself, we consider we-intentions as focusing more on the social behavior within the team. We-intentions represent intentions articulated either in the form, "I intend that we act jointly" (Bratman, 1997), or in the form, "I intend that our group performs group activity X" (e.g., Tuomela, 1995). Therefore, we-intentions mirror the intention of a person identifying him- or herself as a social category, acting as an individual actor but in concert with his or her team members. In line with this, some studies (e.g., Bagozzi and Dholakia, 2002) show how positive anticipated emotions and social identities affect we-intentions. Therefore, under these conditions, team members are psychologically tied to social foci such as goals (Klein et al., 2001; Herscovitch and Meyer, 2002; Morrow, 1993), as well as to their work groups (Becker et al., 1996; Bishop and Dow Scott, 2000; Siders et al., 2001). A collective intention to learn fosters the development of team members' competences and master of tasks, as result of their intrinsic interest in the innovative task which gives them the means to improve their skills and knowledge. This increases the likelihood that team members will decide to devote their efforts to complex tasks in situations where there are no extrinsic rewards (Dweck and Sorich, 1999). In addition, intrinsic motivation to perform the innovation task fosters a deeper and more serious effort to learning which often leads to creative behaviors (Amabile, 1996) and a better attitude to undertaking difficult and stimulating tasks (VandeWalle, 1997). Under these conditions, individuals will invest their efforts in acquiring new knowledge and realizing "deep-processing strategies" needed to tackle complex tasks (Elliot and McGregor, 2001).

A we-intention demonstrates individual intention to be involved in a joint activity not as an individual action but as contributing to group performance or group action as a member of the group. In this case, the individual looks at the group activity holistically in order to identify his or her part in a social representation (Bagozzi and Lee, 2002). We-intentions to perform a group act are promoted by (i) individual reasons to perform the group act (e.g., attitudes to conducting a joint activity with others); (ii) interpersonal pressure to perform a group act (e.g., subjective norms); (iii) group norms to perform a group act, and (iv) social identity related to a group act (Bagozzi and Lee, 2002). Therefore, all learning activities— within the team and related to direct experience—can occur vicariously by observing others' behaviors and their consequences (Bandura, 1986; Rosenthal and Zimmerman, 1978)

However, individuals learn and increase their knowledge and skills based on the information carried on by modeling influences constituted by team norms. In this setting, vicarious learning can also occur:

"By observing a model of the desired behavior, an individual forms an idea of how response components must be combined and sequenced to produce the new behavior. In other words, people guide their actions by prior notions rather than by relying on outcomes to tell them what they must do" (Bandura, 1977, p. 35).

Based on this reasoning, we analyze the role of team social norms for predicting team learning and innovation. We argue that an important part of a team's self-regulated learning and innovation activities stems from established team conduct, which acts as source of influence that guides team members' behaviors.

3.3   TEAM NORMS

Norms can be seen as informal standards of appropriate behavior pre-scribing how the members of a group should act (Argote, 1989). Social norms both catalyze and direct action in significant ways (Aarts and Dijksterhuis, 2003; Cialdini et al., 1991; Darley and Latané, 1970; Kerr, 1995; Terry and Hogg, 2001). Thus, social norms can be seen as the most influential control mechanism regulating self-managing team behavior (Hackman, 1992). However, norms are multidimensional: they can be described through different content and structural dimen-sions related to the many ways and situations they give evidence of themselves (Gibbs, 1965; Jackson, 1966; Jasso and Opp, 1997; Marini, 2000; Opp, 1982). Consequently, different conceptualizations of norms are equally legitimate (Gibbs, 1965; Jasso and Opp, 1997). Beyond the dimension of content, norms can be determined based on their structural aspects where the structure (or "strength") of norms is defined in terms of intensity and consensus (Jackson, 1966; Jasso and Opp, 1997). Inten-sity is related to how firmly team members adhere to, and the degree of relevance members give to these norms. Consensus refers to the extent to which norms are diffused among team members and show their col-lective agreement with and acceptance of them. The closer the adher-ence to and stronger acceptance of norms among team members, the more intense is the motivational force guiding behaviors (Hackman, 1992; Marini, 2000).

Norms can be voluntary and spontaneously created within the team (Barker, 1993) or they can be induced and originate externally to the team (Feldman, 1984; Flynn and Chatman, 2003; Opp, 1982). In many case management plays a crucial role in building team norms (Annosi et al., 2015; Ehrhart and Naumann, 2004; Feldman, 1984).

Induced and spontaneous norms are qualitatively different in their functionality, idiosyncrasy, and specificity of content (Marini, 2000). First, management in an attempt to align the team with the organizational goals may impose norms that are more functional than voluntary norms (Celani et al., 2010; Doherty et al., 2004; Ehrhart and Naumann, 2004; Hoegl and Gemuenden, 2001; Munroe et al., 1999; Wageman, 1995). Second, organizationally induced norms deriving from a single source (i.e., management) rather than from each team, are less team idiosyncratic in their content than voluntary norms. Third, organizationally induced norms are general (i.e., less specific) than voluntary norms, in the range of the behaviors they prescribe.

3.3.1 ENACTMENT OF NORMATIVE CONTROL INSIDE TEAMS

When team members belong to a group and feel that being a group member is important to them, they will align their behaviors with the group's norms and standards, in line with the normative controls imposed by their peers in the team. Thus, consistently with the following definition of control, normative control can be seen as a force that "comes from the knowledge that someone who matters to us is paying close attention to what we are doing and will tell us if our behavior is appropriate or inappropriate" (O'Reilly and Chatman, 1996, p. 161). As a result of peer normative control, members of self-managing teams are transformed into "someone" accountable for monitoring and influencing other members to coordinate work (Barker, 1993; Manz and Sims, 1987; Tompkins and Cheney, 1985).

Normative control relies on a sense of belonging and attachment promoting social pressure for the individual to comply with the group or organizational standards. Desire to feel part of a community motivates the individual to achieve the goals endorsed by the group and to avoid behaviors that the collective considers undesirable (Sorrels and Kelley, 1984). This motivational state is tied to the processes of social identification (Ashforth and Mael, 1989) and social categorization (Tajfel, 1982), and acts such that normative control leads to the internalization of group standards (MacNeil and Sherif, 1976; Pollis et al., 1975). Within self-managed teams, peer-based normative control is a motivational state originating from the perceptions of individuals of influence from teammates through the forces of social inclusion and internalization.

Thus, normative forms of peer-based control mirror emergent states that affect motivated teams' behaviors since they (a) are manifest as shared beliefs regarding what is valued in the environment, and (b) constitute proximal influences for individual and collective investments of effort by directly shaping goals and their pursuit (Chen and Gocus, 2008; Chen and Kanfer, 2006).

3.3.2   TEAM'S DESCRIPTIVE AND INJUNCTIVE NORMS

In considering normative influences on behavior, it is relevant to differentiate between the "is" (descriptive) and the "ought" (injunctive) meaning of social norms, since each refers to a distinct origin of human motivation (Deutsch and Gerard, 1955). Descriptive norms define what is typical or normal. They represent what most people do promoting adaptive action. Descriptive norms provide an information-processing opportunity to achieve a decisional shortcut in deciding which behavior to adopt in a given situation (Cialdini, 1988). Research shows that the perception of what others are doing shapes others' behaviors inducing similar behavior when the behaviors are morally as neutral as selecting a consumer product (Venkatesan, 1966)

Injunctive norms are related to rules or beliefs about morally approved or disapproved conduct. Descriptive norms define what is done, and injunctive norms describe what ought to be done. Unlike descriptive norms which provide information about others' actions, injunctive norms demand action based on the promise of social sanction. Since what is approved is usually what is normally done, it is easy to confound these two meanings of norms. However, they are conceptually and motivationally distinct, and it is important for a proper understanding of normative influence to keep them separate, especially in situations where both are acting simultaneously.

Discriminating between injunctive and descriptive norms is important since both types can be present at the same time in a social context and can have a consistent or a conflicting effect on social behavior (Cialdini et al., 1991). Moreover which of these norms is salient at a particular time will shape individual emergent behavior (Cialdini, 1993). Thus, in a social context where descriptive normative information might generate an undesirable boomerang effect, it is possible to combine descriptive norms with an injunctive message showing that the desired behavior is approved.

The purpose of the current research is to advance our understanding of how normative information, distributed within teams' descriptive and injunctive norms, may differentially affect self-managing teams' social behavior such that it influences teams' self-regulated learning strategies, and consequently team's innovation performance. In responding to the call for a more nuanced explanation of team innovation, we analyzed the joint impact of (descriptive and injunctive) norms and their related peer pressure on their self-regulated learning strategies. We adopt the perspective of social identity and stakeholder theories to clarify the content and structural dimensions of injunctive norms in teams and to emphasizes the role of the sources of both types of norms distinguishing in-group (i.e., the group to which the individual belongs) or out-group (i.e., other groups in the surrounding social environment such as stakeholders and managers) sources. This allows us to highlight the role of the team's executives and leaders, and to examine a new approach to managerial organizational controls, as crucial determinants of the functioning of organizational units and firm performance (Loughry and Tosi, 2008; De Jong et al., 2014) as opposed to close monitoring and supervision in social-ideological modes of control. Combining the effects of different types of norms with the derived peer pressure allows analysis of the joint and complementary interaction of different control mechanism—an area where research is scarce. Analyzing multiple mechanisms not only allows a more reliable evaluation of the role of each mechanism but also allows development of alternative justifications for how control combinations influence self-regulated learning choices, and consequently innovation performances

Our contribution to theory lies in our successful combining of different related logics to provide a systematic description of the complex system of controls which may be complements and which regulate team behavioral choices, and formulating a theory on the specific macro and micro organizational mechanisms responsible for the activation of these controls

3.4 AGILE SOFTWARE DEVELOPMENT

We provide a short description of the Agile Scrum methodology which is the most frequently used method in the organizations studied. We also review the current literature on the effect of about Agile methods on team innovation.

3.4.1 *AGILE SOFTWARE METHODOLOGIES AND SCRUM*

Agile software development methods such as XP (eXtreme Programming), Scrum, DSDM (Dynamic Systems Development Method), and FDD (Feature-Driven Development) are different sets of practices created with the intent to improve a software team's abilities to embrace and respond to changing requirements (Beck and Andres, 2005; Coad et al., 1999; Schwaber and Beedle, 2002; Stapleton, 1997). They were developed as a reaction to plan-driven, structured approaches since the agile practices focus more on lean processes and dynamic adaptation than on detailed front-end plans and heavy documentation (Nerur and Balijepally, 2007).

Software development agility is the ability of the team to respond efficiently and effectively to changes in user requirements. It is crucial to Agile development methods, which embed the ability to respond rapidly, and flexibly to changes in the business and technical domains (Henderson-Sellers and Serour, 2005; Highsmith and Cockburn, 2001). It also includes such aspects as lightness or leanness (i.e., minimal formal processes) (Cockburn, 2007) and related notions such as nimbleness, quickness, dexterity, suppleness, and or alertness (Erickson et al., 2005). In essence, Agile software methodologies propose a 'light' approach that promotes maneuverability as well as speed of response (Cockburn, 2007). Hence, the business value is created by delivering working software to customers at regular, short intervals (Dingsøyr et al., 2012). At the core of Agile practices, is the idea of self-organizing teams implementing Agile practices, designed to allow changes in requirements at any stage in the development process and to involve customers (or their representatives) in the whole development process. Teams are the basic units responsible for implementation of Agile practices in order to realize effective outcomes and eliminate waste and inefficiencies (Conboy, 2009) while sustaining organizational learning (Lyytinen and Rose, 2006).

A number of studies and practitioners in the information systems community, report the increasing popularity of Agile development methods and the implications of their diffusion (e.g., Conboy, 2009; Sarker et al., 2009). According to Forrester Research (West et al., 2010), Agile development methods have achieved wide adoption. A Forrester/Dr. Dobbs Global Developer Technographics® survey administered in Q3 2009 to IT professionals shows that 35% responding to describe their development process as Agile, with Scrum the most frequent Agile methodology.

The Scrum development process was introduced by Schwaber (1995) and is derived from the new product development methodology described in Takeuchi and Nonaka (1986) which was presented as a new approach to increase speed and flexibility. Scrum methods foresee delegation of decision making authority to the operational layer in the organization, and reliance on self-managing teams and a focus on reciprocal trust and respect, and the ability to self-organize to respond to problems (Cockburn and Highsmith, 2001). Feedback loops are key to this process, and Scrum results in a context where it is difficult to plan ahead (Dyba and Dingsør, 2008). In Scrum the software is implemented incrementally (in sprints) starting with a planning session and ending with a review. The items to be developed are prepared by the product owner and listed in the product backlog. Daily stand up meetings are held to coordinate the team's work. One team member, acting as Scrum master, is responsible for solving the problems preventing the team from working effectively.

3.4.2 AGILE SOFTWARE DEVELOPMENT IN THE INNOVATION DOMAIN

Innovation is often considered the main motivation for using Agile methodologies (Highsmith, 2004), since self-managing teams provide the appropriate preconditions for successful innovation activity (Hoegl and

Parboteeah, 2006; Takeuchi and Nonaka, 1986). The importance of creativity is acknowledged and supported by the whole Agile movement (Cockburn and Highsmith 2001; Highsmith, 2002, 2004), promoting the belief that only through creativity is it possible to deal with complex software development problems (Cockburn and Highsmith, 2001), and proposing Agile methods as supporting for firms faced with changes in complex product development. It also discloses the malfunctions and inhibits organization from reaching their true value (Rubin, 2012). Agile software development methods are indicated specifically for exploring new fields and for supporting the goals of innovation and creativity (Highsmith, 2002). However, despite claims that Agile can help to deliver innovation in uncertain situations, there is no confirmatory evidence. Despite the increasing popularity and relevance of Agile methods, few studies empirically analyze their related core concepts and implicit theoretical relationships (Baskerville, 2006; Boehm and Turner, 2004; Larman, 2004), or the conditions under which Agile development is effective for the adopting organizations (Fruhling and De Vreede, 2006; Moe et al., 2008).

Some studies assume that Scrum is based largely on Nonaka's theory of knowledge creation (see for example, Sutherland, 2010), and aimed at effective and efficient knowledge creation in the organization (Beedle et al., 1999) which is at the base of the ideation process. This theory is the basis of some of the core characteristics of Scrum, for example, the creation of new knowledge through direct interaction among people in teams, emphasis on tacit knowledge, feedback from working software, and significant information sharing (Beedle et al., 1999; Sutherland, 2010). In addition, Scrum prescribes the implementation of different routines enabling knowledge sharing, knowledge creation, and learning through software development activities, and sustaining a flexible and collaborative organizational approach (Nerur et al., 2005).

However, the research on Agile methodologies focuses mostly on the introduction and adoption phases (Dybå and Dingsøyr, 2008) rather than the long-term effects of Agile implementation on innovation (Abrahamsson et al., 2009). Dybå and Dingsøyr (2008) find that the available evidence cannot be considered reliable due to differences in data collection procedures and analyzes, and call for more and better quality studies. Thus, the effectiveness of principles and practices of Agile development is mainly anecdotal. The development of Agile needs theoretical underpinnings and concrete evidence of its declared benefits and core principles (Erickson et al. 2005).

3.5   INFLUENCE OF TEAM DESCRIPTIVE NORMS

This section identifies descriptive norms within self-managing teams to describe the strength of the descriptive norm-intention relation and to examine potential moderators and antecedents to the descriptive norm intention relation to explain why team members individually embrace a weak self-regulated learning strategy. By intentions we mean individual motivation to act in a specific manner and demonstrate the individual's level of commitment and the time and effort devoted to performing a behavior.

The above approach originates in an understanding of the experience of team members within their teams, and proposes a broad range of attributes associated with innovation in teams in order to capture relevant social factors related to innovation in self-managing teams. Since we want to identify the dimensionality of the descriptive norms related to innovation, we provide some quotes from team members and other organizational functions that interact with the teams which might result in informally created standards that might influence innovation in the teams. Following a thorough review of the quotes, we identified a few items that were representative of the full range of items mentioned that were frequently described by the groups of team members and organizational roles involved. These items reflect the behavior of others, by reporting information on the "normal" way to behave within the team. Perceptions of others' behavior may be particularly influential for motivating behavior among team members. Indeed, several researchers show that the social influence of peers is the most important predictor of behavior (Kandel, 1980; Oetting and Beauvais, 1986, 1987). Social learning theory (e.g., Bandura, 1977) informs us that this effect is due to imitation of the behaviors of those who have lived the environment before them since "people guide their actions by prior notions rather than by relying on outcomes to tell them what they must do" (Bandura, 1977, p. 35). Thus, all learning encompassed by the team may be based on watching others' behaviors and their results (Bandura, 1986; Rosenthal and Zimmerman, 1978).

The following items represent perceptions of organizational phenomena and implementation of internal policies, as well as clear normative statements. These data were collected from interviews with team members engaged in completing various assignments including development of component-testing programs, development of systems-level integration projects, design of engineering audit procedures, and failure analyzes.

I can see no innovation within my team. We don't produce any ideas. [Team member]

They focus a lot on the features they are implementing and not too much on learning and expending their competence. [Team member]

It is acceptable to spend time in learning, stop working, but no one is doing it (at least it happens in a very limited way). [Team member]

Teams don't spend time on digging the product, people are just making features. [Team member]

To assess the relationship between description norms and the individual intention to innovate and to devote time to learning, the following items were sampled to report on the individual intention to embrace learning and innovation activity. These results provide strong support for the relationship among the descriptive norms for creativity and group innovation.

Hence, I feel there is not that much space or possibilities for innovation, because you have to know a concept really good to understand its limitation. If you are new to an area, then you cannot see the limitations. To know where you want to go, you have first to realize where you have been. [Team member]

I think as we work, it's hard to have innovation opportunities. [Team member]

I don't think I have thought about innovation but I think at least that we have a little bit more freedom to do innovation now, if the team find something it would like to do, for small improvements, we can just do them without asking. For bigger improvements it still has to be agreed as before by others, there has to be discussion and decision by manager and project leader, as we did in the previous way of working. [Team member].

In line with Astrom and Rise (2001), who show that group norms influence adult intentions only among those who identify strongly with the salient reference group, the strong individual identification with team concepts and goals seems to favor the influence of group norms on team members' intentions.

We are usually under a lot of stress to handle tasks. Thus, we have never had time to develop our competence as individuals. [Team member].

I think it is tough, all people work on features and features, and it is hard to come up with innovation. We don't have time to be innovative; previously people had time especially if you were responsible for one or two block. Pressure about the deadline is the barrier to innovation. [Team member]

Hence, we can stipulate the following:

Research Proposition 1: *The team's descriptive norms for creativity and group innovation are positively related to the intention to trigger innovative initiatives inside the team.*

Since behavior may also be guided by a desire to do the "right" thing, we need to know more about the influence of injunctive norms on individual intention. The following extracts show the underlying effects of injunctive norms on descriptive norms.

I don't think we have managed to incorporate innovation in our way of working yet. There is lot of talk about that, a lot of focus on that. We are trying to find a way that allows the teams to be able to innovate and work on improvements and new ideas and so on. I don't think we are mature enough, we have to learn and figure out how to do, teams don't have instructions to have innovation incorporated in their way of working. It's a little bit early I think, but it's something that we really try to address. [Line manager]

The systems we work with are very complex, it takes a lot of time to learn new areas. A team member competent in one area may find themselves taken up with work in that area, meaning they have no time to learn other areas and no time to teach their area to others. If the company wants people to gain new competence this needs to be planned, time needs to be set aside for mentoring, otherwise it won't happen in any big amount. [Team member]

I think you have to do innovation in everything you do. It's hard to say that we should work 30% with innovation, it should be talked that we do it on daily bases, it could small things or the way of working, in some cases it could be larger impact, but it's very hard to say what innovation is. [Team member]

We learn only what it is needed for completing the task. [Team member]

So they are trying to build the competence, at least based on what they want to understand to be able to do the work for this feature. During this time, they study the feature, they pick some user stories to be able to implement them. If they understand the whole things, they don't need to have this spike to do some investigation. But if they don't know, for instance, about ROAM, the RNC part of an impact, they do want to have some competence build up to be able to do the next user story, because they are preparing to understand what to do in the next user stories. So if the team doesn't have that competence, then they plan to have competence build up, at least one sprint before the actual work should be done. [Team leader]

Hence, we stipulate the following:

Research Proposition 2: *Descriptive norms about group innovation are positively related to individual intentions within the team and the magnitude of this association increases as injunctive norms increase*

However, Ajzen and Fishbein (1980) suggest that the threat of social sanction is not considered necessary for norms to influence individual behavior. Norms are indicated as enacting influence because individuals use important referents to guide their actions (Ajzen and Fishbein, 1980). Thus, from the perspective of social norms, team members may perform an action because they think that relevant others expect them to do so (subjective norms), or because failure to do so could result in social sanctions (injunctive norms). The common element in these types of influences is that behavior is driven by expectations about others' beliefs. Individuals often have clear knowledge about what others want them to do, and consequently they can elaborate their perception about injunctive norms using experience of others' reactions to their behaviors.

The daily stand-up meetings used in the Scrum methodology can act as a relevant enforcing mechanism for the establishment of social norms for several reasons. First, in these stand-up meetings, team members and relevant team stakeholder and managers are invited to attend, although team stakeholder and managers can only listen, and are not allowed to speak. During the meetings, team members describe the results achieved the previous day, set out plans for the current day including potential obstacles, which provide a plan and guidance for the whole team. The presence of stakeholders and managers legitimizes the team's work and gives team members the perception that they are acting in response to current organization goals.

However, team members' acknowledgment of legitimacy reflect individuals' beliefs that important referents recognize a correspondence between the team's behavior and "and [their] shared (or assumedly shared) beliefs" (Suchman, 1995, p. 574)

Hence we stipulate the following:

Research Proposition 3: *Within the Agile Scrum routines of daily standup, descriptive and injunctive norms are enacted having as important referents the team's manager and stakeholders*

Research Proposition 4: *The magnitude of the relationship between descriptive norms related to group innovation and behavioral intention grows as outcome expectations become stronger.*

Additionally, making the team's activities and planning public known to managers and stakeholders, constitutes an important mechanism to improve individual identification with the organization. Dutton et al. (1994) suggest that the visibility of the affiliation with an organization is a moderating factor in the relationship between attractiveness of a perceived organizational identity and organizational identification, since this visibility underlines individual affiliation within the organization. On the other hand, the visibility of team's participation in the realization of stakeholders' objectives, generates an enhanced cognitive elaboration of the organizational social identity of the stakeholders.

Elaboration of the team's social identity favors and becomes the prerequisite for the formation and the enactment of peer control which is a form of normative control (injunctive) enacted by peers. In fact, there is a robust link between the microtechnique of discipline and employees' identification with the organization. In line with this, Barker and Cheney (1994: 30) argue that disciplinary mechanisms are more powerful when *"they are grounded in highly motivating values that appeal to the organization's actors."* Knoke and Wood (1981) provide similar evidence that an employee's commitment can be best understood by narrowing the focus to the extent to which he or she internalizes organizational norms and values. A high level of team identification allows for higher norm consensus which is helpful in clarification of what the context demands. Expectations about team members' behaviors are made more explicit, and their salience increases. The negative consequences of not engaging in productive team work acquire more impacts by the team members. This process prevents any autonomous decisions about putting effort into the team task, thereby eliminating any motivational barriers that could lead team members not to participate in productive and collaborative team work (Cooper and Withey, 2009).

In addition, as Foucault (1977) notes, when team members identify so strongly with organizational values, they do not have the critical distance necessary to judge the fairness of the microtechniques they have generated collectively or in which they have been involved. Specifically, team members who identify strongly with their teams should feel better about themselves when they accomplish identity-relevant norms compared to when they violate these norms. On the other hand, individuals with no identification with the group will exhibit emotional responses to conformity versus violation (Christensen et al., 2004).

Hence, injunctive norms, having a moral aspect, and define what people should do, acting as self-standards that determine whom the individual would like to be or whom they ought to be (Higgins, 1987; Moretti and Higgins, 1999; Schwartz, 1977; Schwartz and Fleishman, 1978).

Hence we stipulate the following:

Research Proposition 5: *Greater group identification increases the use of team injunctive norms as behavioral standards for group members.*

Consistent with our discussion, we stipulate the following:

Research Proposition 6: *Descriptive norms about group innovation are positively related to individual intentions inside the team and the magnitude of this association increases as group identification increases.*

3.6   INFLUENCE OF TEAM INJUNCTIVE NORMS

Other relevant aspects for predicting individual intentions are the individual's perceived degree of control over performed behavior (perceived behavioral control, e.g., "Engaging in a binge drinking session is entirely under/

outside my control" (Rivis and Sheeran, 2003, p. 218), and people's evaluations of the consequences of this behavior or their attitudes (e.g., "For me, engaging in a binge drinking session would be wise/foolish," Rivis and Sheeran, 2003, p. 219). The perceived behavioral control refers to the perceived ease or difficulty of performing the behavior and is assumed to reflect both past experience and anticipated impediments and obstacles.

This view of perceived behavioral control is aligned mostly with Bandura's (1977, 1982) concept of perceived self-efficacy which "is concerned with judgments of how well one can execute courses of action required to deal with prospective situations" (Bandura, 1982, p. 122). Much of the current knowledge about the impact of perceived behavioral control derives from the systematic research program of Bandura and his associates (e.g., Bandura et al., 1977; Bandura et al., 1980). Their research reveals that people's behavior is strongly affected by their confidence in their ability to perform it (i.e., by perceived behavioral control). In this context, the theory of planned behavior indicates three conceptually independent antecedents to individual intention. The first is attitude toward the behavior which as already mentioned, is related to the extent to which the individual has a favorable or unfavorable evaluation of the behavior in question. The second predictor is the subjective norm which is the perceived social pressure to enact or not to enact the behavior. The third determinant is the degree of perceived behavioral control. According to the theory of planned behavior, the more positive people's attitudes and subjective norms, and the greater their perceived behavioral control regarding a behavior, the more likely they will intend to perform that behavior. Similarly, the stronger people's intentions, the more likely they will perform the behavior.

The following quotes were extracted from the interviews to give evidence of this.

People Beliefs About Innovation
Learning is not as important as developing and delivering features so we don't spend time on learning. [Team member]

Group Subjective Norms
We are usually under a lot of stress to handle tasks. Thus, we have never had time to develop our competence as individuals. [Team member]

Perceived Behavioral Control

Earlier we worked in a certain area, but now our features strike on every subsystem, and we don't have enough knowledge about it so it's difficult. [Team member]

Thus, in line with the literature, team members' beliefs about the relevance of the innovative behavior and their individual self-efficacy are positively related to team injunctive group norms and we stipulate the following:

Research Proposition 7: *Perceived behavioral control towards an innovative activity mediates the relationship between the attitude to the innovative activity and the injunctive norms to perform (or not) that innovative activity and the individual intention to embrace it.*

Pressure to "get the job done" is common within Agile teams. It is related to the subjective social norm and affects the individual's potential to gain approval or suffer sanction from significant others such as the Agile team's relevant stakeholders as product owner and line manager, for engaging in a behavior. Below are reported relevant quotations from team members.

Some people are proactive about attending learning days and courses, others are less so but when there is on, and we feel that we are getting delayed attendance at learning days is reduced. We need to plan properly time for learning. [Product Owner]

They struggled with that all the time because they're focused on delivering features all the time but they also see they need to help each other, the testers need to help with design as well and vice-versa but it's a challenge for them. I do have to keep reminding them during the sprint planning. They tend as default to get finished the feature. [High level manager]

As reported in Annosi, Magnusson, Martini and Appio (2015), perceived time pressure is influenced by: (i) team's attitude to revealing the importance of project tasks to team members; (ii) the characteristics of specific Agile routines imposing constraints and rules on people's actions as in the implementation of boundary control systems (Simons, 1991, 1994); (iii) concertive control from peers enacting pressure to get the job done; and 4) implementation of diagnostic controls (Simons 1991, 1994) in the form of goals and feedback loops.

Some extracts related to these constructs are reported in the following subsections.

Team Members' Attitude

My view about the main problem is that we need to be more efficient to produce more and then to be able to innovate. Becoming more efficient is a condition to have innovation in place, [...] it is hard to get things into the product because the demand is there but the capability was low. [High level manager]

Our team learning opportunity is not much, we have been working with two features at the same time, we had pressure to deliver those features and we don't have much time to dedicate to learning. It is not the priority as developing and delivering features so we don't spend time on learning. [Team member]

Boundary Control Systems

In Agile we are in quite regular mode, working in a regular and constant time box, which is called sprint, three weeks long. At the beginning of each sprint we have half day meeting called sprint planning, where the Agile team members are looking at the sprint backlog. As team, we know our capacity and according to our estimation of it, we take items in the product backlog, pulling out user stories. Among the user stories we have also some bonus. It deals with normal work as a normal user story, but differently from it, it represents something for which team does not take a specific commitment to implement by the end of the sprint [...] It aims to full use the team's capacity if some spare time occurs. [Scrum master]

Diagnostic Control Systems

I get updated info through several ways: weekly reports about the progress and then I have to report their progress to other forum like the release project." [Product owner]

Normally the teams have, according to the Scrum, meetings every day in the morning in which they discuss about the progresses, we try to be present to this meeting to listen what it is going on. [Line manager]

Concertive Control

Now we are working with new products and we have to learn how they work—at least so much that we can see where and how to do the implementations. But to really understand the product (to be able to make improvements) that takes time. Before you have knowledge about the product, now you even don't know if you can propose/do any improvements— spending time on investigation without any outcome isn't so popular I guess... Teams don't spend time on digging the product, people are just making features. [Team member]

Specifically, team attitudes mirror the values transmitted through line management together with their social environment and represent the basic values which drive team intentions. In Agile, team members consider the priority to be the development of features not innovation and learning. As a result, they prioritize project deadlines which they feel adds pressure, and do not implement strategies to foster learning. Identification with a social group may increase the importance of an attitude if the team's rights are considered to be a stake (Key, 1961; Modigliani and Gamson, 1979).

Hence we stipulate the following:

Research Proposition 8: *Team members' attitudes about the importance of group innovation are positively related to injunctive norms about group innovation.*

Research Proposition 9: *Team members' attitude to the importance of group innovation mediates the relationship between group identification and injunctive norms about group innovation.*

In an Agile context, the effects of boundary control systems, defined as the formal systems used by top management to establish obligatory limits and rules (Simons, 1994), are to impose complex Agile routines/ceremonies that apply to team members. Among these, product backlog seems to limit the team's freedom to allocate time to anything not clearly included in the specific time-period (or sprint). The following quotes are illustrative:

[It is] very difficult to get time for competence development, very tight time schedule [Team member].

Transparency of the organization means that even small prioritization issues are quickly escalated. There are no buffers since product management keeps the teams 100% busy. This means that small additional tasks require the involvement of product management for decisions. [Team member]

Diagnostic control systems are defined as formal feedback systems used to monitor team outcomes and correct deviations from preset performance standards (Simons, 1994). They are represented by the short feedback loops in the Agile framework. Examples of feedbacks include daily standup meetings, continuous integration activities, three-weekly demo and retrospective, frequent meetings with product owners to track team progress, and information radiators to constantly monitor team competence. The presence of these short feedback loops ensures a correct focus and allocation of time to team activities but generates stress and pressure among team members. Consistent with this one informant told us:

Concerning the stress you feel, in Agile the way of working is stressful. Management wants us to deliver code every day for testing, to find out if new code breaks legacy functionality. But the delivery process is not good enough. When people make mistakes, you have to roll back and many people are waiting for you. This way of working is not so effective. It should be modified somehow. [Team member]

Barker (1993) defines concertive control systems for self-regulating teams as normative controls that become restrictive for individual team members, creating high levels of stress. The effect of concertive control is that people feel they are being watched and their contribution to team goals checked up on. They feel unable to divert to activities not strictly related to those of other team members and the project. There is implicit pressure to finish the task as soon as possible in order to start on the next one. The following statement highlights this situation:

You have this tight control on what you are doing. As soon as you are ready, you go to the board and take a new task. So there is pressure to go through this kind of work packages as quickly as possible. And there is also "peer" pressure—if you are in a team, everyone knows what everyone else is doing. [Team member]

In order to clarify the impact and the relevance of these constructs on the team's injunctive norms, we need to introduce the concepts of goal desirability and goal feasibility as norms concerned with the desirability of the means and goals. Goal desirability and goal feasibility are two constructs to explain goal-directed behavior. They have been described as key concepts (e.g., Atkinson, 1964, Liberman and Trope, 1998; Gollwitzer, 1990). They have been related to the concepts of desire and belief in the philosophy of action (Mele, 1997), and goal desire in turn has been defined as "the valence of an action's end state, whereas belief regards the ease or difficulty of reaching the end state" (Liberman and Trope, 1998, p.7).

Specifically, goal desire indicates desire for a behavior, while goal perceived feasibility is perceived as behavioral control (Perugini et al., 2000). Hence, an increase or decrease in the desire for a goal should lead to an increase or decrease in the desire for the behavior functionally tied to the goal. At the same time, an increase in perceived goal feasibility should produce an increase in perceived behavioral control and the influence of perceived goal feasibility on perceived behavioral control should very high given the functional link between goals and behaviors (Perugini and Conner, 2000). Thus, as behaviors are selected based on their usefulness for achieving a goal, a certain level of perceived easiness of the goal should induce a choice of behaviors perceived to be at a corresponding level of feasibility and personal control (Perugini and Conner, 2000). According to Perugini and Conner (2000) the motivation and the volition to perform a given behavior is usually a function of both distal (e.g., the desired goal) and proximal variables (e.g., perceived control over a given behavior). Based on the above, we can assume that collective injunctive norms in teams are determined by the diagnostic controls, contributing to the goal desirability and limited by the boundary control related to the implementation of Agile methodologies combined with the interpersonal pressure imposed by the concertive control which simultaneously influences the formation of perceived control. Boundary and concertive controls contribute to the perception of goal feasibility within the team and act to limit team members' actions.

Hence we stipulate the following:

Research Proposition 10: *Injunctive norms about group innovation in self-managing teams are determined by the implementation of diagnostic controls, which contribute to the desire for innovation action by imposing continuous monitoring on the team's work*

Research Proposition 11: *Injunctive norms are influenced by the team's perception of feasibility of the innovation activity, which is determined by the related concertive control and boundary controls defining* *the constraints on team's actions and impacting the perceived behavioral control of team members.*

3.7 CONCLUDING DISCUSSION

The objective of the study described in this chapter was to identify the social factors involved in influence on team's collective intention to undertake learning and innovation activity. Our findings show that team members' attitudes and team's subjective norms (descriptive and injunctive) significantly influence the behavioral intention to take innovative action. Additionally, in line with Terry and Hogg (1996) for the I-intention, we proposed that group identity reinforces the power of group norms (descriptive and injunctive) that influence the we-intention. We discussed the relationships clarifying how identity-relevance of the team and different types of norms interact to predict team members' behaviors. We also proposed a qualitative evaluation of the strength of the relationship between descriptive norms and group intentions and highlighted possible relevant moderators. Moreover, we identified the proximal determinants of injunctive norms by looking at the way the team's work is organized and the social context in which the team operates.

Team's injunctive and descriptive norms about group innovation act help to predict the we-intention to innovate. These concepts were modeled together to represent team norms and to allow for a holistic view of possible managerial interventions. This discussion revealed other social influences. For example, we found outcome expectations to be important resources to better sustain the we-intention to innovate. Studies by Cialdini et al. (1990) and Kallgren et al. (2000) demonstrates the influence of moderating factors such as outcome expectation, group identity, and injunctive norms, on the effect of descriptive norms on behaviors.

We extended these results to the case of self-managing teams operating in a permeable social environment transmitting teams the perception of managerial expectations building on the implementation of Agile routines. The perception of managerial expectations induces beliefs that enacting a particular behavior will provide the desired benefits (Bandura, 1986). More specifically, outcome expectations can be considered to be the result of the individual's mental calculus about the benefits of embracing certain actions and the associated costs (Rogers, 1975; Rosenstock, 1974). They can be thought of as the beliefs that drive behaviors (Aizen and Fishbein, 1980), and can treated as contributing to individual attitudes to a behavior. On the other hand, we found team members' attitudes have an important impact on the perceived behavioral control of team members which in turn, influences the team's injunctive norms related to group innovation.

We found a prevalence of the impact of group identification for influencing the effects of both descriptive and injunctive norms on team behaviors. This is in line with Christensen et al., (2004) who suggest that identity relevance in the case of both norms is a crucial factor for predicting whether norms are adopted as standards against which individuals can assess their behavior. Research on nominal groups underlines that identification plays a crucial role in an in-group member's capacity to influence peers within the group (Wilder, 1990). Thus, in the absence of identification, there is no way for the group identity to affect individuals' behavioral choices. However, if the individual perceives that the prevalence of a behavior among his or her reference group is common and if the individual's identification with the group is strong, the group member will be more likely to engage in that same behavior (Rimal and Real, 2005). On the contrary, if group members experience strong affinity with the group, and at the same time believe that a behavior is not acceptable to the other group members, then they will be less likely to engage in this less acceptable behavior. Similar to outcomes expectations, group identity is socially constructed and Annosi et al. (2015) highlight the role of organizational entities, managers and team stakeholders, their dynamic relationships and some specific team routines produce the mechanisms at the base of organization and identity formation. This result has a number of implications for managerial practice; interventions should be aimed at reducing the prevalence of efficiency behaviors and the opportunity costs of innovation and learning behaviors.

Regarding the exchange and inculcation of injunctive norms, we propose that this could be accomplished in multiple and enforcing ways which differ in their level of intentionality. Injunctive norms are created through a system of goals and feedback controls applied to a team's work with the purpose of shaping goal desirability. Also, norms are deliberately transmitted through active instructions and rituals (Allison, 1992;

Lumsden, 1988) deriving from the boundary control systems implemented with the adoption of specific Agile routines. Additionally, norms can be transmitted more passively through nonverbal behaviors (Allison, 1992; Lumsden, 1988) emanating from the enactment of interpersonal pressure exercised by peers inside the teams. This is enabled by communication whose critical role is highlighted in Latané's (1996) and Latané et al.'s (1994) dynamic social impact theory. Nu adopting the common components of social impact theory (Latané, 1981), the strength of the source's personal influence, the physical proximity of the target to the source, and the number of sources can be take into account.

Our proposal of norms transmission requires to be tested empirically; however, this chapter provides a description of the process through which organizational and team norms are spread and may vary.

KEYWORDS

- **controls**
- **innovation**
- **norms**
- **self-managing teams**

REFERENCES

Aalbers, H. L., Dolfsma, W., Koppius, O. Individual connectedness in innovation networks: On the role of individual motivation. *Research Policy*, 2013, 42(3), 624–634.

Aarts, H., Dijksterhuis, A. The silence of the library: environment, situational norm, and social behavior. *Journal of Personality and Social Psychology*, 2003, 84(1), 18–28.

Abrahamsson, P., Conboy, K., Wang, X. 'Lots done, more to do': the current state of Agile systems development research. *European Journal of Information Systems*, 2009, 18, 281–284.

Aizen, I., Fishbein, M. *Understanding Attitudes and Predicting Social Behavior.* Prentice-Hall. Englewood Cliffs, NJ, 1980.

Allison, P. D. The cultural evolution of beneficent norms. *Social Forces*, 1992, 71(2), 279–301.

Amabile, T. M. A model of creativity and innovation in organizations. *Research in Orga-nizational Behavior*, In: B. M. Staw & L. L. Cummings (Eds.), Greenwich, CT: JAI Press, 1988, 10, 123–167.

Amabile, T. M. *Creativity in Context*. Boulder, CO: Westview, 1996.

Amabile, T. M. *The Social Psychology of Creativity*. New York: Springer, 1983.

Ancona, D. G., Caldwell, D. F. Bridging the boundary: External activity and performance in organizational teams. *Administrative Science Quarterly*, 1992, 634–665.

Anderson, N. R., West, M. A. Measuring climate for work group innovation: Development and validation of the team climate inventory. *Journal of Organizational Behavior*. 1998, 19(3), 235–258.

Annosi, M. C., Foss, N. J., Magnusson, M., Brunetta, F. *The Interplay Between the Pre-existing Managerial Control Systems and Stakeholder's Networks in Self-Managed Team's Identities* in EGOS 2015 Conference, 2015.

Annosi, M.C., Magnusson, M., Martini, A., Appio, F. P. Social conduct, learning and inno-vation: an abductive study of the dark side of agile software development. *Creativity and Innovation Management*, early view. 2016.

Argote, L. Agreement about norms and work-unit effectiveness: Evidence from the field. Basic and *Applied Social Psychology*, 1989, 10(2), 131–140.

Argyris, C. *Knowledge for Action: A Guide to Overcoming Barriers to Organizational Change*. Jossey-Bass Inc. Publishers: San Francisco, CA, 1993.

Ashforth, B. E., Mael, F. Social identity theory and the organization. *Academy of Manage-ment Review*, 1989, 14(1), 20–39.

Astrom, A. N., Rise, J. Young adults' intention to eat healthy food: Extending the theory of planned behavior. *Psychology and Health*, 2001, 16(2), 223–237.

Atkinson, J. W. *An Introduction to Motivation*. Princeton, NJ: Nostrand Co., 1964.

Baer, M., Leenders, R. T. A., Oldham, G. R., Vadera, A. K. Win or lose the battle for cre-ativity: The power and perils of intergroup competition. *Academy of Management Journal*, 2010, 53(4), 827–845.

Bagozzi, R. P., Dholakia, U. M. Intentional social action in virtual communities. *Journal of Interactive Marketing*, 2002, 16(2), 2–21.

Bagozzi, R. P., Lee, K. H. Multiple routes for social influence: The role of compliance, internalization, and social identity. *Social Psychology Quarterly*, 2002, 226–247.

Bandura, A. Self-efficacy mechanism in human agency. *American Psychologist*, 1982, 37(2), 122.

Bandura, A. *Social Foundations of Thought and Action: A Social Cognitive Theory*. Pren-tice-Hall, Inc., 1986.

Bandura, A. *Social Learning Theory*. Englewood Cliffs, NJ: Prentice Hall, 1977.

Bandura, A., Adams, N. E., Beyer, J. Cognitive processes mediating behavioral change. *Journal of Personality and Social Psychology*, 1977, 35(3), 125.

Bandura, A., Adams, N. E., Hardy, A. B., Howells, G. N. Tests of the generality of self-efficacy theory. *Cognitive Therapy and Research*, 1980, 4(1), 39–66.

Barker, J. R. Tightening the iron cage: Concertive control in self-managing teams. *Admin-istrative Science Quarterly*, 1993, 408–437.

Barker, J. R., Cheney, G. The concept and the practices of discipline in contemporary orga-nizational life. *Communications Monographs*, 1994, 61(1), 19–43.

Baskerville, R. L. Artful Planning. *European Journal of Information Systems*, 2006, 15(2), 113–115.

Becker, T. E., Billings, R. S., Eveleth, D. M., Gilbert, N. L. Foci and bases of employee commitment: Implications for job performance. *Academy of Management Journal*, 1996, 39(2), 464–482.

Beedle, M., Devos, M., Sharon, Y., Schwaber, K., Sutherland, J. Scrum: a pattern language for hyperproductive software development. In: *Pattern Languages of Program Design*, N. Harrison (Ed.), Boston: Addison-Wesley, 1999, pp. 637–651.

Bishop, J. W., Dow Scott, K. An examination of organizational and team commitment in a self-directed team environment. *Journal of Applied Psychology*, 2000, 85(3), 439.

Boehm, B. W., Turner, R. *Balancing Agility and Discipline: A Guide for the Perplexed.* Boston: Addison-Wesley, 2004.

Bratman, M. E. Responsibility and planning. *The Journal of Ethics*, 1997, 1(1), 27–43.

Burningham, C., West, M. A. Individual, climate, and group interaction processes as predictors of work team innovation. *Small Group Research*, 1995, 26(1), 106–117.

Celani, A., Tasa, K., Schat, A. C. H. An examination of collectivistic group norms in relation to collective efficacy and team performance. *Academy Management Annual Meeting, Montreal*, 2010.

Chen, G., Gocus, C. I. *Motivation in and of Teams: A Multilevel Perspective.* In: R. Kanfer, G. Chen, & R. D. Pritchard (Eds.), Work Motivation: Past, Present, and Future. New York, NY: Routledge Academic, 2008, pp. 285–317.

Chen, G., Kanfer, R. Toward a systems theory of motivated behavior in work teams. *Research in Organizational Behavior,* 2006, 27, 223–267.

Christensen, P. N., Rothgerber, H., Wood, W., Matz, D. C. Social norms and identity relevance: A motivational approach to normative behavior. *Personality and Social Psychology Bulletin*, 2004, 30(10), 1295–1309.

Cialdini, R. B. Altruism or egoism? That is (still) the question. *Psychological Inquiry*, 1991, 2(2), 124–126.

Cialdini, R. B. *Influence: Science and Practice* (2nd ed.). Glenview, IL: Scott, Foresman, 1988.

Cialdini, R. B. *Influence: The Psychology of Persuasion.* New York: Morrow, 1993.

Cialdini, R. B., Kallgren, C. A., Reno, R. R. A focus theory of normative conduct: A theoretical refinement and reevaluation of the role of norms in human behavior. *Advances in Experimental Social Psychology*, 1991, 24(20), 1–243.

Cialdini, R. B., Reno, R. R., Kallgren, C. A. A focus theory of normative conduct: recycling the concept of norms to reduce littering in public places. *Journal of personality and Social Psychology*, 1990, 58(6), 1015–1026.

Cialdini, R. B., Trost, M. R. Social influence: Social norms, conformity and compliance, 1998.

Coad, P., De Luca, J., Lefebre, E. Java Modeling in Color, Englewood Cliffs, NJ: Prentice Hall, 1999.

Cockburn A, Highsmith, J. Agile software development: the people factor. *Computer* 2001, 34(11), 131–133.

Cockburn, A. *Agile Software Development: The Cooperative Game.* Boston: Addison-Wesley, 2007.

Collyer, S., Warren, C., Hemsley, B., and Stevens, C. Aim, fire, aim—Project planning styles in dynamic environments. *Project Management Journal*, 2010, 41(4), 108–121.

Conboy, K. Agility from first principles: reconstructing the concept of agility in information systems development. *Information Systems Research*, 2009, 20(3), 329–354.

Cooper, W. H., Withey, M. J. The strong situation hypothesis. *Personality and Social Psychology Review*, 2009, 13(1), 62–72.

Darley, J. M., Latané, B. Norms and normative behavior: Field studies of social interdependence. *Altruism and Helping Behavior*, 1970, 83–102.

De Jong, B. A., Bijlsma-Frankema, K. M., Cardinal, L. B. Stronger Than the Sum of Its Parts? The Performance Implications of Peer Control Combinations in Teams. *Organization Science* 2014, 25(6), 1703–1721.

Deutsch, M., Gerard, H. B. A study of normative and informational social influences upon individual judgment. *The Journal of Abnormal and Social Psychology*, 1955, 51(3), 629.

Dingsøyr, T., Nerur, S., Balikepally, V., Moe, N. E. A decade of agile methodologies: towards explaining agile software development. *Journal of Systems and Software*, 2012, 85(6), 1213–1221.

Doherty, A., Patterson, M., Van Bussel, M. What do we expect? An examination of perceived committee norms in nonprofit sport organizations. *Sport Management Review*. 2004, 7(2), 109–132.

Drach-Zahavy, A., Somech. A. Understanding team innovation: The role of team processes and structures. *Group Dynamics: Theory, Research, and Practice*, 2001, 5(2) 111–123.

Drucker, P. F. *Innovation and Entrepreneurship.* Newbridge: Newbridge Communications, 1985.

Dutton, J. E., Dukerich, J. M., Harquail, C. V. Organizational images and member identification. *Administrative Science Quarterly*, 1994, 239–263.

Dweck, C. S. Self-theories: *Their Role in Motivation, Personality, and Development.* Hove: Psychology Press, 2000.

Dweck, C. S., Sorich, L. A. *Mastery-Oriented Thinking.* Coping: The psychology of what works. New York: Oxford University Press, 1999.

Dweck, C., Molden, D. C. Self theories. In *Handbook of Competence and Motivation*, Elliott, J. A., Dweck, C. (eds.). London: The Guilford Press, 2005, 122–140.

Dybå, T., Dingsøyr, T. Empirical studies of Agile software development: A systematic review. *Information and Software Technology*, 2008, 50(9), 833–859.

Ehrhart, M. G., Naumann, S. E. Organizational citizenship behavior in work groups: a group norms approach. *Journal of Applied Psychology,* 2004, 89(6), 960–974.

Elliot, A. J., McGregor, H. A. A 2×2 achievement goal framework. *Journal of Personality and Social Psychology,* 2001, 80(3), 501.

Erickson, J., Lyytinen, K., Siau, K. Agile modeling, agile software development, and extreme programming. *Journal of Database Management*, 2005, 16(4), 88–100.

Feldman, D. C. The development and enforcement of group norms. *Academy of Management Review*, 1984, 9(1), 47–53.

Flynn, F. J., Chatman, J. A. "What's the norm here?" Social categorization as a basis for group norm development. In *Research on Managing Groups and Teams*. Polzer, J., ed. Stanford, CA: JAI Press, 2003, 135–160.

Foucault, M. *Discipline and Punish: The Birth of the Prison*. Vintage Books, 1977.

Fruhling, A., De Vreede, G.-J. Field experiences with eXtreme programming: developing an emergency response system. *Journal of Management Information Systems*, 2006, 22(4), 39–68.

Gibbs, J. P. Norms: The problem of definition and classification. *American Journal of Sociology*, 1965, 60(5), 586–594.

Gollwitzer, P. M. Action phases and mind-sets. *Handbook of Motivation and Cognition: Foundations of Social Behavior*, 1990, 2, 53–92.

Hackman, J. R. *Group Influences on Individuals in Organizations*. Consulting Psychologists Press, 1992.

Hargadon, A., Sutton, R. I. Technology brokering and innovation in a product development firm. *Administrative Science Quarterly* 1997, 42(4), 716–749.

Harrison, S. H., Rouse, E. D. Let's dance! Elastic coordination in creative group work: A qualitative study of modern dancers. *Academy of Management Journal*, 2014, 57(5), 1256–1283.

Henderson-Sellers, B., Serour, M. K., Creating a dual-agility method: the value of method engineering. *Journal of Database Management* 2005, 16, 1–23.

Herscovitch, L., Meyer, J. P. Commitment to organizational change: extension of a three-component model. *Journal of Applied Psychology*, 2002, 87(3), 474–487.

Higgins, E. T. Self-discrepancy theory: A theory relating self and affect. *Psychological Review*, 1987, 94, 319–340.

Highsmith, J. A. *Agile Software Development Ecosystems (Vol. 13)*. Addison-Wesley Professional, 2002.

Highsmith, J. *Agile Project Management*, Boston: Addison-Wesley, 2004.

Highsmith, J., Cockburn, A., Agile software development. 1. The business of innovation. IEEE Computer 2001, 34, 120–127.

Hirokawa, R. Y. The Role of Communication in Group Decision-Making Efficacy A Task-Contingency Perspective. *Small Group Research*, 1990, 21(2), 190–204.

Hirst, G., Van Knippenberg, D., Zhou, J. A cross-level perspective on employee creativity: Goal orientation, team learning behavior, and individual creativity. *Academy of Management Journal*, 2009, 52(2), 280–293.

Hoegl, M., Gemuenden, H. G. Teamwork quality and the success of innovative projects: A theoretical concept and empirical evidence. *Organization Science*. 2001, 12(4), 435–449.

Hülsheger, U. R., Anderson, N., Salgado, J. F. Team-Level Predictors of Innovation at Work: A Comprehensive Meta-Analysis Spanning Three Decades of Research. *Journal of Applied Psychology*, 2009, 94(5), 1128–1145.

Imai, K., Nonaka, I., Takeuchi, H. *Managing the New Product Development Process: How Japanese Companies Learn and Unlearn*. Division of Research, Harvard Business School, 1984.

Jackson, J. A conceptual and measurement model for norms and roles. *Pacific Sociology Review* 1966, 9(1), 35–47.

Jasso, G., Opp, K. D. Probing the character of norms: A factorial survey analysis of the norms of political action. *American: Review of Sociology*. 1997, 62(6), 947–964.

Kallgren, C. A., Reno, R. R., Cialdini, R. B. A focus theory of normative conduct: When norms do and do not affect behavior. *Personality and Social Psychology Bulletin*, 2000, 26(8), 1002–1012.

Kandel, D. B. Drug and drinking behavior among youth. *Annual Review of Sociology*, 1980, 235–285.

Kerr, N. L. Norms in social dilemmas. In: S*ocial Dilemmas: Perspectives on Individuals and Groups*. D. Schroeder (Ed.), Westport, CT: Praeger, 1995, pp. 31–48.

Key, V. O. *Public Opinion and American Democracy*. New York: Knopf, 1961.

Klein, H. J., Wesson, M. J., Hollenbeck, J. R., Wright, P. M., DeShon, R. P. The assessment of goal commitment: A measurement model meta-analysis. *Organizational Behavior and Human Decision Processes,* 2001, 85(1), 32–55.

Knoke, D., Wood, J. R. *Organized for action: Commitment in voluntary associations*. Rutgers University Press, 1981.

Larman, C. *Agile and Iterative Development: A Manager's Guide*. Boston: Addison-Wesley, 2004.

Larson, J. R., Christensen, C. Groups as problem-solving units: Toward a new meaning of social cognition. *British Journal of Social Psychology*, 1993, 32(1), 5–30.

Latané, B. Dynamic social impact: The creation of culture by communication. *Journal of Communication*, 1996, 46, 13–25.

Latané, B. The psychology of social impact. *American Psychologist*, 1981, 36(4), 343–356.

Latané, B., Nowak, A., Liu, J. H. Measuring emergent social phenomena: Dynamism, polarization, and clustering as order parameters of social systems. *Behavioral Science*, 1994, 39(1), 1–24.

Liberman, N., Trope, Y. The role of feasibility and desirability considerations in near and distant future decisions: a test of temporal construal theory. *Journal of Personality and Social Psychology*, 1998, 75(1), 5–18.

Lindvall, M., Basili, V., Boehm, B., Costa, P., Dangle, K., Shull, F., Tesoriero, R., Zelkowitz, M. Empirical findings in Agile methods. *Proceedings of the XP/Agile University 2002; Second XP Universe and First Agile Universe Conference*, Chicago: Springer-Verlag, 2002.

Locke, E. A., Latham, G. P. *A Theory of Goal Setting and Task Performance*. Prentice-Hall, Inc., 1990.

Loughry, M. L., Tosi, H. L. Performance implications of peer monitoring. *Organization Science*. 2008, 19(6), 876–890.

Lumsden, C. J. Psychological development: Epigenetic rules and gene-culture coevolution. In *Sociobiological Perspectives on Human Development*. Springer New York, 1988, pp. 234–267.

Lyytinen, K., Rose, G. M. Information System Development Agility as Organizational Learning, *European Journal of Information Systems* 2006, 15(2), 183–199.

MacNeil, M. K., Sherif, M. Norm change over subject generations as a function of arbitrariness of prescribed norms. *Journal of Personality and Social Psychology*, 1976, 34(5), 762.

Maier, N. R., Solem, A. R. Improving Solutions By Turning Choice Situations Into Problems. *Personnel Psychology*, 1962, 15(2), 151–157.

Manz, C. C., Sims Jr., H. P. Leading workers to lead themselves: The external leadership of self-managing work teams. *Administrative Science Quarterly*, 1987, 106–129.

Marini, M. M. Social values and norms. In *Encyclopedia of Sociology*, Borgata, E. F., Montgomery, R. J. V., eds. Macmillan, New York, 2000, 2828–2840.

Martin, R. C. *Agile Software Development: Principles, Patterns, and Practices*. Prentice Hall PTR, 2003.

Mele, A. R. Understanding and explaining real self-deception. *Behavioral and Brain Sciences*, 1997, 20(1), 127–134.

Modigliani, A., Gamson, W. A. Thinking about politics. *Political Behavior*, 1979, 1(1), 5–30.

Moe, N. B., Dingsøyr, T., Dybå, T. Understanding self-organizing teams in agile software development. *Proceedings of the Australian Software Engineering Conference—ASWEC*, 2008.

Moretti, M. M., Higgins, E. T. Own versus other standpoints in self-regulation: Developmental antecedents and functional consequences. *Review of General Psychology*, 1999, 3(3), 188.

Morrow, P. C. *The Theory and Measurement of Work Commitment*. Jai Press, 1993.

Nerur, S., Balijepally, V. Theoretical Reflections on Agile Development Methodologies, *Communications of the ACM* 2007, 50(3), 79–83.

Nerur, S., Mahapatra, R., Mangalaraj, G. Challenges of migrating to agile methodologies. *Communications of the ACM*, 2005, 48(5), 72–78.

O'Reilly, C. A., Chatman, J. A. Culture as social control: Corporations, cults, and commitment. *Research in Organizational Behavior*, 1996, 18, 157–200.

Oetting, E. R., Beauvais, F. Common elements in youth drug abuse: Peer clusters and other psychosocial factors. *Journal of Drug Issues*, 1987, 2, 133–151.

Oetting, E. R., Beauvais, F. Peer cluster theory: Drugs and the adolescent. *Journal of Counseling and Development*, 1986, 65, 17–22.

Oldham, G. R., Cummings, A. Employee creativity: Personal and contextual factors at work. *Academy of Management Journal*, 1996, 39(3), 607–634.

Opp, K. D. The evolutionary emergence of norms. *British Journal of Social Psychology*, 1982, 21(2), 139–149.

Perugini, M., Conner, M. Predicting and understanding behavioral volitions: The interplay between goals and behaviors. *European Journal of Social Psychology*, 2000, 30(5), 705–731.

Pollis, N. P., Montgomery, R. L., Smith, T. G. Autokinetic paradigms: A reply to Alexander, Zucker and Brody. *Sociometry*, 1975, 358–373.

Rimal, R. N., Real, K. How behaviors are influenced by perceived norms a test of the theory of normative social behavior. *Communication Research*, 2005, 32(3), 389–414.

Rivis, A., Sheeran, P. Descriptive norms as an additional predictor in the theory of planned behavior: A meta-analysis. *Current Psychology*, 2003, 22(3), 218–233.

Rogers, R. W. A protection motivation theory of fear appeals and attitude change. *The Journal of Psychology*, 1975, 91(1), 93–114.

Rosenstock, I. M. The health belief model and preventive health behavior. *Health Education Monographs*, 1974, 2(4), 354–386.

Rosenthal, T. L., Zimmerman, B. J. *Social Learning and Cognition*. New York: Academic Press, 1978.

Rubin, K. S. *Essential Scrum: A Practical Guide to the Most Popular Agile Process*. Addison-Wesley, 2012.

Sarker, S., Munson, C., Chakraborty, S. "Assessing the Relative Contribution of the Facets of Agility to Distributed Systems Development Success: An Analytic Hierarchy Process Approach, *European Journal of Information Systems* 2009, 18(4), pp. 285–299.

Schwaber, K., Beedle, M. *Agile Software Development with Scrum*, Upper Saddle River, NJ: Prentice-Hall, 2002.

Schwaber, K., *Scrum Development Process*, OOPSLA'95. Workshop on Business Object Design and Implementation. Springer-Verlag, 1995.

Schwartz, S. H. Normative Influences on Altruism. *Advances in Experimental Social Psychology*, 1977, 10, 221–279.

Schwartz, S. H., Fleishman, J. A. Personal norms and the mediation of legitimacy effects on helping. *Social Psychology*, 1978, 306–315.

Searle, J. R. Collective intentions and actions. *Intentions in Communication*, 1990, 401.

Shalley, C. E., Zhou, J., Oldham, G. R. The effects of personal and contextual characteristics on creativity: Where should we go from here? *Journal of Management*, 2004, 30(6), 933–958.

Shin, S. J., Kim, T., Lee, J., Bian, L. Cognitive team diversity and individual team member creativity: A cross-level interaction. *Academy of Management Journal*, 2012, 55(1), 197–212.

Siders, M. A., George, G., Dharwadkar, R. The relationship of internal and external commitment foci to objective job performance measures. *Academy of Management Journal*, 2001, 44(3), 570–579.

Simons, R. How new top managers use control systems as levers of strategic renewal. *Strategic Management Journal*, 1994, 15(3), 169–189.

Simons, R. Strategic orientation and top management attention to control systems. *Strategic Management Journal*, 1991, 12(1), 49–62.

Sorrels, J. P., Kelley, J. Conformity by omission. *Personality and Social Psychology Bulletin*, 1984, 10(2), 302–305.

Stapleton, J. *DSDM: Dynamic Systems Development Method*, Harlow, England: Addison Wesley, 1997.

Stewart, G. L., Manz, C. C., Sims, H. P. *Team Work and Group Dynamics*. New York, NY: J. Wiley, 1999.

Suchman, M. C. Managing legitimacy: Strategic and institutional approaches. *Academy of Management Review*, 1995, 20(3), 571–610.

Sutherland, J. *The Roots of Scrum. How the Japanese Experience Changed Global Software Development*, 2010, Online: http://www.gbcacm.org/sites/www.gbcacm.org/files/slides/5%20-%20Roots%20of%20Scrum.pdf (Accessed on 20 February 2014).

Swieringa, J., Wierdsma, A. Becoming a learning organization. *Beyond the Learning Curve*. Wokingham: Addison-Wesley, 1992.

Taggar, S. Individual creativity and group ability to use individual creative resources: A multilevel model. *Academy of Management Journal*, 2002, 45(2), 315–330.

Tajfel, H. Social psychology of intergroup relations. *Annual Review of Psychology*, 1982, 33(1), 1–39.

Takeuchi, H., Nonaka, I. The new product development game. Harvard Business Review 1986, 64(1), 137–146.

Terry, D. J., Hogg, M. A. Attitudes, behavior, and social context: The role of norms and group membership in social influence processes. In: J. P. Forgas & K. D. Williams (Eds.), *Social Influence: Direct and Indirect Processes*. Philadelphia: Psychology Press, 2001, pp. 253–270.

Terry, D. J., Hogg, M. A. Group norms and the attitude-behavior relationship: A role for group identification. *Personality and Social Psychology Bulletin*, 1996, 22(8), 776–793.

Tompkins, P. K., Cheney, G. Communication and unobtrusive control in contemporary organizations. *Organizational Communication: Traditional Themes and New Directions*, 1985, 13, 179–210.

Tuomela, R. *The Importance of Us: A Philosophical Study of Basic Social Notions*. Stanford University Press, 1995.

VandeWalle, D. Development and validation of a work domain goal orientation instrument. *Educational and Psychological Measurement*, 1997, 57(6), 995–1015.

Venkatesan, M. Experimental study of consumer behavior conformity and independence. *Journal of Marketing Research*, 1966, 384–387.

Wageman, R. Interdependence and group effectiveness. *Administrative Science Quarterly* 1995, 40(1),145–180.

West, D., Grant, T., Gerush, M., D'silva, D. Agile development: Mainstream adoption has changed agility. *Forrester Research*, 2010, 2, 41.

West, M. A. *Reflexivity and Work Group Effectiveness: A Conceptual Integration*. In: M. A. West (Ed.), Handbook of work group psychology. London: Wiley, 1996, pp. 525–579.

West, M. A., Farr, J. L. *Innovation and Creativity at Work: Psychology and Organizational Strategies*. Chi Chester: Wiley, 1990.

Wilder, D. A. Some determinants of the persuasive power of in-groups and out-groups: Organization of information and attribution of independence. *Journal of Personality and Social Psychology*, 1990, 59(6), 1202–1213.

Williams, L., Cockburn, A. Guest Editors' Introduction: Agile Software Development: it's about feedback and change. *Computer*, 2003, 36(6), 39–43.

Woodman, R. W., Sawyer, J. E., Griffin, R. W. Toward a theory of organizational creativity. *Academy of Management Review*, 1993, 18(2), 293–321.

CHAPTER 4

DIGITAL OPPORTUNITIES FOR FIRST-YEAR UNIVERSITY STUDENTS' MOTIVATIONAL ENHANCEMENT

DACE RATNIECE

Distance Education Study Centre, Riga Technical University, Kronvalda Boulevard 1, Riga, LV 1010, Latvia; Faculty of Sciences and Engineering, Liepaja University, Liela Str.14, Liepaja, LV-3401, Latvia

CONTENTS

ABSTRACT

Young people, who are the fundamental asset of our economies and societies across the world, face a real and increasing difficulties in finding a decent job with each day. Three additional merging factors are worsening the youth employment crisis even further, causing challenges while transiting to decent jobs, namely (i) numbers of discouraged youth, in other words, young people, who are neither in education nor in employment or training (NEETs) are increasing, (ii) unemployment among university graduates of tertiary education in general are rising and (iii) potential NEET group students, especially in the 1st year, who, apart from reduced study fees, require extra motivation and moral support from educators. The study aim—to find the e-learning and conventional learning as the optimal ratio for 1st year students to increase motivation. Research methods—during two academic years (2013/2014th and 2014/2015th.) the first year students of the course "Entrepreneurship (Distance Learning e-course)" were tested about quality of this course using different research methods. Students had been tested by: (i) survey about the course on "Entrepreneurship" (Distance Learning e-course) assessment; (ii) psychologist M.Lusher color test, based on the method of projection individual's emotional state of the diagnosis; (iii) the degree of risk appetite according to Schubert's method of success; (iv) motivation after T.Elersa methods, failure avoidance motivation in correlation with T.Elersa method; (v) survey about optimal proportion between traditional and e-learning studies. The chapter contains analyzes of these results.

4.1   INTRODUCTION

Twenty-first century higher education paradigm is based on the teacher-student mutual cooperation and direct-to-student. Unfortunately, Latvian for the sixth consecutive year, the number of students experiencing a downward trend. 2012/2013 academic year, together studied 94,474 students at the Latvian higher education institutions. Compared to last year the number of students has decreased by 6% (Progress report on the Latvian National Reform Program in the context of implementation Strategy "Europe 2020"). The number of students has decreased over the last four years due to demographic factors (demographic pit), as well as the economic crisis and the general economic emigration, suggesting a decrease in access to higher education for economic reasons.

It is important to note that Latvian National Action Plan aims by 2020 to ensure 34–36% of the population (30–34 age group) in higher education. Ministry of Education and Science is responsible for the following key policies and measures with higher education population increase:

- modernization of higher education;
- the modernization of material and technical resources and resource efficiency in higher education institutions;
- higher education equal access opportunities;
- studies and research quality improvement activities;
- attraction of foreign students (Kapenieks, 2012).

European Commission document 'Opening up education: innovative teaching and learning for all through new technologies and open educational resources' /COM/2013/0654/ highlights that today's students want to personalized treatment, greater cooperation and better links between formal and nonformal education, which can largely be implemented by school learning using digital technologies. In addition, in this respect, the European Union (hereinafter EU) risk falling further behind other regions of the world. United States and some Asian countries are investing in ICT strategies to transform education and training. These countries are transforming their education systems, modernize and make it international, achieving remarkable results in schools and universities in access to education and the cost of teaching practice and the teaching institutions globally renowned reputation or brand promotion. An example would be that a large portion of digital content provided by market participants from outside Europe, including educational institutions that offer training programs on a global scale through massive open online courses (hereinafter—the MOOC) (Progress report on the Latvian National Reform Program in the context of implementation Strategy "Europe 2020", 2013).

In addition to increasing access to education, greater use of new technologies and open educational resources that can help reduce the costs of educational institutions and students, particularly disadvantaged groups. Thus MOOC should use the opportunity to:

- studies in universities embarked on, but unfortunately due to higher earning leavers students who work all day;
- school leavers NEET group of students (NEET—not in employment, education or training—a person who is not employed and

is not involved in the educational process) (Progress report on the Latvian National Reform Program in the context of implementation Strategy "Europe 2020", 2013);

- school prospective NEET group, especially in the 1st year, students who have no cost-cutting is a great need for motivation and moral support from educators.

All three target groups linked by a common need to deal with the problem—as soon as possible to gain experience or to provide educational opportunities to live and work stably. Are there any initiatives to remedy this situation, or so far they have been a success? Of course, there are also extreme making choices—the opportunity to migrate, but if it helps in the long run?

The 2013 summer EU higher education modernization high-level working group came up with 16 recommendations of teaching and learning to improve the quality of higher education in universities of the EU modernization of high-level working group teaching and learning and improve the quality of the recommended use of new technologies. Latvian institutions of higher education new technologies are used in various stages of development, but with university and government support for the EU is trying to help teachers to develop their teaching skills and online teaching and learning forms that have become available right now, in the digital era.

Higher education institutions should be encouraged, supported and also take into account the students' feedback, if it could help detect problems in time teaching and learning environment, and quickly and efficiently to improve the environment. As noted by the majority of respondents from industry, higher education already takes into account student feedback on teachers' work, for example, through surveys. Other recommendation requires that training programs should be developed and monitored by teaching staff, students, university graduates and labor market participants of discussing and cooperating. New teaching and learning methods in need of skills required facilities to help students find a job. Recommendation to improve the skills of university teachers to teach their subjects, to learn new teaching methods, forms and implement an interdisciplinary approach to the development of students' innovative thinking entrepreneur, organized by each higher education institution in Latvian. Each teacher develops individual study methods of teaching.

The goal of the chapter is to make 1st year Higher Educational institutions students' problem analysis in order to understand their motivation to engage in distance learning process.

Research methods—a study was carried out in the lectures and final exam of course "Business (Distance Learning e-course)" during the 1st year students (respondents) participating on a voluntary basis. The following Empirical data extraction method where used:

- a survey about course on "Entrepreneurship (Distance Learning e-course)" assessment, developed by D.Ratniece;
- psychologist M.Lüscher color test based on the method of projection of the individual psychoemotional diagnosis (Ņikiforovs, 2008);
- methods for diagnostics of the degree of risk preparedness (Schubert), motivation to success (methods of diagnostics of the person on the motivation for success T.Elersa) and motivation to avoiding failures (methods of diagnostics of the person on the motivation for avoiding of failures T. Elersa) (Ņikiforovs, 2008).

4.2 LATVIAN STUDENTS' DESIRE TO USE SOCIAL NETWORKS TO THE LEARNING PROCESS—A GOOD INCENTIVE TO CARRY OUT SUCH RESEARCH IN UNIVERSITIES

"Samsung's future school" student survey, which took place in February 2014, found that 75% of Latvian students in favor of using social networks to communicate not only with friends but also with teachers and learning useful information. This survey was conducted teacher training programs in digital "Samsung School Future" program (2014). Online "Draugiem. lv" filled in a 713 pupils aged 12 to 18 years.

The most common social network "Facebook," "Twitter," "Draugiem. lv" and another networks see the benefits of training of students in situations where for various reasons have impeded school hours and follow up remotely. In this way students can quickly learn the latest study material, get advice, teacher comments and information about homework. Also, students would like to build a virtual environment of like-minded groups, discussions and "brainstorming," discussing the subject matter and the common class entertainment. Almost a quarter of or 36% of the students assess the social networks as a good platform to look for learning useful reading material, view videos, photos and listen to audio reflections, or "podcasts." A similar number of respondents in the social networks choose to play educational computer games, participate in after-school counseling and contact with different fields of expertise. However, only 13% of the students themselves are interested in building a digital learning materials.

Learning digital skills teachers can diversify teaching methods and to develop creative, innovative and curiosity-enhancing training materials. The students are interesting to perform tasks online and to operate in an unusual environment. Social networks help to motivate students to learn, and that is also good for data selection training, formulation of evaluation and opinion. The challenge of teachers, however, is a task of social networking evaluation system developing, otherwise the pupils' interest fades. Although students will be happy to communicate with teachers, social networks and one-third choose to follow his teacher, but the majority of students (67%) would not want teachers to keep track of them. About a quarter of students surveyed believe that social networks have their private space, not intended for teachers and students do not want them to reveal their thoughts and views on personal issues.

Some years ago, U.S. researchers conducted a study on the basis of the results and concluded that the best way to build a digital technology-based learning environment (Kim, 2009). Methods, which integrate digital technology may vary depending on the types of technologies available, teachers 'expectations of pupils' needs and academic research purposes. In a study designed to assess the fifth and eighth grade students' reading skills, it was discovered that some students of literary and linguistic skills performance has improved, thanks to the enhanced use of digital technology (Kim, 2009).

4.3   PRACTICAL EVALUATION METHOD AND RESULTS

From October till December of academy year 2013/2014th and academy year 2014/2015th author as the Assistant of Riga Technical University Professor A.Kapenieks, who provided the course "Business (Distance

Learning e-course)," supplementing the lecture content, presenting her study entitled "Use of Social microblogging to motivate young people (NEETS) to participate in distance education" to 1st year students. From October till December the course "Business (Distance Learning e-course)" was taken within two home works—"Business Ideas searches on the Internet" and "Your business idea." The course was taken through Riga Technical Universities e-learning environment ORTUS. Author evaluated all home works in the e-learning environment ORTUS, added comments, encourage and motivate students to prepare business plans better till the final exam at the end of the semester. Each comment was prepared according to the content analysis. The assessment of the student homework was done by author concerning the seven criteria: (i) actuality or viability of idea; (ii) technological solution or how to enforce; (iii) marketing—promotion of goods or services in the market; (iv) competition; (v) financial security (e.g., planned revenues, expenses, financial support for the company's start-up and ongoing development (bank loan, other resources, etc.); (vi) the company's ability to realize the idea; (vii) the potential risks.

Here are some author's comments, contained in the RTU ORTUS e-learning environment after assessment of two home works of 130 students:

"It is a good idea and a good understanding of LV local economic problems and possible solutions."

"The idea is great, your involvement and knowledge is felt. Description well-structured and well founded. Good luck to implement plans! If you intend to implement the idea in Latvia urge timely improvement Latvian language. Based on your good vision I could not be left uncorrected Latvian spelling errors. I hope it will be a good support for your business plan. "

"Cannot be assessed, possibly innovative creative ideas, due to the stingy information. Please summon one's strength and prepare the business plan more seriously!"

"The idea is very innovative, as long as it has not been known before. Before two years one high school student team participated to the Junior Achievement Latvia competition with this great business idea. This student team received a favorable assessment. As the company has fared forth, is not known. Have a good luck for you too!"

"You have already submitted almost a complete business plan! Good luck in implementing the ideas! Note that this region is largely popular among hunters organizations, which could be your potential customers will stay for a reasonable price."

"Excellent idea in people's everyday needs, while saving time and ensuring a truly preferred diet, finding the opportunity to learn about its health. Very wisely points out the potential risks. Just do not use the word 'tablet' of the Latvian language in the text, as there may be a misunderstanding. Consistently sticking to the same wording in Latvian. Have a nice time with this innovation to conquer the world, painting business image of Latvia!"

The author's comments were made in positive, supportive and motivational manner supporting each student. During this period, RTU ORTUS e-learning environment could well be traced to the original falls for 1st year students. About one-third did more first homework than the second homework.

In order to establish whether and what are the factors hindering the continuing education of students, in the middle of the first semester of academy year 2013/2014th, the author carried out the above 1st year student testing under a Swiss psychologist M.Lücher color test based on the method of projection of the individual psychoemotional diagnosis. Before testing of student, the author visited the lectures "Social psychology course" of associate professor O.Ņikiforovs in Baltic International Academy for the design and preparation of test forms (Ņikiforovs, 2008).

The Lüscher color test is a psychological test invented by Dr. Max Lüscher in Basel, Switzerland. Max Lüscher believed that sensory perception of color is objective and universally shared by all, but that color preferences are subjective, and that this distinction allows subjective states to be objectively measured by using test colors.

Lüscher believed that because the color selections are guided in an unconscious manner, they reveal the person as they really are, not as they perceive themselves or would like to be perceived (Ņikiforovs, 2008).

He believed that personality traits could be identified based on one's choice of color. Therefore, subjects who select identical color combinations have similar personalities. In order to measure this, he conducted a test in which subjects we shown 8 different colored cards and asked to place them in order of preference. On the other hand each color position in the color line are analyzed. In this case, the first position of color down human goals and aspirations, but at last—the repressed needs and impulses. Test data results was sent to each student personally. After the collection of RTU's color test data results it can be concluded that this test is necessary for the first year students to enhance motivation. Then, in time to determine the appropriate educational support the need for change in the learning process, balancing the traditional and e-learning form the volume to students that they can be customized according to the psychoemotional condition moment.

4.4   YOUNG PEOPLE MOTIVATION TO ENGAGE IN DISTANCE LEARNING PROCESS

Methods for diagnostics of the degree of risk preparedness (Schubert), motivation to success (methods of diagnostics of the person on the motivation for success T.Elersa) and motivation to avoiding failures (methods of diagnostics of the person on the motivation for avoiding of failures T. Elersa) have been tested for all students three times in the course in 2014/2015th academic year: at the beginning, in the middle of course and at the end. There was correlation between risk level preparedness and course evaluation at the beginning 0.734, at the middle 0.633 and at the end 0.654. Coefficient decreasing and after raising characterizes that students in the beginning are higher motivated than in the middle of the course.

Many respondents indicate the success of the course learning objective and self-critically evaluated in the course gain the skills and knowledge of the business plan. A number of contributions respondents highlight lectures existing friendly atmosphere, teacher through knowledge, positive attitude, responsiveness, interesting narrative. Tables 4.1 and 4.2 of the study about the use of the form efficiency is reflected in the students' support for both traditional forms of study, as well as e-learning

Respondents very carefully study the two kinds of form of negative and positive aspects, since the completion of the training time personally felt, why learning requires direct contact, and situations in which use

TABLE 4.1   Student Evaluation of the Course Business (Distance Learning Course) During the Study Assessing the Effectiveness of the Form (2013/2014th Academic Year)

Form of study	Low rating			Average rating				A high rating		
	1	2	3	4	5	6	7	8	9	10
Lecture				3	6	16	34	29	11	6
Discussion			2	3	5	13	18	35	21	8
Homework preparing and inserting in ORTUS system			1		7	11	19	35	15	17
Teacher comments in ORTUS system			1	2	7	12	15	33	17	18
e-Portfolio utility	9	5	6	3	10	16	26	16	10	4

TABLE 4.2   Student Evaluation of the Course Business (Distance Learning Course) During the Study Assessing the Effectiveness of the Form (2014/2015th Academic Year)

Form of study	Low rating			Average rating				A high rating		
	1	2	3	4	5	6	7	8	9	10
Lecture	1	1	2	1	1	10	25	18	12	8
Discussion		1	1	1	1	3	13	24	18	17
Homework preparing and inserting in ORTUS system			1	3	4	5	15	20	15	16
Teacher comments in ORTUS system	1		1	2	4	4	9	14	12	31
e-Portfolio utility	1	2				4	17	24	12	19

e-learning opportunities. This questionnaire respondents reflected comments for e-learning balance:

"E-learning is not a substitute for traditional studios at the moment, but they can be a good tool for learning."

"E-learning is useful because it can get a lecture files and, if never been to a lecture, it's a great help."

"E-learning suitable for cost reduction and to provide a compelling learning environment. Traditional forms necessary to maintain interest in the course."

"Traditional forms of studies must be more, because the presence of asking the teacher can better understand the subject matter."

"E-learning should be available for all subjects, because it is very convenient."

Respondents indicate that e-learning and traditional forms of study needs to be balanced, because e-learning provides a great advantage to learn anywhere, anytime, and successful conduct of the study process and quality education are important, however, is the work of a teacher. Respondents' assessment of the teacher's three core competencies are generally as follows:

- responsive, intelligent, good contact with the students, generous, sociable, demanding adequate heights of their knowledge, understanding, the ability to listen, motivate, etc.;
- wise with the knowledge economy, the ability to lead discussions, the ability to appeal to, the ability to prepare a training plan, a comprehensive understanding of different areas, a teaching of the subject with interest, etc.;
- is a specialist in their field, with good experience in his field, a great life experience, knowledge of foreign experience, etc.

The first competency among the three main teacher or educator competencies respondents indicate positive character traits, suggesting the need for the learning process to develop positive communication. Only then, as the next teacher competence, mostly referred to the professional qualities and experience.

Very important information is provided by respondents concerning data about student previously graduated from an educational institution. To above examination in RTU marked an interesting trend. RTU electronics and telecommunications specialty is studying by number of the same educational institution graduates. So for a good and excellent education quality is preciously to mention a number of general secondary and secondary vocational educational establishments.

Author participated two times in the 1st year examination of students of three specialties. For that exam named "Commercial (Distance learning e-course)" students prepared presentations. Author evaluated content of students' presentation and presentation skills. During the exam, the author conducted a survey of students, asking her to fill out a questionnaire prepared by the 5 key questions:

- the course rating knowledge gained professional context of assessing the low (by 1–3 points), moderate (4–7 points) or high (8–10 points), as well as adding a comment;

- during the course of studies assessing the effectiveness of a form 10-point rating system, by adding a comment;
- e-learning desired balance, indicating the relationship between traditional forms of study and e-learning forms, as well as adding a comment;
- the three main teacher competence, adding a comment;
- reference for a few details about yourself-gender, age, graduated educational institution.

During the exam are issued 107 questionnaires in 2013/2014th academic year, 69 questionnaires in 2013/2014th academic year. All questionnaires was filled by all respondents. Tables 4.1 and 4.2 includes the students' evaluation of the course "Business Training Course (Distance Learning e-course)."

4.5   CONCLUSIONS

Higher education paradigm is based on the teacher-student mutual cooperation, which urges for personalized treatment of students, greater cooperation and better links between formal and nonformal education, which can largely be implemented by school learning using digital technologies.

According to learning and teaching quality assessment made by students, it can be concluded that using of traditional forms and e-learning opportunities is necessary in similar proportions. Higher education institutions should take into account the students' feedback. They could help to detect problems in teaching and learning environment, as well as faster and more efficiently to improve the environment.

The determination of risk motivation degree is recommended for Higher Educational institutions' 1st-year students. That is necessary to be able to predict the pedagogical support, balancing traditional and e-learning form of quantity.

First year students of psychoemotional condition for the determination of recommended M.Lücher color test at the beginning of the study, to allow timely and appropriate educational support to identify the need for change and balance the traditional and e-learning form the amount that students could be customized according to their psychoemotional state of necessity.

Educational institutions should be applied to traditional forms of study and e-learning, as an e-learning provides a great advantage to learn anywhere, anytime. Quality education play an important role in obtaining a teacher to direct contact with students.

ACKNOWLEDGMENT

This work was partly funded by European Social Fund, project "The development of doctoral studies in the University of Liepaja," grant No. 2009/0127/1 DP/1.1.2.1.2./IPIA/VIAA/018.

KEYWORDS

- **digital options**
- **e-learning**
- **NEET group**
- **quality of education**
- **teacher's competence**

REFERENCES

Kapenieks, A., Žuga, B., Štāle, G., Jirgensons, M. Internet, Television and Mobile Technologies for Innovative e-Learning. Society. *Integration, Education: Proceedings of the International Scientifical Conference, May 25–26th Rezekne: Rezekne Higher Education Institution*, 2012, Vol. I, pp. 303–311, ISSN 1691–5887.

Progress report on the Latvian National Reform Program in the context of implementation Strategy "Europe 2020". 2013, Riga, pp. 56–57, Retrieved on 19 November 2014 from http://ec.europa.eu/europe2020/pdf/nd/nrp2013_latvia_lv.pdf.

Ratniece, D. Social microblog TWITTER use to motivate young people (NEETs) to involve in distance education. *Society, Integration, Education: Proceedings of the International Scientifical Conference, May 24–25th, 2013*, Vol. II, Rezekne: Rezekne Higher Education Institution, 2013, pp. 449–464, ISSN 1691–5887, Retrieved on 22 May 2015 from http://www.ru.lv/ckfinder/userfiles/RAweb/Saturs/zinatne/zinatniskie_instituti/personas_socializacijas_petijumu_instituts/izdevumi/2013/II%20da%C4%BCa.pdf.

Kim, H. Y. A review of "interactive literacy education": Facilitating literacy environments through technology. *Language and Education,* 2009, 23(3), 287–290.

Judson, E. Improving technology literacy: Does it open doors to traditional content? *Education Technology Research and Development,* 2010. 58(3), 271–284.

Nikiforovs, O. Social Psychology. The Course, Baltic International Academy. Riga, 2008, 6 p.

Samsung School for the Future, 2014, Riga https://www.linkedin.com/pub/eva-mezite/23/1a9/a6b.

CHAPTER 5

BUILDING A SUCCESSFUL INNOVATION PLATFORM FOR AFFORDABLE MEDICAL TECHNOLOGY IN LOW RESOURCE SETTINGS

RAMAKRISHNA PAPPU[1] and JAGDISH CHATURVEDI[2]

[1]*Business Associate, InnAccel, 5th Floor, Aanand Towers, Municipal No. 4, Rajaram Mohan Roy Road, Ward No. 77, Sampangiramanagar, Bangalore–560025, India*

[2]*Director Clinical Innovations, InnAccel, 5th Floor, Aanand Towers, Municipal No. 4, Rajaram Mohan Roy Road, Ward No. 77, Sampangiramanagar, Bangalore–560025, India*

CONTENTS

ABSTRACT

The chapter emphasizes the need for an innovation platform for successful accomplishments and taking the example of healthcare innovations, explores the different facets that need to be brought together to create an innovation platform in the Medical Technology space and its use today to enable affordable medical technology in low resource settings.

The authors use various case studies of innovation platforms accessible to healthcare innovators and highlight the thought process behind developing such platforms (Stanford Biodesign, John's Hopkins innovation platform, CAMtech innovation platform, InnAccel acceleration program, Government run incubation programs, etc.).

The chapter details a stage-wise process that begins with the identification of gaps in the ecosystem through feasibility studies to setting up a physical Medical Technology innovation platform. Further, the authors highlight the need for incorporation of structured processes for needs identification and product development embedded within innovation platforms. An overview of how this is being used today in different settings are described.

5.1   INTRODUCTION

"Innovation platforms are ways to bring together different stakeholders to identify solutions to common problems or to achieve common goals." CGIAR and ILRI, in their brief on innovation platforms, provide a succinct definition of the terminology as it has come to be used today.

"An innovation platform is a space for learning and change. It is a group of individuals with different backgrounds and interests. The members come together to diagnose problems, identify opportunities and find ways to achieve their goals" (http://r4d.dfid.gov.uk/pdf/outputs/Water-foodCP/Brief1.pdf).

Innovation platforms are used in various fields from agriculture to networks to medical technology to innovate new solutions, products, and technology to address problems faced by the community at large. These innovation platforms tackle challenges and opportunities at different levels—from a city or across a country in a geographic setting, or through a value chain in an economic sector, and hence can be thought of as working on several levels. A platform based approach often works well in areas of high complexity—where the solutions to problems need a multidisciplinary approach, such as in medical technology innovation.

Innovation platforms are created by different types of institutions and individuals. These could be in the private sector, by the government, or even by developmental nonprofits. Typically, innovation platforms have a focus that would bring different kinds of people together. The focus could vary from a specific technology to an industry vertical. Often, an important component of a successful innovation platform is the capacity building ability and opportunities available. These could be from basic training to develop its members skills to a programs that teach more complicated processes. But the goal is to enable more of its members and stakeholders to become problem-solvers to make the platform succeed.

Innovation platforms can be thought of as dynamic agents for systematic attempts to enable change in the ecosystem. At its core, innovation platforms, facilitate dialog and understanding among stakeholders and provides space to create a common vision and mutual trust (http://r4d. dfid.gov.uk/pdf/outputs/WaterfoodCP/Brief1.pdf). Innovation platforms allow groups to come together to identify the problems faced by the community in the chosen focus area and to together develop solutions that would be beyond what an individual could themselves typically hope to accomplish. It can be argued that innovation platforms lead to better informed decisions in the innovation process as a result of more members' contributions. These lead to opportunities to create wider impact for the benefit of the community through demand-driven approaches to innovative research and development. Innovation platforms enable collective contribution of its members to be greater than the sum of its members' individual contributions.

Innovation platforms can't be considered the solution to all problems, and could deter innovation in certain contexts and situations. The progress of the innovative work, through such innovative platforms, typically requires the buy-in of all the members in the group. Homann-Kee Tui et al. state that 'members have to be willing to work together and trust each other. Social and institutional conflicts, lack of political will, and power structures can hinder the growth of the innovation platform' (http://r4d.dfid.gov.uk/pdf/outputs/WaterfoodCP/Brief1.pdf). Innovation platforms often require a long-term perspective in its workings to become successful in its outputs. It could be difficult to monitor and evaluate such platforms systematically.

Hence, the appropriateness of innovation platforms to foster innovation in different areas would depend on the circumstances. Sometimes "other approaches, such as more traditional research coordination meetings, stakeholder consultations, or participatory research methods, may be more appropriate... (and) these methods can be used in conjunction with innovation platforms" (http://r4d.dfid.gov.uk/pdf/outputs/WaterfoodCP/Brief1.pdf).

One such innovation platform was created by InnAccel, a medical technology accelerator based in Bangalore, India. InnAccel is India's first medical technology acceleration company focused on innovation for low and mid-income markets. It has built a proprietary innovation platform, and forged partnerships with national and global entities, to support startups and entrepreneurs. InnAccel is led by an experienced management team and advised by industry leading experts (http://www.innaccel.com). However, before such an innovation platform was set up, the company conducted a feasibility study to understand the demand, the market, the stakeholders and the ecosystem at large, which would enable it to provide the most value to the members of its innovation platform.

The Feasibility Study done by InnAccel was conducted by an external consultancy firm called Strategic Development Services that specializes in such infrastructural projects. It was conducted over 8-months and included extensive secondary as well as primary research. The primary market research included 35 in-depth, one-on-one interviews with a broad cross-section of stakeholders, and 15 focus group participants. Stakeholders from academia, clinics, hospitals, government agencies, investors as well as large and small MedTech CEOs were interviewed from October 2012 through April 2013.

The outcome of the research was that requisite services and infrastructure specific to MedTech innovation did not exist in India, and that there was a tremendous pent-up demand for such an ecosystem by MedTech startups. The respondents indicated that the ecosystem was suboptimal with key gaps that were barriers to success for MedTech startups. Some of the key gaps identified are in the Table 5.1.

Further analysis of the results revealed some of the key elements that InnAccel would need to provide in its innovation platform to be successful. These key elements from the Feasibility Study are stated in Table 5.2.

The findings from the Feasibility Study were revalidated by the respondents, and viewed as barriers to success for start-up MedTech ventures. The study indicated that InnAccel would be filling a huge gap in the market, and providing a sorely needed resource for innovators. An initial concept of the working of the innovation platform devised was tested out by different respondent groups. Further, a 100% of all respondent groups reacted positively to the concept and validated the demand for a MedTech Accelerator. Not only the concept, but also the business model along with the revenue model was tested out on the so-called 'customers' of the accelerator—the startups and entrepreneurs working in Medical Technology. These startups and entrepreneurs provided strong validation for InnAccel's fee + equity stake model for acceleration services, with more than 90% of respondents reacting favorably to the model, when accompanied with access to capital.

TABLE 5.1 Gaps Identified in the Indian Medical Technology Ecosystem

1. Access to clinical partners and technical resources.
2. Access to capital.
3. Product engineering, development, and regulatory expertise.
4. Access to labs and equipment.
5. Lack of ideas and understanding of clinical needs.
6. Lack of good team members and managers.

Source: Feasibility Study for a MedTech Accelerator, Strategic Development Services. June 2013.

TABLE 5.2 Key Elements for a Successful MedTech Accelerator in India

1. Clinical, academic and technical partner networks.
2. Capital and access to capital.
3. Product design, development, and regulatory support.
4. Physical lab infrastructure (including prototyping facilities).

Source: Feasibility Study for a MedTech Accelerator, Strategic Development Services. June 2013.

Strategic Development Services, based on its expertise and experience, even provided a recommendation to InnAccel based on its analysis of the data collected from the study. It said, "Based on historical success in other geographies as well as our experience and information developed during the course of this study, we believe that the for-profit, investment portfolio model is best suited to the vision and mission of InnAccel." It even identified that the experience, reputation and domain expertise of the principals was the key success factor, which it described as the 'most critical element of success.'

Once it was concluded that the development of a MedTech Accelerator was not only feasible, but also sorely needed, some of the other recommendations included are Table 5.3.

InnAccel then tried to understand the MedTech ecosystem in India and its extent. It found emerging MedTech clusters in several parts of India, and a growing interest in MedTech commercialization and innovation by most academic institutions. There was some evidence of nascent cluster development in all of the major population centers, but Bangalore continually emerged as the most logical choice for the initial location. Bangalore has a concentration of research institutions (both public and private), as well as the most advanced entrepreneurial culture in India, and a GDP of $83 billion. Bangalore is also recognized globally as a technology hub, and is one of the top preferred entrepreneurial locations in the world. About 70% of the top venture capital firms in India have a presence in Bangalore.

TABLE 5.3   Strategic Development Service's Key Recommendations

1. Development of a 15–20,000 square foot accelerator facility, which will accommodate, and provide lab infrastructure, to 15–20 early stage MedTech firms.

2. Provide an engineering and prototype development platform.

3. Continue to develop strategic partnerships with sources of IP.

4. Provide MedTech-specific business support services.

5. Serve as the focal point for MedTech networks (mentors, advisors, clinicians, service providers) and cluster development.

6. Provide additional sources regarding access to capital.

Source: Feasibility Study for a MedTech Accelerator, Strategic Development Services. June 2013.

InnAccel decided that it would be highly selective regarding tenants for the Accelerator. Sources of potential tenants were to come primarily from academic and research institutions initially, and subsequently augmented by various sources such as potential investors, hospitals, corporate spin-outs, independent research institutions, community MedTech entrepreneurs and to a lesser degree, start-ups attracted from outside the Karnataka region.

InnAccel has taken a holistic approach to MedTech innovation, and provides a complete bouquet of services and infrastructure specific to the MedTech industry. The pillars of its innovation platform are in Figure 5.1:

InnAccel provides an 18–36 month acceleration program to selected entrepreneurs and teams. It helps teams convert ideas and concepts to market-ready and regulatory compliant medical products. It aims to do so while minimizing risk, cost, and time to market for the startup. InnAccel offers lab infrastructure at its Bangalore Accelerator, along with experienced management support, and access to capital to help the startups succeed. The model for this innovation platform is to partner with entrepreneurs and provide physical infrastructure, clinical, engineering, and

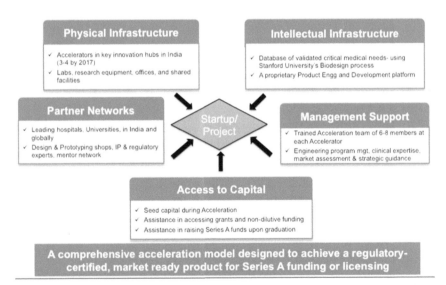

FIGURE 5.1   Multi-pronged acceleration model (*Source*: InnAccel's Corporate Deck October 2015).

business expertise along with access to capital in exchange for an equity stake in the company.

InnAccel has formed strong partnerships and strategic relationships with a number of national and global entities including medical colleges and hospitals in various regions that enable startups to gain clinical input, conduct fieldwork, and carry out early testing of products. InnAccel's relationships with leading academic institutes in the country provide access to students as well as strong engineering and technical expertise to our startups. In addition, the global partnerships enhance the flow of ideas, funds, and entrepreneurs to the innovation platform built in Bangalore. InnAccel's Acceleration process is outlined in Figure 5.2.

The pathway to successful device development is cyclical and iterative as ideas are prototyped, tested, improved, retested, optimized and finalized. InnAccel has built a proprietary Product Engineering and Development Platform, which coupled with acceleration support, enables startups to undergo the product development path successfully, identifying and managing risk effectively during execution.

One of the key elements of such an innovation platform is the selection of appropriate entrepreneurs and projects. Criteria such as in Table 5.4 could be used to guide the selection process for an innovation platform.

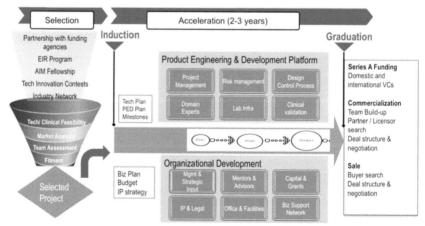

FIGURE 5.2   InnAccel's Acceleration process (Source: InnAccel's Corporate Deck October 2015).

TABLE 5.4   InnAccel's Selection Criteria For Acceleration

1. Clinical need you are solving.
2. The technology solution you have developed, including Intellectual Property information.
3. The market and business opportunity estimates.
4. The team composition with team members' backgrounds.
5. And the current status of the project.

One of the key facets of a successful innovation platform is capacity building. InnAccel, through its Entrepreneur in Residence program aims to train passionate individuals in this regard. InnAccel looks to support entrepreneurs who have a passion to transform healthcare through MedTech innovation. Entrepreneurs could explore an innovative idea, clinical area, or preidentified clinical needs in a structured fashion. The Entrepreneur-in Residence program is custom designed for entrepreneurs—either working alone or in an existing team, and is typically completed in 4–6 months. This program helps entrepreneurs achieve a comprehensive understanding of the clinical need and environment, explore different solutions to the identified need, and develop a viable business plan to develop and commercialize their solutions. The program culminates in a presentation of the business plan to InnAccel's management team, which evaluates the entrepreneur for acceleration. The selected entrepreneurs are accepted into InnAccel's acceleration program and become eligible for seed funding for their venture.

Another such innovation platform is CAMTech, which is the Consortium of Affordable Medical Technologies, based out of the Massachusetts General Hospital in Boston. The CAMTech India program focuses on technologies for Reproductive, Maternal, Newborn, and Child Health (RMNCH). It follows a public-private-partnership model that is "designed to accelerate medical technology innovation in order to improve RMNCH outcomes around preventable deaths in India and other low- and mid-income countries" (http://www.massgeneralcenterforglobalhealth.org/camtech/#mission). The program is funded by USAID, Bacca Foundation, and Omidyar Network. CAMTech works with multiple stakeholders in the Indian Medical Technology ecosystem to not only develop new technologies in RMNCH but also to build local entrepreneurial capacity.

CAMTech has a similar program in Uganda, with similar goals targeting the African ecosystem (Figure 5.3).

CAMTech conducts Clinical Summits, Medical Hack-a-thons, Innovation Awards, along with setting up Co-Creation Labs. In addition, it has setup an Online Innovation Platform that aims to address a critical gap in the 'MedTech ecosystem by providing expertise, resources and targeted support to global health innovators.' This Online Innovation Platform would bring innovators in touch with experts, investors, clinical opportunities, other partners and resources necessary to accelerate the development of the technology (http://camtechmgh.org/about) (Table 5.5).

Other successful innovation platforms in MedTech includes the Biodesign Program, which was created in 2001 at Stanford University using an unmet clinical need approach to drive innovation. It is a medical device innovation program and process that has been taught to 141 Fellows, 900+ students, and 100 executives over the years. 38 companies have been formed by those trained in the Biodesign process, creating more than 600 jobs. These companies have raised close to $362 million in external capital (Figures 5.4 and 5.5).

An example is Kerberos Proximal Solutions, which has created a device that removes blood clot material in the treatment of coronary and peripheral artery blockages, reducing stroke complications and neurological deficits. The company was acquired by Foxhollow Technologies for around $32 million in 2006. Another is Acumen Medical, which has created a device for visualization and cannulating the coronary sinus to

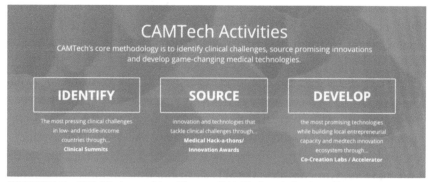

FIGURE 5.3 CAMTech activities (*Source*: CAMTech website: http://www.massgeneralcenterforglobalhealth.org/camtech/).

TABLE 5.5   Description of CAMTech's Activities

What is a Clinical Summit?

The CAMTech Clinical Summit brings together physicians, nurses, healthcare workers, government and public health experts to identify pressing clinical needs and best practices in RMNCH care. This event serves as a pivotal activity to drive affordable medical technology innovation, including a "Technology Showcase" to preview early stage and newly marketed technologies that have the potential to improve healthcare.

What is a MEDTech Hack-A-Thon?

CAMTech's hack-a-thons crowd-source solutions for critical clinical challenges in LMICs and foster entrepreneurship in the Medtech Space. Medtech hack-a-thons are two-day events that bring together engineers, clinicians, entrepreneurs and end-users to develop disruptive innovations to improve health in LMICs. Hack-a-thons provide a platform for engineers, clinicians, entrepreneurs and end-users to come together to advance knowledge-sharing across disciplines and catalyze better innovations for resource-constrained settings.

What is the CAMTech 100k Innovation Award Program?

The CAMTech Innovation Awards are part of a growing portfolio of health technologies supported by CAMTech's mission to build entrepreneurial capacity and accelerate medical technology innovation for LMICs. Awards provide one year of research, development and/or commercialization support to a research institution, NGO, or for-profit company. Through a competitive request for proposal process, CAMTech has generated a growing pipeline of technologies that have been evaluated across public health impact, technical innovation, and commercial viability.

What is an Accelerator?

CAMTech incubates medical technologies with targeted technical assistance to identify the fastest and most viable path to commercialization. For its portfolio technologies, CAMTech provides resources and identifies partners at critical stages of Medtech development.

Source: Recreated based on inputs from CAMTech's website http://www.massgeneralcenterforglobalhealth.org/camtech/

facilitate LV Lead delivery. Medtronic acquired the company in 2009 for about $370 million. Oculeve, another Stanford Biodesign startup with a device to treat moderate to severe dry eye, was acquired by Allergen in 2015 for $125 million.

The products developed by the Stanford Biodesign companies have together treated over 500,000 patients. The Stanford Biodesign program has sprung out 5 Global Programs, with 39 global fellows and 6 global faculty conducting these programs across the world in countries like Japan,

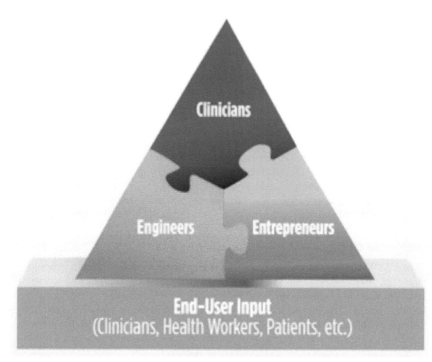

FIGURE 5.4 *Source*: http://www.massgeneralcenterforglobalhealth.org/ camtech/

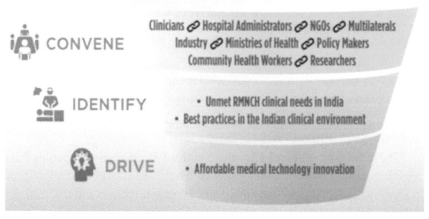

FIGURE 5.5 *Source*: http://www.massgeneralcenterforglobalhealth.org/ camtech/

Ireland and Singapore. One such program is in India—the Stanford India Biodesign Program.

The Stanford Biodesign, in its global avatar, launched the Stanford India Biodesign Program (SIB) in 2007 in New Delhi. SIB is jointly run by AIIMS, IIT-Delhi, the Dept. of Biotechnolgy, and Stanford University and has trained 32 fellows since inception. Till date, it has led to the formation of 6 companies working on India-specific unmet clinical needs. An example is Consure, which has developed a device to manage fecal incontinence in bedridden patients. It recently raised Series A funding of $4.5 million at a valuation around $15–20 million. The program has also led to the development of 7 other technology solutions that have been licensed out to industry players. Thorashield, a novel device for safer pleural tapping was licensed to MecMaan Healthcare in December 2013 for development, and is currently making initial limited sales to hospitals in North India. Another innovative technology, Bioscoop—for liver biopsies, was licensed to IndioLabs in 2013 for further development, and is currently undergoing safety testing at the beta-prototype stage.

The outputs of some of the successful medical technology incubators is captured in Table 5.6. Among 53 companies incubated by these incubators, a little more than half, went on to get acquired by others and nearly 10% went public. The combined capital raised by these companies is a staggering $1.6 billion, and the impact created by the medical device solutions on the healthcare systems around the world is significant.

ExploraMed in mountain view, California, is a private medical device incubator set up in 1995, largely to develop Dr. Josh Makower's ideas into commercial entities. ExploraMed has led to the creation of 6 companies that have collectively raised close to $700 million in venture funding. Three of these companies have been acquired by other medical device companies, including Acclarent in the ENT space—that was sold to Johnson & Johnson in 2010 for around $785 million. Another ExploraMed company—transvascular, which developed several revascularization technologies, was bought by Medtronic in 2003 in a stock swap deal valued at around $59 million at that time. ExploraMed's venture partner for all its companies is new enterprise associates.

Incube Labs was set up in 1995 in San Jose, California, by Mir Imran, one of the most prolific medical device innovators who holds over 250

TABLE 5.6   Successful medical technology incubators outputs

MedTech Incuba-tors:	Year Founded	# of Cpys Incu-bated	# of Cpys Acquired	# of cpys IPO	Capital Raised by cpys ($MM)	Signature Acquisitions
Explo-raMed	1995	6	3	0	700	Acclarent to J&J for $785 MM in 2010
Incube Labs	1998	22	11	4		Vidamed to Medtronic for $326 MM in 2001
The Foundry	1998	15	9	1	500	Ardian to Medtronic for $800 MM in 2011
The Inno-vation Factory	1999	10	4	0	460	AqueSys to Allergan for $300 MM in 2015
Total		53	27	5	1660	

Source: Table recreated based on information from individual incubator websites.

patents. It has sprung out 22 companies over the years, with 11 companies acquired and 4 companies that went public. An example is Percu-Surge, which allows cardiologists and interventional specialists to capture embolic debris during interventional procedures to prevent vessel blockage and damage to the heart, was acquired by Medtronic for $225 million in 2000. Another company, Physiometrix, which made noninvasive devices such as EEGs, raised around $20 million in an IPO in 1996 and was subsequently acquired by Hospira in 2005 for about $23 million. Medtronic also acquired another Incube Lab company—Vidamed, for around $326 million in 2001, when it was already public (IPO in 1995). Incube Labs is backed by Incube Ventures and VentureHealth and currently has three companies in its portfolio that are in the market, and five that are in the premarket stage.

The Foundry was set up in Menlo Park, California in 1998. Since then, it has incubated 15 MedTech companies, 9 of which have been acquired by larger medical device companies, and 1 has gone public. Collectively, these companies are valued at over $2 billion in the market. One of its incubate companies, Concentric Medical, which made products to treat acute ischemic strokes, was acquired by Stryker Medical for $135 million in 2011. Another company, Xtent, which made drug-eluting stent systems, went public in 2007, raising $75.2 million. It later sold its technology to JW Medical in 2009 that continued development. The Foundry, through its companies, has created employment for over 500 people since inception. It is backed by Venture Capital Funds such as Domain Associates, Morgenthaler Ventures, and Versant Ventures.

The Innovation Factory is a MedTech focused incubator in Duluth, Georgia. It was established in 1999 and has incubated 10 MedTech companies since. Its companies have collectively raised around $460 million in external funding till date. Four of these companies have been acquired by other medical device companies. LipoSonix, which uses ultrasound technology to noninvasively bust up fat in the body, was sold to Medicis Pharmaceutical in 2008 for $150 million. As recently as September 2015, another of its companies, Aquesys, which makes surgical devices for the treatment of glaucoma, was acquired by Allergan for close to $300 million. TIF's venture partners include Accuitive Medical Ventures, Versant Ventures, and SV Life Sciences.

India, and most other developing nations today, face a key constraint in delivering affordable, quality healthcare to its citizens. This constraint is medical technology—or the devices, diagnostics, and equipment used to deliver healthcare. In India, like elsewhere, Western imports make up over 65% of the medical technology market- and serve only the high-income, Tier 1, "global Indian" consumers. These technologies are not only unaffordable by most Indians, but are also misaligned with the healthcare ecosystem (infrastructure, skill levels, etc.) prevailing outside of our Tier 1 cities. What can the government do to support such innovation platforms in MedTech in India?

The government can enable the creation of this ecosystem, and catalyze a whole wave of innovation, entrepreneurship and manufacturing in medical technology, in partnership with industry and academia. This process can be initiated by the creation of a task force to assess the potential of this sector, and examine global best practices, to create an *Assessment and Policy Support Report*. This Report can be prepared by engaging an external agency with experience in this sector. The Report should provide concrete policy recommendations, backed by extensive analysis, to create an innovation-led, medical technology industry in India. The Report should also provide a road-map to make India the R&D and manufacturing hub of affordable medical technology, preferably under a *Public-Private-Partnership* model.

A preliminary analysis of policy initiatives in Israel and Singapore, backed by learning's from other healthcare systems, suggest 6 near-term initiatives. These initiatives should ideally be managed by a dedicated entity (like the Office of Chief Scientist in Israel) to make quick decisions for investing, facilitating, and coordinating the recommended activities and programs. This autonomous entity would work in tandem with the Ministry of Health, the Department of Science and Technology, and the Ministry of Commerce and Trade, and be the nodal agency tasked with creating a thriving MedTech industry in India. These initiatives, described below, would require a total public investment of INR 1,200 crores (~USD 200 Million) over 7 years. Most of this investment would generate attractive returns (@10–12% per annum) if the initiatives are successful. Much more importantly, this investment will catalyze the emergence of a thriving indigenous MedTech sector, which will transform healthcare for millions of Indians, reduce the import intensity (and the resultant foreign exchange burden) of our MedTech market, contribute to the nation's Make in India thrust, and become an export powerhouse to rival the IT and pharma sectors over the coming years.

1. Set up world-class medical technology incubators in India:
Set up 6 world-class medical technology incubators in India, in partnership with nationally recognized academic or medical institutes, at key innovation clusters. These incubators would be 15,000–20,000 sq.ft. facilities, with state-of-the-art R&D infrastructure, product engineering and prototyping facilities, and office space for 15–20 startups.

Target: 6 dedicated medical technology incubators by 2017, with capacity to support 100 companies at a time.

2. Set up a grant funding mechanism for early stage MedTech research:
Create a dedicated mechanism to fund idea-stage research (preproof of concept) in priority areas of medical technology. This fund should be for individuals, research teams, and small companies, and should be adequate to support 6–8 months of early stage research.

Target: 200 grants awarded for research in high-priority medical areas.

3. Provide seed-stage capital to incubated Startups:
Besides research infrastructure, and strong incubation support, MedTech startups also need seed funding (typically INR 2–3 crores or USD 300,000–500,000) to develop well-engineered products for Indian needs, and raise venture capital for product launch and commercialization after incubation. The government should provide this funding, in partnership with private investors.

Target: Significant seed-funding with private investors in 100 Incubated startups.

4. Support the creation of dedicated MedTech VC funds:
Dedicated MedTech venture capital funds, with the requisite investment expertise and the right timeframe, are missing in the investment ecosystem in India today. The government can enable creation of such funds by acting as an anchor investor, and partnering with private fund managers to set up dedicated MedTech funds.

Target: INR 2000 crores (~USD 300 million) of venture capital raised to fund MedTech innovation.

5. Kickstart MedTech manufacturing in India by setting up manufacturing for 10–20 high-impact products in PPP mode:
The government can, in mission mode, identify several high-value and high-impact products that are primarily imported today, and are unaffordable for 90%+ of potential consumers. These could include high-tech medical imaging equipment (fMRIs), electromechanical implants (cochlear implants, LVADs, deep brain stimulators), or surgical systems (robotic surgery platforms). Identify global MedTech leaders to partner with the government, and develop and manufacture these products for emerging markets from India, in a PPP mode.

Target: Indigenous manufacturing of 20 high-impact products for Indian and other emerging markets globally by 2020.

6. Support industry through tax breaks and preference in public procurement:

The indigenous MedTech industry can be supported through a favorable tax regime, much like the software sector was supported through STPI. Domestic manufacturing of products should be supported through subsidies, and through rationalization of duty structures. Finally, preference in public procurement can be considered for indigenous MedTech companies—with some budgetary allocation for novel, IP-protected, products developed by Indian companies.

Target: Provide procurement support to 50 innovative, indigenous, products through public health procurement by 2022.

The government should target exiting the programs in 7 years, having created an ecosystem that can be completely driven by private investment. Aligning with the government's focus on outcomes vs. outlay, the above-mentioned initiatives should be evaluated on the basis of outcomes achieved.

Table 5.7 shows the tangible outcomes that the preliminary list of proposed outcomes that the government can use to measure the success of the initiatives.

This nascent industry can be supported through tax incentives, preferential procurement in the public healthcare system, and manufacturing subsidies. Additionally, the government can Kickstart high-tech MedTech manufacturing by selecting 20 high-technology, high-impact products for domestic development and manufacturing, in partnership with global MedTech leaders. This would build domestic manufacturing expertise in the high-tech area of medical products, and support the Government's Make in India initiative.

Globally, small private companies that have been funded through venture capital and research grants have led medical technology innovation. It is estimated that of the 10,000 unique product categories in MedTech, small private companies have developed two- thirds. Larger public companies have a very active licensing and company acquisition strategies

TABLE 5.7   Proposed Outcomes To Measure Success

1. The setup of 6 dedicated medical technology incubators across the country by 2017.

2. Making 200 grant awards (INR 25 Lakh each or USD 50,000) for research in high-priority areas by 2022.

3. Creating dedicated VC funds with INR 2000 crores of capital (~USD 300 million) by 2017.

4. Incubating and funding 100 incubated startups by 2022, and successful graduation of >50 companies to Series A funding.

5. Launch of 50 indigenously developed, novel, products in the Indian market, from incubated startups, by 2025.

6. Launch 20 high-tech, high-impact global products for Indian and other emerging markets, in partnership with global MedTech leaders, by 2020.

7. Emergence of 5–10 domestic MedTech giants (with market capitalization of over $1 billion each) by 2025.

to get access to these innovations and leverage their sales and marketing expertise to bring them to market.

This trend is particularly evident in the United States. The five years from 2007–2012 saw over 1,000 acquisitions of small private companies by global MedTech players. The industry is supported by a vibrant venture capital industry, which invests billions of dollars in startups that have identified an unmet need and are developing innovative products to meet the identified need. Technology incubators at universities, or private medical technology accelerators support many such startups. It is estimated that over a 1,000 such medical technology incubators and accelerators support companies each year.

Israel has also developed a thriving medical technology industry over the last 20 years. This was achieved by a comprehensive government program to drive innovation and research by setting up 24 technology incubators to support startups in this space. These incubators were placed under private management and substantial early stage funding was made available for startups at these incubators through liberal grant funding, and technology venture capital funds. Today, Israel has a thriving MedTech sector, with over a 1,000 companies developing innovative products for the US and Western markets. Now, Singapore is replicating the Israeli model through it's A*STAR program to create a research-led MedTech industry.

Technology incubation, supported by research grants, and ample high-risk venture capital for early stage, research-led companies, has been the model that has successfully created these global hubs of MedTech innovation. This model can be effectively deployed in India to create the world's first ecosystem for affordable MedTech innovation in 5–7 years, and tap the emerging global opportunity in affordable medical technology.

KEYWORDS

- acceleration
- biodesign
- InnAccel
- innovation platform
- medical technology

REFERENCES

"CamTech: Consortium For Affordable Medical Technologies." *www.Massgeneralcenterforglobalhealth.org*. N.p., 2016. Web. 12 Mar. 2016.

"CamTech Innovation Platform: Platform To Accelerate Disruptive Healthcare Innovations." *www.Camtechmgh.org*. N.p., 2016. Web. 12 Mar. 2016.

"InnAccel." *www.Innaccel.com*. N.p., 2016. Web. 12 Mar. 2016.

APPENDICES

APPENDIX 1:

InnAccel's Proprietary Product Engineering and Development Platform Structure

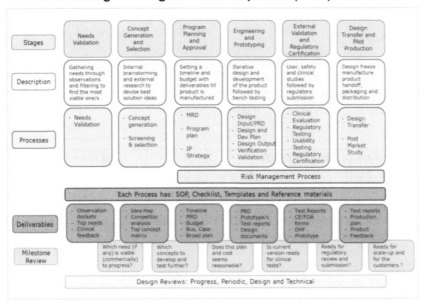

Product Engineering and Development (PED) Platform

APPENDIX 2:

InnAccel's Vision, Mission, and Goals.

Vision
To be the global leader in enabling Affordable MedTech Innovation for India and other emerging markets

Mission
To provide a world-class technology acceleration platform to startups developing innovative medical devices and diagnostics for India and emerging markets

Goals
- Accelerate 100+ startups through a national network of Medical Technology Accelerators
- Deploy INR 1000 crores in these startups towards research, product development, and commercialization
- Deliver 25+ transformational medical technologies to low and mid-income consumers in India and globally

APPENDIX 3:

The following key needs were identified in the Feasibility Study in terms of what services InnAccel should provide, along with the number of respondents mentioning each service:

What InnAccel Should Provide	# of Respondents
Clinical, Academic and Technology Partner Networks	14
Physical Laboratory Infrastructure and Prototyping Facilities	10
Collaborative Working Environment for Clinicians and Entrepreneurs	9
Access to Capital	9
Product Design, Development and Regulatory Support	6
Commercialization Support	6
Mentoring and Strategic Support	6

InnAccel proposed to provide all of the above services and support, either internally or outsourced. Although InnAccel cannot single-handedly develop the nascent MedTech cluster, it could act as a catalyst for more rapid development of the cluster in both the near and long-term.

In the focus group interviews, attendees were asked what types of business assistance did you need, do you need, or do you expect to need? They were then asked to indicate the level of importance with 5 being very important, 1 being least important. (Responses are ranked in order of perceived value:

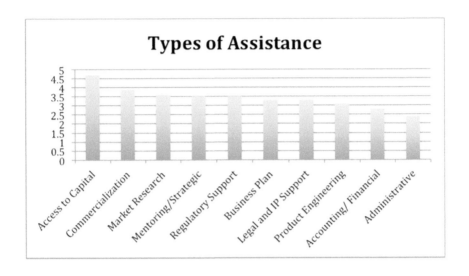

APPENDIX 4:

CAMTech's Innovation Platform in Graphical Depiction.

Source: http://www.massgeneralcenterforglobalhealth.org/camtech/

CHAPTER 6

SOFT-FACTORS ENABLING INNOVATION

CHRISTINE G. KAPP

*DataPsy, Inc., 1503 Ross Ave, Kissimmee, Florida 34744, USA,
E-mail: ckapp@DataPsy.com*

CONTENTS

6.1   INTRODUCTION

"Man cannot discover new oceans unless he has the courage to lose sight of the shore."

—André Gide

Process Models, idea generation platforms, and cognitive products are all necessary to improve an organizational innovation management process. However, many soft factors provide the real key to innovation success. It's hard for any person to discover or notice something new, when they are embedded within current organizational operating processes, when they have worked on the same problem for many years, or when their role has been designed to be 95% reactive. This chapter describes some of the factors inherent in people and organizations that can inhibit innovation.

Companies have to nurture [creativity and motivation]—and have to do it by building a compassionate yet performance-driven corporate culture. In the knowledge economy the traditional soft people side of our business has become the new hard side.

— Gay Mitchell
Executive VP, HR, Royal Bank

This chapter begins by describing the *art of innovation* as an analogy that shows the exponential level of complexity when scaling innovation management processes from personal innovation to visionary-led innovation and finally to enterprise/ecosystem innovation. Soft Factors to the innovation process are explained at each level, with the chapter emphasis being on enterprise-level factors with suggestions for overcoming them.

6.2   METHODS

The method used for developing this chapter was to leverage observation from personal management consulting history and entrepreneurial experience. The observations were cleansed so individual clients cannot be identified, and common factors to innovation are documented. These observations were then organized, and grouped and practical examples added by including references to additional research and popular articles and providing additional references that illustrate current thought leadership on the innovation management process.

6.3   THE ART OF INNOVATION

"Art is how I practice innovation. I see inspiration, then I imagine something and then I create it."

—Violet

When stated this way, innovation seems amazingly simple, yet many organizations today struggle to innovate.

"There is no other organizational capability with such a gap between importance and performance. In the 2015 BCG survey, 70% of executives replied that innovation was either the company's top priority or among the top three. Other surveys by IESE, KPMG and The Conference Board confirm these numbers. Executives consider innovation as the most critical capability for the future success of their companies.

But when asked about their satisfaction with the performance of innovation, less than 20% of the executives was happy based on a survey of our clients."

—London School of Economics and Political Science, 2016

Using the artistic innovation process as a reference is one way to create a framework within which you can design a successful organizational innovation process. It is a clean, simple example of a self-contained innovation management process where one person is under complete control.

"When I create a new sculpture, I find something that I like and connect some concepts and things that I see in a sketch to guide the rest of the design. When I imagined "Sugar Dolphin," I combined my love of Sugar Skulls with the concept of happiness and play. Sugar Dolphin is an 8 foot high creation made of metal bits and pieces inspired by Mexican Sugar Skulls on dia de los muertos. Water turns into confetti and the dolphin leaps in joy over confetti"

—Violet

6.4   PERSONAL INNOVATION PROCESS

A personal innovation process is always the same, whether you are creating a new work of art, or whether you are personally imaging a new business offering that combines new technologies such as Natural Language Processing with eCommerce to improve customer engagement with your website. You, the individual designer are in complete and total control of your personal process. The output of your success process is limited, however, and it is only as good as the time you contribute to it without any input other than external influences (Figure 6.1).

6.4.1   SOFT FACTORS

1. Person's mental framework has creativity, creates ides, and has willingness and passion to deliver on them.
2. Physical ability or personal funding needs to be able to produce the product or service.

6.5   VISIONARY-LED INNOVATION PROCESS

A visionary leader drives innovation by leveraging teams of skilled people. This can be illustrated by understanding at how a great artist works. Louis Comfort Tiffany leveraged organizations of skilled artisans to achieve his goals instead of personally creating art. He created prototypes, and guided the creative direction. In this way, he scaled up his innovation power to

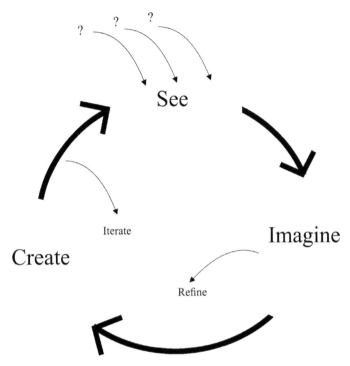

FIGURE 6.1   The personal innovation process.

use existing technologies that had been used in common practice to make new things.

> "Louis Comfort Tiffany (1848–1933) began his work in glass with the same tools and ingredients that had been used by artisans for thousands of years before him. Tiffany took the science of glass-making, however, and elevated it to an art form of new brilliance and beauty. Under his watch, teams of talented designers and crafts-people translated Tiffany's all-encompassing vision into some of the most memorable glass creations of our time. Tiffany's studio system was not a simple enterprise; he needed specialized employ-ees—a hierarchy of artists and artisans—to accomplish his goals."
>
> —(Morse Museum of Art, 2016)

"Innovative leaders are creative visionaries who have big ideas and, most importantly, can motivate people around them to turn those ideas into reality."

—(InnmovationManagement.se, 2015).

This level of innovation is limited by the mental process of this individual, inspirational leader *and* their ability to recognize or imagine great ideas, then act to inspire and drive people in the organization they lead to validate, then create their vision. This is illustrated in (Figure 6.2) as the questions and ideas are formed by the visionary leader, driven down into the organization to create, and then the organization produces the result.

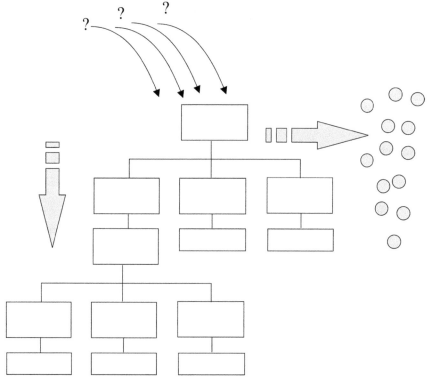

FIGURE 6.2   The visionary-led innovation process.

6.5.1 REAL-WORLD MEDIUM SIZED COMPANY EXAMPLE

Many descriptions of innovation refer to obvious, famous entrepreneurs, such as Steve Jobs as visionary leaders. However, there are many visionary leaders performing this function within smaller organizations on a regular basis. The pattern of the process is the same for all visionaries.

The next example illustrates visionary leadership within a medium-sized information technology consulting company and creation of a regenerative innovation management process to sustain this business even as the world changed around it after 9/11. This leader's role was to plan how to streamline a $27 million company that had been formed through a roll-up of 20 disparate IT consulting companies. The Service offerings in the companies included managed network services, web development, custom application development and distance learning. She observed the companies slow response to proposals, and inconsistent delivery ability after winning a proposal. She imagined a different situation, where any sales person or any area service manager would have at their fingertips the credentials and skills of anyone else in the company. Any sales person in any region would have access and knowledge of detailed information about other regions' "wins," and any technical person could easily find a more informed expert to collaborate with to sell a deal. She also imagined a situation where all of the needed resources would be easy and quick to locate to respond to customer requirements. Not just the letters showing the technical people's ability to fit into the box of a particular job role, but knowledge of their ability to think cognitively and deliver solutions. She designed a system comprised of people, processes, and information systems to support this consulting company's continuous ability to respond to changing technology and customer demands, and define or refine service offerings to continue to be successful. This system was a complex system.

In order to achieve this, she elicited ideas from the area service managers and sales people to learn what they needed, and found ways to provide what the teams needed to participate in the system. As a result, many of the tools that the company operated changed: Job Descriptions, Compensation Plans, and Support Systems were all modified to encourage revenue renewal and collaborative selling. A regenerative process was created to continually gather feedback from the regions and incorporate it into the shape of the overall company service offerings on an ongoing basis. The success of the overall process depended on participation of all of the regional leaders, their consultants, and their sales people. It was refreshing to many staff, to be able for the first time to have resources available to create innovative regional business plans and consistently be able to deliver.

6.5.2   SOFT FACTORS

There are several factors to success in this form of innovation management.
1. The leader has to have the capability to recognize or imagine actionable ideas
2. The leader needs to be able to motivate the organization to deliver on the idea.
3. The leader needs to create an innovation management process in order to keep the actionable ideas and new products/services flowing out.
4. The organization needs the resources to be able to deliver on the idea such as funding, human capital, and physical assets.

6.6   ENTERPRISE INNOVATION PROCESS

Enterprise innovation management processes are exponentially more complex than Visionary-led innovation management processes. The number of actors that participate in the overall innovation management process is far greater, and the leadership skills required to define the means for the actors to collaborate requires higher-level business and human capital management skills.

"The innovativeness of a company is defined as the proven capability to systematically collect ideas, inventions, and other input from a broad range of versatile channels, and to exploit this information, together with the company internal/external competencies, in order to find a new solution to a problem, based on which, to bring up commercially new products and/or services, or other valuable gains with measurable impact, in a timely manner."

—(Rintala, 2011)

Breaking down this definition still shows that the overall innovation management process remains simple, even though it is exponentially more complex to implement than the prior two leadership approaches to innovation (Table 6.1).

The vision in an enterprise innovation process now comes from the entire organization, instead of from a single person. The leader needs to transform into an organizational coach, innovation management process facilitator, or and guide. Figure 6.3 illustrates how multiple ideas, questions and inspiration flow into all contributors in the organization, combine together, then other parts of the organization work together to deliver the new product or service. This is a regenerative process, since when fully operating, it will continually renew itself, even as the individual actors, participants and organizational structure continues to change and improve.

As a different frame of reference, imagine that the organization is a living being, with a collective consciousness. It would be able to leverage all of the knowledge in all of the minds contained within in the organization and their trusted partners, as well as to exploit their openness and perception of the new external forces they collectively see. The organiza-

TABLE 6.1   The Simple Process Within the Complex Enterprise Innovation Process

Enterprise Innovation Management Definition	Simple Definition
Proven ability to systematically collect ideas, inventions, and other input from a broad range of versatile channels.	Seeing the idea
Exploit this information, together with the company internal/external competencies.	Refine, design, fund in the organization's context
Find a new solution to a problem, based on which, to bring up commercially new products and/or services, or other valuable gains with measurable impact, in a timely manner.	Create

Adapted from Source: Rintala, Pekka. Agile Innovation Management—A Proposal for an Express Assessment Tool. Master's Thesis, Helsinki Metropolia University of Applied Sciences, Helsinki, Finland, 2011. With Permission.

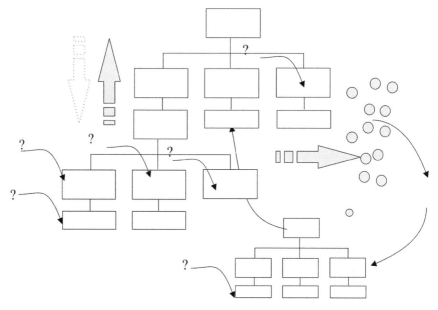

FIGURE 6.3   A regenerative innovation management process.

tion would be capable of connecting ideas from multiple perspectives and departments together with inspiration from outside sources to create new ideas. It would also be able to test them out, break them down, and then recombine them into a new solution.

But today, organizations are not living beings and they don't have collective consciousness.

6.6.1   SOFT FACTORS

There are key success factors that lead to an innovation process. "The analysis suggests that fundamental building blocks for a successful innovation process can be categorized under five leading themes. First, a culture and climate that support innovation; second, a strategy that facilitates the innovation process to serve a purpose; third; resources that enable implementation of the plan; fourth, networks that link the internal and external realities; and fifth, the process that brings structure, measurability and controllability into the system (Rintala, 2005).

TABLE 6.2 Building Blocks Cross Referenced to Soft Factors and Structural/Process Elements

Building Block	Soft Factor
Culture and Climate that support innovation	Factor 1: Type of Leadership
	Factor 2: Culture and Climate
	Factor 3: Human Mindset
Strategy that facilitates the innovation process	Factor 4: Innovation Management Process Design Capability
Resources that Enable Implementation of the Plan	Structural and process elements, such as Job Descriptions, Governance Structure, Organization Structure, Compensation Plans, Contracts, Human Capital Management
Networks that link the internal and external realities	Factor 6: Contracts
Process that brings structure, measurability and controllability into the system	Factor 4: Innovation Management Process Design Capability

Adapted from Source: Rintala, Pekka. Agile Innovation Management—A Proposal for an Express Assessment Tool. Master's Thesis, Helsinki Metropolia University of Applied Sciences, Helsinki, Finland, 2011. With Permission.

Table 6.2 associates building blocks to the soft factors that support innovation. There are more things associated with each building block, such as tools that would enable networks, or business strategy definition and some of these are also illustrated.

6.7 FACTOR 1: TYPE OF LEADERSHIP

The best executive is the one who has sense enough to pick good men to do what he wants done, and self-restraint to keep from meddling with them while they do it."

—(Theodore Roosevelt)

In many organizations, leaders have been trained to create a vision, request budget and then leverage their subordinates to achieve their vision. In a sense, they are trained to be visionary leaders. When creating a sustainable ecosystem that will lead to innovation, a different type of leader is required.

In the book "Collective Genius the authors illustrate that "truly innovative groups are consistently able to elicit and then combine members' separate *slices of genius* into a single work of *collective genius.* Creating and sustaining an organization capable of doing that again and again is what we saw our leaders do (Hill, et. al., 2014)." A major lesson stated in the book was, "You can't plan for innovation or tell people to innovate, but you can organize for it. Leading innovation is about building an organization where individual slices of genius come together to create collective genius through collaboration, discovery-driven learning, and integrative decision making (Hill et al., 2014)." They further state that the leader needs to create an environment with a sense of shared purpose, values, and create a situation where people are able to do the work of innovation.

This observation of success is echoed by Sarah Miller Caldicott, MBA in her Power Patterns blog. She relates an observation of Dr. Carol Pletcher, former Chief Innovation Office at Cargill (PowerPatterns.com, 2009). "Cargill's experience has been that recognizing innovation at the highest management levels and creating a networked program that reaches deep into the grass roots of the organization delivers a high index of success over the long-term." As she states "The challenge in organizational innovation is in creating the environment that permits the multiple people to come together and create new, operationally sound ideas."

6.8   FACTOR 2: CULTURE AND CLIMATE

The culture and climate of the organizations and the individual participants in the innovation process is vital to the overall process operation. "Designate intrapreneurs. Create models and practices that don't just encourage novel thinking but also offer channels and forums to openly challenge leadership." (Steep, 2014)

Google uses a 70/20/10 model as support for their innovative culture. 70% of their projects are dedicated to their core business, 20% of the projects are related to their core business, and 10% of the projects are unrelated to the core business. They use this to support a culture of "yes" or "how can I?"

Culture is not one of those soft matters to be dealt with when the real business is done. Culture is a complement to the formal, established rules of doing business. An understanding of and commitment to the organization's mission will guide employees when confronted by the unexpected for which no rules exist.

It is all too easy for organizations to fall into the analysis trap and focus on left-brain skills like process, measurement, and execution. Sustained innovation enterprises embrace right-brained skills: creativity, imagination, analogy, and empathy. Unlike most organizations that separate these individuals into silos (such as marketing versus engineering), innovative enterprises build teams that morph as new processes and ideas unfold. This results in the creation of focus during ideation and analytical emphasis as market growth accelerates. (Google, 2016).

Table 6.3 shows climate characteristics of organization as created by Ekvall (Rintala, 2011) The characteristics of innovative organizations are

TABLE 6.3 Climate characteristics of more and less innovative organization (Innovation Centre, Europe, 2011)

Innovative	Stagnated
More open and trusting relationships	Fewer open and trusting relationships
Fewer personal conflicts	Higher frequency of personal conflicts
Higher frequency of debates and discussion about ideas	Fewer debates and less discussion
More likely to take risks (e.g., introducing new procedures	Less likely to take risks
More personal freedom in doing the job	Close and conspicuous supervision
More time to spend in idea generation/evaluation	Less time to spend in idea generation/evaluation
New ideas received favorably by senior people and encouraged	New ideas ignored or discouraged
Committed people highly involved in their work	Less commitment and involvement
More fun	Less fun
Workplace more exciting/dynamic	Workplace less exciting/dynamic

Source: Rintala, Pekka. Agile Innovation Management—A Proposal for an Express Assessment Tool. Master's Thesis, Helsinki Metropolia University of Applied Sciences, Helsinki, Finland, 2011. With Permission.

TABLE 6.4   Dolphin Index Innovation Climate Dimensions (Innovation Centre, Europe, 2011)

Dimension	Description
Commitment	The extent to which people are committed to the organization and work is viewed as stimulating and engaging.
Freedom	High freedom work environments are those in which people are empowered to make their own decisions, for example about prioritizing their work. In low freedom environments there is close and conspicuous supervision.
Idea Support	Refers to organizational support and encouragement for the development of new ideas and suggestions for improvements.
Positive relationships	Refers to the extent to which there are positive, trusting, friendly, interpersonal relationships between people, rather than negative (e.g., hostile, conflicting ones).
Dynamism	Refers to whether work is exciting and dynamic, or static and boring.
Playfulness	Refers to levels of light-heartedness and fun in the work place. Work environments low on playfulness may be seen as dour and humorless.
Idea Proliferation	Refers to the extent to which other people in the work environment are perceived as having innovative ideas about, and varied perspectives towards, their work.
Stress	High stress work environment are defined as those in which other individuals are observed to be highly stressed and encountering heavy workloads.
Risk Taking	High risk taking environments are thought to promote the speed at which new ideas are implemented. Low risk taking environments are likely to be characterized by excessive use of formal rules and procedures.
Idea Time	Refers to the extent to which employees perceive that there is time for producing and developing new ideas.
Shared View	Refers tot the extent to which there are open and adequate communications between more and less senior employees. Work environment where there is an 'us' culture rather than an 'us and them' culture.
Work Recognition	Do people feel that they receive credit and praise for their achievements? Or do they feel undervalued?
Pay Recognition	Refers to satisfaction with pay and conditions. Do people feel fairly remunerated for their work—or at worst, feel exploited.

representative of a collection of open minds, while a stagnated climate exhibits more symptoms of a trust-less environment.

In fact, the Dolphin Index contains a number of dimensions that measure the organizations' internal culture (Table 6.4). If the innovation ecosystem contains multiple enterprises, then each of them would need to have similar characteristics in order for the collaboration endeavor to be sustainable over time.

6.9   FACTOR 3: HUMAN MINDSET

It isn't the incompetent who destroy an organization. The incompetent never get in a position to destroy it. It is those who achieved something and want to rest upon their achievements who are forever clogging things up.

— F. M. Young

Innovation is dependent on open and creative idea flow. In the collective consciousness model, the minds participating in the collaboration need to develop the skills to know how to interact on a personal level with others in addition to whatever governance model guides and supports their participation in the process.

6.9.1   *PERSONAL RESPONSIBILITY TO REMAIN OPEN TO NEW IDEAS*

Responsibility means being accountable for what we each personally think, say, and do. Personal responsibility involves working on our own character and skill development instead of blaming others for situations and circumstances.

Although corporate executives have responsibility to create the cultural environment that produces and sustains a more innovative environment, it is each individual participant's responsibility to contribute within that framework to the overall goal of innovation.

When someone is seeking," said Siddhartha, "It happens quite easily that he only sees the thing that he is seeking; that he is unable to find anything, unable to absorb anything, because he is only thinking of the thing he is seeking, because he has a goal, because he is obsessed with his goal. Seeking means: to have a goal; but finding means: to be free, to be receptive, to have no goal. You, O worthy one, are perhaps indeed a seeker, for in striving towards your goal, you do not see many things that are under your nose."

—*Hermann Hesse, Siddhartha*

6.9.2 CERTIFICATIONS

Certifications are an excellent measure of competence. They measure people's knowledge and skills against industry- and vendor-specific benchmarks to prove to employers that they have the right mix of skills, knowledge, and expertise to perform a specific task. Using the information technology world as an example, certifications such as PMP for Project Managers, Certified Scrum Masters, or Agile Certified Practitioners are prevalent. So are ITIL certifications for support organizations, and architecture certifications such as TOGAF, Zachman or the IASA Foundation. There are at least ten cloud computing certifications. Certifications save organizations time and money in evaluating candidates and help human resource departments identify the right people for the roles.

However, rewarding job-specific knowledge alone has a detrimental effect on innovation because it narrows the field of thought for a particular individual who is part of the collaboration.

We all operate in two contrasting modes, which might be called open and closed. The open mode is more relaxed, more receptive, more exploratory, more democratic, more playful and more humorous. The closed mode is the tighter, more rigid, more hierarchical, more tunnel-visioned. Most people unfortunately spend most of their time in the closed mode. Not that the closed mode cannot be helpful. If you are leaping a ravine, the moment of takeoff is a bad time for considering alternative strategies. When you charge the enemy machine-gun post, don't waste energy trying to see the funny side of it. Do it in the "closed" mode. But the moment the action is over, try to return to the "open" mode—to open your mind again to all the feedback from our action that enables us to tell whether the action has been successful, or whether further action is need to improve on what we have done. In other words, we must return to the open mode, because in that mode we are the most aware, most receptive, most creative, and therefore at our most intelligent.

— John Cleese

6.10 FACTOR 4: INNOVATION MANAGEMENT PROCESS DESIGN CAPABILITY

Within an organization that knows how to innovate, *an innovation management process* exists. The process may have developed accidentally, because of the way the organizational leaders operated, or it could have been designed intentionally, by a complex system designer skilled in business, people and technology. In this chapter, we are referring to the initial design of the innovation management process as the *innovation process management process (IPMP)*

Just like any large complex system, the IPMP will have an initial startup phase, after which time it will reach steady-state operation. Steady-state operation will include the ability to continuously respond and improve with respect to changes inside the organization, or changes outside the organization.

By design, business outcomes that include new products and services will occur as a result of the innovation process management activities that do not exist in the original design of the organization or even in the *innovation process management process*. As time moves forward, the participants in the process change, the organization changes, and external market forces and technology change.

There is not yet a prescriptive design methodology on exactly how to design an IPMP, however, it is useful to think of an IPMP as a complex system of systems. The field of System of System (SoS) design provides us with a design starting point. "Two primary traits, evolutionary and emergent behavior are highlighted since they call attention to a network-of-systems, dynamic-behavior focus as opposed to an individual system, static-behavior focus (DeLaurentis, 2005)." Table 6.5 provides some distinguishing traits of System-of-Systems (DeLaurentis, 2005) that have been correlated with soft factors enabling innovation and aspects of IPMP design process. This table has been augmented with some of the innovation factors that are related to the SoS traits.

TABLE 6.5   Traits of System-of-Systems and Innovation Management Systems

Trait	Description	Soft Factor
Operational and Managerial Independence	Constituent systems are useful in their own right and generally operate independent of other systems (i.e., with unique intent provided by the owner/operator)	Factor 1—Type of Leadership
Geographic Distribution	Constituent Systems are not physically colocated; but, they be in communication	Factor 4—Innovation Management Process Design Capability
Evolutionary Behavior	The SoS is never completely, finally formed, constantly, changes and has a "porous" problem boundary; i.e., is a living system	Factor 4—Innovation Management Process Design Capability
Emergent Behavior	Properties appear in the SoS that are not apparent (or predicted) from the constituent systems	Factor 4—Innovation Management Process Design Capability
Networks	Networks define the connectivity between independent systems in the SoS through rules of interaction	Factor 6—Contracts and Agreements (business and technical)
Heterogeneity	Constituent systems are of significantly different nature, with different elementary dynamics that operate on a different time scale	Factor 6—Contracts and Agreements
Trans-Domain	(Proposition) Effective Study of SoS requires unifying knowledge across fields of study: engineering, economy, policy, operations	Cross-Functional knowledge Factor 3—Mindset

Adapted from Source: DeLaurentis, Daniel. Understanding Transportation as a System-of-Systems Design Problem, 43rd AIAA, Aerospace sciences meeting, Reno, Nevada, January 10–13, 2005; AIAA-2005-0123. With Permission.

The IPMP needs to be designed so that it will simultaneously produce ideas within an ecosystem comprised of one or more organizations. Components of the system will include organization structure, well defined roles and responsibilities, ways to reinforce collaboration between organizational units, ways to require collaboration by suppliers bound by contracts, and any information technology or physical support systems needed for the whole process to work.

Importantly, this innovation strategy must have consistent management support throughout all business cycles, and it should also cover alternative paths for ideas that have merits but do not fit the prevailing corporate strategy. Next, the process must be clearly defined and communicated. Furthermore, the process must have owners and coaches. Well-structured incentive plans are also an important element, if any longer lifetime and support for the process is desired; but careful planning is vital. Incentives are obviously linked to metrics, but these seem to be very company and time specific, and defining generally valid and useful metrics is not considered to be a relevant or even possible target.

—(Rintala, 2011).

Consider what makes innovation managers successful. "We have seen CIOs continue to act as guardians of the stage gate process and related metrics, all things which most of the companies do pretty well and where the leverage for impact is minimum. Companies are really struggling on capabilities for discontinuous innovation. Successful leaders create the right environment for discontinuous ideas to be generated across the company and to nourish them up to the concept stage when the risk is lower and the idea/project can be transitioned back to the business units and standard development process."

—(Di Fiore, 2016).

Some say they see poetry in my paintings. I see only Science.

—Georges Seurat

The struggle to innovate can be alleviated if the leaders take a step back and look at their organization from the outside. Start with a high-level view of interactions between the organization in context of its interactions with its customers, suppliers, competitors provides a simple view of and changing technological innovations. Then drill down into the interactions between each organization and its supporting systems. Then think about how to make that system innovate. Taking a look from that perspective makes the high-level IPMP process visible. A simple way to get the concept is to go to a museum and look at Georges Seurat pointillism painting. In this painting style, the picture is comprised of tiny dots of color, which when viewed from a distance provide "the big picture." Looking up close, all you see is dots, stepping back, all you see is a beautiful painting.

6.10.1   PROTO METHOD RELATED TO IPMP DESIGN

The soft skills related to the ability to designing a complex system-of-systems environment require the ability to see all of the component parts, as well as the interactions between them.

A system-of-systems is an assemblage of components which individually may be regarded as systems, and which possess two additional properties:

Operational Independence of the Components: If the system-of-system is disassembled into its component systems the component systems must be able to usefully operate independently. That is, the components fulfill customer-operator purposes on their own.

Managerial Independence of the Components: The component systems not only *can* operate independently, they *do* operate independently. The component systems are separately acquired and integrated but maintain a continuing operational existence independent of the system-of-systems (Maier, 1998).

A starting point to think about how to design a system that supports innovation is borrowed from a proto-method System-of-Systems lexicon (DeLaurentis, 2005). Table 6.6 leverages two columns from this lexicon, categories and descriptions, and shows business entities and processes whose contributions need to be considered in the initial design.

TABLE 6.6 Key Categories, and Descriptions Correlated with Fundamental Building Blocks of Innovation Management Systems

Categories	Descriptions	Innovation Management Systems
Resources	The entities (systems) that give physical manifestation to the system-of-systems	Supporting information systems
Economics	The nonphysical entities (stakeholders) that give intent to the SoS operation	Companies, partners, suppliers, competitors, funding sources
Operations	The application of intent to direct the activity of physical & Non-physical entities	Operational Leadership
Policies	The external forcing functions that impact the operation of physical and nonphysical entities	Governance and Contracts

Adapted from Source: DeLaurentis, Daniel. Understanding Transportation as a System-of-Systems Design Problem, 43rd AIAA, Aerospace sciences meeting, Reno, Nevada, January 10–13, 2005; AIAA-2005-0123. With Permission.

6.11 FACTOR 5: CONTRACTS

Many organizations have now adopted outsourcing models where all or part of their business services are provided by third party companies. This means their ecosystem and their innovation management process, contains other business partners whose objectives are to provide contractual services.

These relationships are typically governed by contract which can include fixed price contracts, time and materials contracts, or joint venture contracts. Measurement of these contracts is performed through measurement of specific service targets depending on the service being measured. Incident response and resolution metrics are common, as are financial penalties to suppliers when measures have not been met.

Sometimes factors to innovation are crystallized within outsourcing contracts. Many information technology outsourcing contracts today are structured based on contractual towers of service management responsibilities (Oshri and Kotlarsky, 2012). Typically in information technology towers are organized around types of technology in the stack, as opposed to a business process delivery process.

6.11.1   EXAMPLE: MULTIVENDOR OUTSOURCED ENVIRONMENT

In this simplistic example, we have organized an information technology organization into three organizations. The Software delivery organization produces new software. The Application Service Management organization manages availability of corporate applications. The infrastructure service management team manages availability of hardware and network services. The Software delivery team uses internal resources and one external vendor. The Application service management team is responsible for monitoring and managing the level of service provided to support existing applications such as ERP, and multiple line of business applications. This application service management team has two MSP's that manage different applications. The *infrastructure team* has two different MSP's that focus on server infrastructure and network infrastructure (Figure 6.4). All of these services are measured by traditional means including root cause analysis, change management success rates, incident handling metrics and more. The contracts for Vendor 1, MSP1, MSP2, MSP3 and MSP4 are all

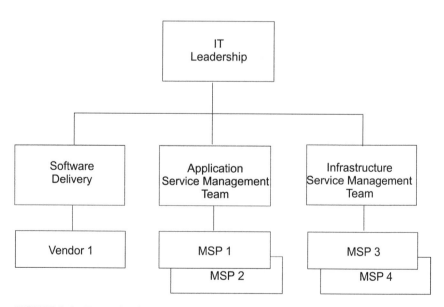

FIGURE 6.4   Example of Corporate Managed Outsourced Services.

on different timeframes, meaning their contract start time and contract end times are different.

6.11.2 INTRODUCING A COMPANY-GENERATED INNOVATION

Now let's introduce an innovation to this structure and look at the response. As a new innovative contribution to the organization, an idea has been created that will leverage natural language processing to be used in dialog with a customer emergency response team. The new customer response mobile and web application will answer questions from customers and provide responses based on what the application "knows" from reading the corporate knowledge base. This will eliminate 80% of the initial calls, so that only the higher skilled customer service agents will be needed in the organization. The technology is implemented in such a way that MSP1 will be supporting the mobile application, but MSP2 will be supporting the part of the application that "knows" the answer to the customer's question. In addition, the solution will be hosted on a cloud platform not yet supported by either MSP3 or MSP4.

In this example, when the innovation comes to fruition, and depending on how the initial contract language was written with MSP1, MSP2, MSP3 and MSP4, there may need to be four new contracts negotiated. While this is not a deal-breaker, it can cause the implementation time of the innovation to increase if not planned for initially.

6.11.3 INHERENT OBSTACLE TO MULTI-SOURCING GOVERNANCE

"The basic obstacle to effective multisourcing governance is the way that outsourcing contracts are traditionally negotiated. Providers tend to focus on their particular scope of responsibility, and to be very specific about what they are and aren't responsible for (CruxialCIO, 2014)." In each contract, metrics are provided to keep the MSP's accountable to the business. MSP's manage their scope of responsibility tightly, because "the vast majority of the firms are using fixed price contracts (78%). Only 42% are using time and materials contracts and 21% are using joint venture with a profit sharing clause (Oshri, et al. 2012)."

Using the same structural example, let's assume that MSP2 is supporting an application that is running on MSP4's hardware and MSP3's network (Figure 6.5). MSP4 is, in turn, dependent on the organizations internal maintenance department to support the facility that MSP4's equipment is located in. One day, the organizations internal maintenance department causes an outage that breaks MSP4's entire hardware infrastructure. This causes the application supported by MSP2 to become unavailable for an extended period of time. Both MSP2 and MSP4 are liable for a penalty because of the service unavailability. However, MSP2 will ask for relief from penalty because it was MSP4's fault, and MSP4 will ask for relief because it was the customers fault. In the end, both MSP's will not be liable for the penalty and much time will have been wasted.

The contractual arrangements create a culture of blame between the MSP's instead of a culture of collaboration. The contracts could be amended to include clauses related to cross-MSP collaboration, not just in a reactive situation like this, but in a situation that requires innovation. Or alternatively, the contracts could be focused around business process

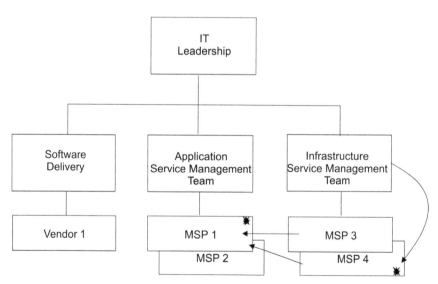

FIGURE 6.5   Illustration of multi-vendor outsourcing responsibility crossing organizational boundaries.

delivery instead of technology stacks. There are many potential solutions to eliminating this factor, which require rethinking in contract structure.

The outsourcing context poses additional challenges to achieving innovation between a client firm and a vendor. One of the main reasons often cited by CIOs for failing to achieve innovation in outsourcing is the uncertainty about the nature of innovation desired from the vendor, and also the inability to design a contract that is on the one hand mitigating client's exposure to be exploited by the vendor and at the same time offers compensation for extra work and innovation delivered by the vendor. Put simply, most outsourcing contracts do not accommodate these often contradicting requirements properly (Oshri, 2012).

6.12 CONCLUSION

In conclusion, this chapter presented the soft factors that impact innovation in the context of three distinct sizes of innovating organizations. Personal innovation is within the individual innovators' control. Visionary innovation requires all of the same factors as personal innovation, but adds the requirement that the visionary be able to direct and manage people towards a goal. With enterprise innovation, the game changes. With enterprise innovation, a process and supporting systems exist or are structured within the organization. An IPMP supports the ability of the people within the organization to collaborate, identify ideas, refine them and produce new marketable products and services, while keeping the lights on every day. Factor management grows exponentially with large-scale leadership and includes the right leadership, the right culture, the right participant's mindset, and the elimination of contractual barriers.

KEYWORDS

- **art of innovation**
- **factors to innovation**
- **innovation**
- **system-of-systems**

REFERENCES

DeLaurentis, Daniel. Understanding Transportation as a System-of-Systems Design Problem, 43rd AIAA, Aerospace sciences meeting, Reno, Nevada, January 10–13, 2005; AIAA-2005-0123.

Google. Creating a Culture of Innovation. Eight ideas that work at Google. https://apps.google.com/learn-more/creating_a_culture_of_innovation.html# (accessed January 25, 2016).

Hill, Linda; Brandeau, Greg; Truelove, Emily; Lineback, Kent. Collective Genius, The Art and Practice of Leading Innovation," Harvard Business Review Press, 2014.

Ilan Oshri, Julia Kotlarsky, Innovation in Outsourcing: A Study on Client Expectations and Commitment, Warwick Business School and Rotterdam School of Management. http://innovationmanagement.se/wp-content/uploads/2012/01/Cognizant-WBS-innovation-report-FINAL.pdf.

Innovation Management. What Is Innovation Leadership? http://www.innovationmanagement.se/imtool-articles/what-is-innovative-leadership/ (accessed January 25, 2016).

London School of Economics and Political Science. What Makes Innovation Managers Successful? http://blogs.lse.ac.uk/businessreview/2016/01/08/what-makes-innovation-leaders-successful/ (accessed January 25, 2016).

Maier, M. W. (1998). Architecting principles for systems-of-systems. Syst. Engin., 1: 267–284. doi: 10.1002/(SICI)1520–6858(1998)1:4<267::AID-SYS3>3.0.CO;2-D.

Morse Museum of Art. Secrets of Tiffany Glassmaking. http://www.morsemuseum.org/on-exhibit/secrets-of-tiffany-glassmaking (accessed January 25, 2016).

Multi-Sourcing Offers Big Rewards, Carries Big Risks. http://www.cruxialcio.com/multi-vendor-outsourcing-can-yield-it-innovation-only-if-its-well-managed-4377 (accessed January 25, 2016).

Oshri Ilan, & Kotlarsky Julia. Innovation in Outsourcing: A Study on Client Expectations and Commitment. Warwick Business School and Rotterdam School of Management, 2012. http://innovationmanagement.se/wp-content/uploads/2012/01/Cognizant-WBS-innovation-report-FINAL.pdf (accessed January 20, 2016).

Power Patterns™ Igniting Innovation. Rewarding vs. Recognizing Innovation—Which is Better. http://powerpatterns.com/Articles/NewsletterArchives/2009_12 (accessed January 20, 2016).

Rintala, Pekka. Agile Innovation Management—A Proposal for an Express Assessment Tool. Master's Thesis, Helsinki Metropolia University of Applied Sciences, Helsinki, Finland, 2011.

Steep, Mike. How to Create Innovation Cultures That Keep Working, Forbes, September 3, 2014. http://www.forbes.com/sites/forbesleadershipforum/2014/09/03/how-to-create-innovation-cultures-that-keep-working/2/#2715e4857a0b754bb7c33fa3.

CHAPTER 7

IOT AND M.E.S.: ARE YOU READY FOR THE NEXT INDUSTRIAL REVOLUTION?

SELEM CHARFI

HD Technology, Europarc du Chкne, 8 rue Pascal-BP90, 69672 BRON Lyon, France, E-mail: Selem.Charfi@hdtechnology.fr

CONTENTS

ABSTRACT

This chapter presents the impact of the Internet of the Things (IoT) concept on the manufacturing systems and the challenges to which will be faced the R&D actors in order to anticipate on the future evolution. The author first present the general concepts related to IoT and Manufacturing Executing Systems (M.E.S.). Then the announced benefits from this exposition are presented. These benefits won't be priceless. We will then present the major challenges to be expected from this change.

7.1   INTRODUCTION

By 2020, experts expect more than 50 billion of sold objects of the internet of things (Sundmaeker et al., 2010). Such revolution is announced as imminent and certain. Then, different field experts and researchers are working to anticipate the related consequences and challenges. The expected impact is anticipated to cover energy, healthcare, manufacturing, public sector, transportation and related industrial systems (IIC, 2015).

One of the areas that will not certainly stay indifferent to IoT wave is the industrial area. In fact, nowadays a new concept that is becoming more and more current: the fourth industrial revolution "Industry 4.0" (Bloem et al., 2014).

Remember that the first revolution occurred by the 18th century by integrating mechanical production (essentially through steam engine). The second was guided by the introduction of the electric engine from the beginning of the twentieth century (assembly line mass production). The third one was dictated by the computing and networking for automating the manufacturing process. The fourth revolution is accelerated mainly by the M2M and the industrial Ethernet.

Note that the Machine-to-Machine (M2M) represents a future where billions to trillions of everyday objects are interconnected and managing a wide range of devices, networks, and servers (Geng et al., 2011). "M2M refers to those solutions that allow communication between devices of the same type and a specific application all via wired or wireless communication networks. M2M solutions allow end-users to capture data about events from assets, such as temperature or inventory levels. Typically, M2M is deployed to achieve productivity gains, reduce costs and increase safety of security" (Höller et al., 2014).

Many works and organization are proposed in order to guide this revolution such is Industrial Internet Consortium (IIC).

The M.E.S., a must part of supervising and optimizing manufacturing process performance, is not immune toward the IoT "tsunami." The main goal of this chapter is to present the resulting challenges and the expected future features of M.E.S.

The remainder of this chapter is structured as follows. First, we introduce the most relevant notions of M.E.S. systems and IoT. Second, we will present the expected M.E.S. evolution in the future. Next, the incoming challenges are introduced. Finally, we conclude this chapter by concluding remarks and some perspectives.

7.2 DEFINITION

7.2.1 M.E.S.: DEFINITION AND CONCEPT

Since their beginning in the mid-1990s, the M.E.S. have been significantly evolving. The M.E.S. were proposed for industrial need for optimizing the manufacturing process reactivity, the manufacturing quality, the standards respect, and mainly reducing cost and deadlines (Ugarte et al., 2009).

They were first intended for only storing and analyzing data for manufacturing and mainly in an offline mode. Then, they are actually operating in real time for storing and analyzing data. They evolved from simple supervision software to integrated software applications at the paste of computing technologies to supporting the manufacturing process from the production order to the delivery of finished products. However, the manufacturing actors are expecting more from M.E.S. to support in the future the planning of future process and to integration functionalities to anticipate in the future possible process deviation.

Note that in 1997, the MESA organization proposed the first step for the standardization of the M.E.S. The MESA defined clearly the expected functionalities from M.E.S. The M.E.S. functional areas are:

1. **Labor management:** Provides the status of different human resources involved in the manufacturing process. It also provides statistics and reporting about the manufacturing staff activities (realized and scheduled). It enables labor tracking and scheduling. The M.E.S. might interact with resources allocation to optimize the manufacturing process.

2. **Resource allocation:** Manages the different manufacturing physical resources: machines, devices, material, tools and other equipment. The M.E.S. can provide documents about the history of each resource. This functionality is important to enable dispatching the work orders on the different physical resources.

3. **Dispatching:** Although dispatching and scheduling the Product Orders on the manufacturing machines is communicated from the Enterprise Resource Planning (ERP), the M.E.S. can dispatch the order differently since it has a better overview of the available machines. The M.E.S. support the manufacturing priorities, the BOM (the recipe for manufacturing), and the production characteristics. Then, the M.E.S. can provide manufacturing alternatives to ERP ones.

4. **Product tracking:** The M.E.S. support the visibility of the production by the time and the physical resource axes. For a given product, the M.E.S. indicate about the material batches used for producing this product (serial number, quantity, etc.), the allocated physical resources for manufacturing this product and the human operators responsible of its manufacturing. These data are stored for a long time, especially for food and drug manufacturing.

5. **Quality management:** This functionality consists of reporting in offline and online analysis of the product quality. This reporting is established via different measurements collected manually or automatically from manufacturing.

6. **Performance analysis:** Provides a real-time overview of actual manufacturing operations' results. This overview can be coupled with historical data in order to establish comparison and for benchmarking purposes. This overview is based on periodically or on demand measurements. The provided analysis can be: production rate, conformance to scheduled manufacturing, availability of raw products, resource status (temperature, pressure, etc.). The analysis can be as numerical data, personalized widgets, control charts, pdf report, web reports, etc.

7. **Process management:** The M.E.S. monitor the manufacturing process to automatically correct or provide decision support to face the process derivation or to improve the manufacturing process.

8. **Scheduling:** To schedule the manufacturing process: the product order, the batches, the scheduled tasks, etc. This functionality consists of dispatching the information received from ERP on the manufacturing resources. As the scheduled work can change at any time, the M.E.S. ensures rescheduling the manufacturing activities.

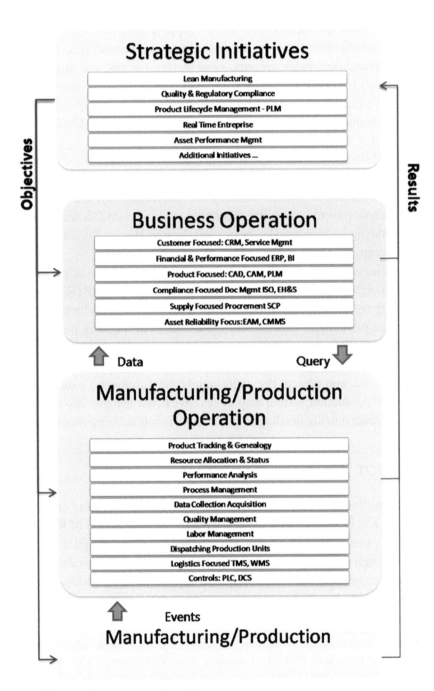

FIGURE 7.1 The M.E.S. functionalities.

9. **Document control**: The M.E.S. support documentation about the manufacturing recipe, the manufacturing instructions, operation procedures, batch records, engendering notices, etc. It considers also factors related to environment, staff safety and health. There are many regulations and recommendations to be considered following the kind of manufacturing sector: The GAMP (2001), 21 CFR Part 11 (2003), etc.

10. **Maintenance management**: In order to maintain a good manufacturing flow, the operator has to proceed frequently with maintenance operations in order to warranty the resource ability, availability and capability to ensure the scheduled tasks. The M.E.S. can manage the maintenance tasks' or prevent the operator for the scheduled or required maintenance task.

Further works were proposed for better standardization, such is the ISA effort in order to formalize the exchange interface with ERP (B2 MML[1]).

Many references define the M.E.S. as an intermediate layer between the office planning systems (mainly the ERP) and the shop floor (Owen and Parker, 1999; Koch, 2001).

In other words, The M.E.S. aims to collect, organize, analyze, integrate, record, and present the data (mainly measurements) issued for the industrial production, so that employees have better insights into processes and can react quickly, leading to predictable manufacturing processes.

7.2.2   IOT

The term "Internet of Things" was used the first time by the end of the 1990 by Kevin Ashton. He used this term concerning the use of RFID tags in Supply chain. Nowadays, it is introduced as a promising field.

Although there is a universal definition about the IoT, the existing definitions define it as a network of physical objects, devices, building, and all things that can be embedded with software's and sensors supporting network connectivity in order to interchange data collected by these objects

---

[1] Business to Manufacturing Markup Language: is an XML implementation of the ANSI/ISA-95 standards (ISA-95). It consists on an XML schema (XSD) to define a common data definition to formalize the exchanged data between ERP and manufacturing systems (MESA, 2016).

without human intervention. The IoT concept is strongly related to the internet and its proliferation is related to the internet proliferation.

7.3   MES AND IOT: THE BENEFITS

In this section, we will present the different benefits for M.E.S. actors through integrating the IoT.

7.3.1   MORE FLEXIBILITY: THE AGILITY OF M.E.S. EXPLOITATION

As the M.E.S. are intended for optimizing the manufacturing process and resources, they have to be connected to the different measurement devices and the different parts of the manufacturing system.

One of the major concerns of M.E.S. actors is how to easily face to the manufacturing environment that were qualified for a long time as a static one and now migrating to a dynamic one to quickly respond to customer and market queries. This change is mainly due to the often the market demand change and the highly competitive atmosphere of the global market. This change is characterized by the increasing frequency of the custom production orders. Then, the traditional M.E.S. systems have to improve their ability to respond easily and quickly to the different changes.

The M.E.S. have to be more flexible in terms of supported functionalities. Two major alternatives are proposed. The first one consists one adopting a full web solution; a solution based as SaaS[2] one. However, this solution presents some inconveniences that are:
- Security aspects of exposing manufacturing data on the net,
- Performance lost as the gathered data has to be uploaded on the net, analyzed and then, and load it to manufacturing dashboard.

The second alternative is the preferred one: the workflow[3]. It has mainly the advantage to integrate flexible alternative for invocating alarms such is

---

[2] Software as a service is a software licensing and delivery model in which software is licensed on a subscription basis and is centrally hosted (Dan Ma, 2007).

[3] Workflow: An automation of a business process, in whole or part, during which documents, information or tasks are passed from one participant to another for action, according to a set of procedural rules (see, WFMC).

the case of mail and Short Message Service (SMS) notifications. However, the actual M.E.S. need further work in order to be adopted by the workflow engine. This alternative is estimated as a promising as it provides the user with the possibility to specify new manufacturing Key Performance Indicators (KPIs)[4] and to adjust the M.E.S. for the possible changes occurring on the shop floor. Furthermore, many M.E.S. actors are working on proposing out-of-the-box versions that can be used immediately by the user without changing the system and without requiring integrators for setting up the M.E.S.

The main area that is intended to be flexible and supported by the workflows are:

1. elementary data storage,
2. the data return,
3. the relevant data selection (KPI),
4. the decision model design,
5. the decision evaluation, and
6. the selection and choice of a solution.

7.3.2   REACTIVITY: FASTER MARKET TIME

The incoming industrial revolution is intended to lead more fluid communication flows. The implicated actors to the manufacturing can access easily to the information. The dashboard is not only, as it had been for a long time, screens including great amount of metrics that are used while operating on the production line. These user interfaces are exported now to innumerable devices (e.g., smart phones, tablets, smartwatch) that offer accessibility to them and consequently contribute to boost the reaction time to potential line state change or client requirement.

In terms of Business Intelligence, the expert can have further information to proceed to a deeper predictive analysis and then to better assist the decision maker in short delays.

The sales management generally introduces the M.E.S. as real time data processing. This is in accordance with the announced objective with the

---

[4] Key Performance Indicator: A type of performance measurement. It enables the evaluation of an organization or an activity.

MESA. However, the reality seems different from the announced objective. In fact, the processing the data is generally articulated through three categories: (i) acquisition from the shop floor and planning systems, (ii) analyzing data, and (iii) saving the data (raw data and/or aggregate data).

The two first categories often take time to be finished and generally the final result needs several seconds or minutes or delay. Comparing the time requested of many ERP, and many old shop floor, the M.E.S. is considered by many as a real time system. One of the expected solution, provided by IoT, is to gather and to analyze data at the same time. This can surely improve the M.E.S. time execution performances.

One related issue to improve the scalability of M.E.S. for better context adaptation to support small and huge manufacturing systems.

7.3.3   SMART FACTORY

Based on cyber-physical systems, the smart factory has been for a long time the dream of the manufacturer as it is intended to provide high flexibility and intelligence. The data processing is distributed following the related resource in real-time (Lucke et al., 2008).

7.3.4   OPTIMIZATION

The IoT universe offers the ability to manufacturer to enable access to the information independently of their geographical location. This lead to faster control process and more effective management and supervision of the manufacturing process.

The concept of Smart Factory was introduced first in 1991 by Mark Weiser. This concept is based on the Ubiquitous Computing one. It was boosted through the mobile phone evolution. It is based mainly on shorter and reactive manufacturing cycles. The smart factory includes designing, setting up, piloting, and supervising the factories. The impact on the M.E.S. will lead to more flexible and configurable M.E.S. to support the flexible aspects of the Smart Factories. The M.E.S. will turn from a static management of the manufacturing system to an adoptive one.

7.3.5   MANUFACTURING IMPROVEMENT

The business and manufacturing leaders are optimists to the idea to improve their business ability by interconnecting simultaneously heterogeneous and dispatched objects over the internet network. The main goal to reach is to support manufacturing process adaptability and flexibility to face the rapid market growth and rapidly changing customer requirements.

By distributing the manufacturing process tasks and subtasks, the manufacturing system is more persistent to communication flows communication temporary shutdown. It promotes offline processing thanks to the smart aspect of manufacturing resources.

7.4   INCOMING CHALLENGES

7.4.1   BIG DATA

Manufacturing environment is evolving from simply physical resource manufacturing system managing to heterogeneous and various information management system. It is mainly due to the last generation of smart sensors and connected devices and machines. Despite improving the manufacturing systems performances, the M.E.S. leaders are according particular interest to the increasing data volume.

Nowadays leading DBMS are reaching high and promising performance dealing with a great amount of data. The new DBMS generation based on NoSQL[5] (Leavitt, 2010) is announced as a promising solution to handle such data. This goal can be reached through the Cloud based application that offer the possibility to store and exploit data more efficiently.

About 70% of manufacturing executives are focusing on plant-floor data initiatives to drive operational and business excellence, faster time to market, and immediate access to data from machines on the factory floor (*see*, Aberdeen Group).

---

[5] NoSql: Not Only SQL: refers to Database Management Systems that are not based on the classical relational architecture.

7.4.2 NETWORKING AND SECURITY

The cloud-based applications are announced as a magic solution for the next information era by providing better connectivity. It enables to interconnect everything to everything. Although the potential of the cloud-based applications and the positive user experience, the customer still feel anxious toward security problems. Despite the many proposed works for improving the security aspect, no one can actually warranty the security aspects.

The existing automation client server protocols are not estimated to be enough sufficient and performant to support the emerging wave of IoT in terms of data quantity and frequency. The isolated and single factories turn to interconnected factories.

In order to adopt and exploit the coming industrial revolution, the M.E.S. have to be more efficient, to handle Big Data, and to provide an opening to the internet (Cloud Computing) to support connectedness and interaction. This leads to new interfaces with other systems and devices.

The fact of interconnecting billions of devices, exponentially raises the questions toward the security aspect. One of the current research efforts concerns the "security and chip."

A major challenge to which are faced IoT promotors is cybersecurity. As there is not any universal solution that does not present any potential threat. This delicate aspect does not clearly motivate manufacturing decision maker to follow the new wave. This is due to the fact that they surely do not want to expose their customer database, their production composition, etc.

7.4.3 CLOUD COMPUTING

The proliferation of Mobile internet in all sectors and the continuous improvement in terms of chipset cost and poser consumption.

Moreover, the factory of the future is not expected as many devices each one acts alone by many devices processing together. This lead to a complex and multivariable processing that is executed as a distributed processing. Handling a huge amount of data, ensuring the processing of several devices, lead making the right decision as fastest as possible certainly lead to the Cloud connected devices. It is even considered of an essential value of the IoT (Geng et al., 2011).

7.4.4 ARCHITECTURE

One of the major barriers of migrated to interconnected manufacturing factories is the warranty about the stability and the effectiveness of such choice. In fact, it requires valid architecture to integrate effectively and easily the different connected objects. The architecture requires greater effort to support an intuitive translation from the physical world to a computerized and logical format that can be easily exploited for better *Industry 4* adoption.

- The architecture has also to distinguish clearly of two layers: the business layer (process) and the physical one (product and resources). This distinction is delicate to establish due the fact that IoT are devices, that when integrated into the manufacturing process, are considered as an integrated sub process.
- Another important aspect is the mapping of two kinds of flows: physical flow and information one.

In Meyer (2013), the authors pointed the lack of modeling concepts to represent sensors and actuators of the IoT in a business process model. They consider it as a significant obstacle to successfully include real-world resources in traditional ERP systems business processes.

7.4.5 PLATFORM INDEPENDENT

The computer science community is often faced to long and endless debates about the computing platform: which is better Linux distribution or Windows one? Which is more reliable in terms of performance Mac OS or Windows?…

Such debates are not frequent in the industrial side: Windows server is a mostly used in manufacturing sites.

One of the advantages of IoT is the fact that they are based on cloud computing architecture and operate independently of the running platform. Such aspect can facilitate the migration and the opening to other platforms easily and not costly (in terms of deployment time, allocated material resources, and required human resources).

7.4.6 *FASTER PROCESSING REQUIREMENT*

No one can deny the fact that users (particular and industrials) are greedier than ever in terms of systems' performances. This is the main engine for the R&D placements in order to attract customer and consumers.

Similarly, as evolving manufacturing environment (c.f 5.1), the manufacturing machine ensured functionalities are evolving too. They evolve from simply executing programmed task to more independent machines endue with more independence, autonomy, collaboration, and intelligence. One promising issue is to process to corrective and preventive action in order to minimize the damages and waste.

7.5 IOT, WHAT ELSE?

7.5.1 *HCC HUMAN COMPUTER CONFLUENCE*

The SCADA dashboards are no more user interfaces, including several metrics for supervising the production process. It evaluates to more usable and useful interfaces. This is essentially motivated by the fact that the User Interface is now a quality factor. The SCADA professionals propose now more accessible and usable user interface by adapting the supervision process into smart phones, tables, user interfaces to offer better interaction.

One of the announced and expected features of IoT is to promote communication and connectivity.

As HCI professionals expect a new HCI era that is presented as Human-Computer Confluence (e.g., wearable interfaces for example, this HCI evolution will surely impact the manufacturing area via new dashboard offering flexibility, connectivity and mainly ease of use for supervision and piloting purposes.

7.6 CONCLUDING REMARKS AND PERSPECTIVES

The present chapter presents an overview about the actual perception of the M.E.S. and the expected evolution in this sector. This evolution will mainly be paced by the fourth industrial revolution. The customer expectation is evolving from a simple tool for gathering, analyzing and storing data to a system taking part of the decision process. Furthermore, the M.E.S. have to be more flexible to easily adopt the different changes having in the manufacturing process or the managerial one.

The new M.E.S. that is announced to support the smart factories and the IoT is expected to be the engine of a revolution in manufacturing areas. However, in many manufacturers this challenge seems to be unreachable since the used physical resources are quite old fashioned and needs huge amounts of money to replace the existing installation with a newer one.

One of the announced perspectives, concerns the Internet of Everything: People, Process, Data, and Things. The IoT is far from to be a final step. It is considered as a departure point for another concept that is the Internet of Everything. In fact, the smart sensors offer the possibility for context awareness and support energy independence. Another factor is promising; it concerns the processing power constant evolution. Then, we can predict the imminent second phase of the fourth revolution: Internet of Everything. It is supposed to combine information related to: people, process, data, and things.

This perspective implicates further work on the mentioned challenged to which are facing the M.E.S. leaders. Indeed, the IoE is presented as a network of networks where we predict trillions of connections related to a manufacturing sector.

KEYWORDS

- **Agile Manufacturing**
- **Big Data**
- **Industry 4.0**
- **IOT**
- **Manufacturing Execution System (MES)**
- **Smart Factory**

REFERENCES

Aberdeen Group [http://www.aberdeen.com/].

Bloem, Jaap, Doorn, M. V. "The Fourth Industrial Revolution." Things to Tighten the (2014).

CFR. Part 11: Electronic Records, Electronic Signatures [http://www.fda.gov/ora/compliance_ref/part11/].

Dan Ma. The Business Model of "Software-As-A-Service," Services Computing, 2007. SCC 2007. IEEE International Conference on 9–13 July 2007, pp. 701–702, doi: 10.1109/SCC.2007.118.

GAMP. The Good Automated Manufacturing Practice Guide for Validation of Automated Systems, GAMP 4 (ISPE/GAMP Forum, 2001), 2001, (http://www.ispe.org/gamp/).

Geng, W., Talwar, S., Johnsson, K., Himayat, N., Johnson, K. D., M2M: From mobile to embedded internet. Communications Magazine, IEEE, 2011, 49(4), pp. 36–43, 2011.

Höller, J., Tsiatsis, V., Mulligan, C., Karnouskos, S., Avesand, D. Boyle: From Machine-to-Machine to the Internet of Things: Introduction to a New Age of Intelligence. Elsevier, 21014, 2014, ISBN 978-0-12-407684-6.

IIC, Industrial Internet Consortium, 2015, http://www.iiconsortium.org/.

Koch, C., Why your integration efforts end up looking like this... CIO Magazine, 2001, 15, 98–108.

Leavitt, N. Will NoSQL databases live up to their promise? Computer, 2010, 43(2), 12–14.

Lucke, D., Constantinescu, C., Westkämper, E. Smart factory—a step towards the next generation of manufacturing. In Manufacturing Systems and Technologies for the New Frontier. Springer London, 2008, pp. 115–118.

MESA, MESA Model [online]. MESA International. Available from: http://www.mesa.org/en/modelstrategicinitiatives/MESAModel.asp [Accessed December 5th 2016].

Meyer, S., Ruppen, A., Magerkurth, C. Internet of Things-Aware Process Modeling: Integrating IoT Devices as Business Process Resources. In *Advanced information systems engineering (CAiSE)*. Vol. 7908. Edited by Camille B. Achour-Salinesi, Moira C. Norrie and Oscar Pastor, 84–98, 7908. Berlin, Heidelberg: Springer, 2013.

Owen, T., Parker, K. One app's ceiling is another app's floor. Manufacturing Systems, 1999, 17(10), 6.

Saenz de Ugarte, B., Artiba, A., Pellerin, R. Manufacturing execution system–a literature review. Production Planning and Control, 2009, 20(6), 525–539.

Sundmaeker, H., Guillemin, P., Friess, P., Woelffle, S. Vision and challenges for realizing the internet of things. European Commission Information Society and Media, Tech. Rep, March 2010. Available from: http://www.internet-of-things-research.eu/pdf/IoT_Clusterbook_March_2010.pdf.

Tenhiälä, A., Helkiö, P. Performance effects of using an ERP system for manufacturing planning and control under dynamic market requirements, Journal of Operations Management, Volume 36, May 2015, pp. 147–164, ISSN 0272-6963.

WFMC, Workflow Management Coalition [http://www.wfmc.org/].

CHAPTER 8

A STRUCTURED PROCESS TO GENERATE IDEAS IN MEDTECH

JAGDISH CHATURVEDI[1] and RAMAKRISHNA PAPPU[2]

[1]*Director Clinical Innovations, InnAccel, 5th Floor, Aanand Towers, Municipal No. 4, Rajaram Mohan Roy Road, Ward No. 77, Sampangiramanagar, Bangalore–560025, India*

[2]*Business Associate, InnAccel, 5th Floor, Aanand Towers, Municipal No. 4, Rajaram Mohan Roy Road, Ward No. 77, Sampangiramanagar, Bangalore–560025, India*

CONTENTS

ABSTRACT

The chapter provides an overview of the various methods used today for identifying unmet needs and developing products. The healthcare domain is chosen as the medium for the description. The Biodesign process as developed at Stanford University is described, along with multiple off-shoots and adaptations of the process; specific to the adoption of the process in various countries is described. Success stories and short-comings of the process with case studies are highlighted. The chapter analyzes other processes—examining the critical factors that lead to the success of these programs. It also analyzes through examples of medical device and medical technology developments, where lack of a structured process has led to 'failures' and the key learning from these case studies.

8.1 INTRODUCTION

The key to MedTech entrepreneurship is to develop a product that addresses a clear unmet clinical need. Identifying and understanding an unmet need requires diligence; comprehensive clinical, technical, and market under-standing. To address this need an appropriate solution concept must be formulated. The concept must take into account different parameters like regulatory considerations, intellectual property, business models and technical feasibility. The conceptualization process will culminate with the selection of the "strongest" solution concept. Transforming the chosen concept into a functional prototype and finally a usable product is the endpoint. Medical Device development has become increasingly complex with the constant influx of newer technologies and stricter regulatory and safety requirements. The final step in the developmental process is ensuring that the product meets all the necessary clinical, safety and user needs.

There is a difference between a "problem" and an "unmet need." For example, the WHO states that 4 million newborn babies die each year. This is a problem. The unmet need here would be for a way to prevent or reduce the number of newborn deaths each year. However, being able to say that a mother's lack of knowledge of newborn warming care is the primary cause of certain number of neonatal deaths due to hypothermia is a more specific and addressable issue. A method (program or tool) to teach pregnant women how to maintain the warm chain for newborns in order to reduce the incidence of mortality from environmentally induced hypothermia could be one of the solutions. Thus it is evident that there is a significant difference between a "problem" and an "unmet need" and a "solution." By addressing real needs many problems can be solved or indeed prevented.

Perspective on Global Medical Technology Innovation—Globally, small private companies that have been funded through venture capital and research grants have led medical technology innovation. It is estimated that of the 10,000 unique product categories in MedTech, small private companies have developed two-thirds. Larger public companies have a very active licensing and company acquisition strategy to get access to these innovations and leverage their sales and marketing expertise to bring them to market.

This trend is particularly evident in the United States. The five years from 2007–2012 saw over 1,000 acquisitions of small private companies by global MedTech players. The industry is supported by a vibrant venture capital industry, which invests billions of dollars in startups that have identified an unmet need and are developing innovative products to meet the identified need. Technology incubators at universities, or private medical technology accelerators support many such startups. It is estimated that over a 1,000 such medical technology incubators and accelerators support companies each year. Israel has also developed a thriving medical technology industry over the last 20 years. This was achieved by a comprehensive government program to drive innovation and research by setting up 24 technology incubators to support startups in this space. These incubators were placed under private management and substantial early stage funding was made available for startups at these incubators through liberal grant funding, and technology venture capital funds. Today, Israel has a thriving MedTech sector, with over a 1,000 companies developing innovative products for the US and Western markets.

Now, Singapore is replicating the Israeli model through it's A*STAR program to create a research-led MedTech industry. Technology incubation, supported by research grants, and ample high-risk venture capital for early stage, research-led companies, has been the model that has successfully created these global hubs of MedTech innovation. This model can be effectively deployed in India to create the world's first ecosystem for affordable MedTech innovation in 5–7 years, and tap the emerging global opportunity in affordable medical technology. As described, the need to follow a process to identify unmet needs in medical technology innovation is self evident. But does everyone in the innovation ecosystem, at least for medical technology, follow a process? That yet remains to be seen.

Broadly, the different stages of an innovation process—either formal or informal, contains several common features looked at by entrepreneurs. More often than not, the innovation and entrepreneurial journey begins with an idea. This idea could be a result of the individual or group of individual's experience of working in a particular industry or field; it could be the result of an observation made by an individual; or it could even be the result of an 'aha' moment where the individual discovers some hitherto undiscovered information.

What is the significance of getting an idea? Why is the idea given so much importance in the innovation process? The idea becomes important as it is addresses or seeks to address an underlying need. This underlying need might be based in reality and factually evident, it might be a perception of the innovator, or it might be something evident to only a few who understand the need's intricacies and complexities. Nevertheless, the idea more often than not seeks to solve a problem that was faced by someone or a group of people.

By just having an idea is never enough is it? The innovator, to be called an innovator, would need to act on the idea—rather, build a solution that would solve this underlying problem. The solution would obviously depend on a whole host of factors—from what is the best technology to use in the solution, to the skills and ability of the innovator, to the resources available to develop this solution, to what is perceived to be required or demanded by the users of this solution—the list goes on. The next stage after identifying an idea, flushing out its details, and building a concept that could work, is to validate it. Often described in different ways—concept validation, proof of concept, etc. The goal is to get evidence of the working of the concept (now more than just an idea). This evidence could be external or internal. Innovators could get feedback from external users, buyers, technical experts, etc.—essentially stakeholders who might provide some feedback on the efficacy of such an idea. The concept could even be validated internally by the innovator, and by that, we mean through a set of laboratory tests designed to show the efficacy of the principle used to support the idea. Often called establishing the proof of concept in engineering terms, this could be done via setting up a test bed, or even using software to determine the workings of the concept in theory.

Validating the concept is not enough for the innovator, is it? The golden million dollar (or billion?) idea is still in a concept stage, though some degree of its efficacy has been established, it still remains as a theoretical phenomenon. The innovator's job is not done yet. Developing the proof of concept to a prototype stage is always a challenge. There are multiple iterations of the prototype and different innovators use differing terminology to describe the various stages of their iterations. Looks-like prototype, alpha prototype, functional prototype, beta prototype, etc. are common ways to describe the stage of development to others—often these terms are used in different ways depending on the engineering background of the audience. However, the point remains that prototype is undergoing change and moving towards what would be essentially a final product. What started out as an idea and was serially changed in aspect, content and shape over time, is heading towards a final product. The essential aspect of this metamorphosis is technology development.

A final product needs to meet certain criteria before it is accepted in the market. Often these criteria vary depending on the type of solution—from regulatory certifications to intellectual property rights. These criteria are important to not only drive adoption by buyers and scale the business, but also to legitimately sell the product in the first place. Regulatory approval, depending on the geography, is essential to be able to market and sell the final product. Especially for medical devices, the safety of the patient is paramount. This is echoed by regulatory bodies, most notably the US FDA and European CE, which sets standards and evaluates the product for use in the clinical setting. In most countries, an innovator (now an entrepreneur), would need the approval of either these regulatory agencies, or the relevant agency of the country to be able to get the final product used in the clinical setting.

Another important aspect in the innovator's journey is to deal with the intellectual property rights and implications of the novel solution being built. Innovators often struggle with questions such as—is what we are doing considered novel by law? Can we file a patent for this? Do we want to file a patent for this? Where do we file a patent? How do we go about it? Is it expensive? Where does the patent apply? Do we have patent rights internationally? The answers to these questions obviously depend on the specific situation that the innovator is in and the plan that the innovator has going forward.

With the final product developed, with regulatory approval considered, with intellectual property implications thought of, is it enough to move forward to the next stage? Somewhere in this development process, the business aspect has to be evaluated. Firstly, at the initial idea stage—does this idea even have a market potential? Does this new technology solution make business sense? Answering some of those questions—either externally or internally, gives the innovator some confidence to move ahead. Given that there is market potential for this new solution, what is the best way to go about it? What is business model? How big is the market in monetary terms? In number of units and buyers? And what strategy does one use to go about ensuring that this idea, nay final product, sees the light of day and is actually used to solve someone's problem?

8.2   STAGES OF AN INNOVATOR'S JOURNEY

Innovation theorists often state that before taking on a technically challenging project to develop a product, it is essential to take a step back and understand what is required. Lenk et al. (2000) state that there are essentially three processes to get from an idea to a product—"concept development, technology development, and product development." These processes are not isolated, but feed directly feed into each other (Figure 8.1).

"Some ideas feed directly into product development, while others require technical development to be feasible. Technology development provides solid technologies for incorporation into the product development process, and it also spurs new ideas. The product development process itself may even generate new concepts or illustrate the need for new technology."

They add that the key to develop successful and innovative medical devices is to understand the unique characteristics of these three processes, how they interact with one another, and to manage them appropriately. This, according to the authors is the key to ensure that the product development process in efficient and capable of producing innovative and successful products.[6]

---

[6] http://www.mddionline.com/article/beyond-product-development-creating-process-drives-innovation

FIGURE 8.1 Stages of an Innovator's Journey.

Innovation in medical devices occurs in the technology innovation of the product, the manufacturing processes, the method of distribution and adoption among others. MedTech innovation comprises of new inventions of medical devices or modifications of existing devices to better serve the patients, doctors, and other stakeholders. Further, these innovations can be considered either radical or incremental. Radical innovations are those that "introduce dramatic new capabilities," while incremental innovations are take place in existing products and processes. Innovation from scratch does take place, but over the years, the definition of innovation has come to include "modifying, upgrading, and improving existing devices." Loosely defined, innovation could also be taken in an adoption context, where "a device that (was) …developed previously… (is) apply(ed)… to a different situation." Innovation can be looked at as a way to apply new scientific research or knowledge, or even as an "engineering problem solving, in which existing knowledge or techniques are applied to newly defined problems."[7]

Typically, innovation in medical devices is "based on engineering problem solving by individuals or small firms, is often incremental rather than radical, seldom depends on the results of long-term research in the basic sciences, and generally does not reflect the recent generation of fundamental new knowledge."[7] But who is it that brings about medical device innovations? In the study published by Edward Roberts, he found that

---

[7] http://www.ncbi.nlm.nih.gov/books/NBK218293/

individuals in the academic and clinical setting, at least in the West, largely dominate MedTech innovation. In addition, he found that the role of the big medical device manufacturers tended to be more 'secondary' with a focus on the distribution and commercialization aspects. However, is this still the case today?

India is an example of an emerging economy with a nascent, albeit fast growing, innovation ecosystem in medical technology. Medical Technology innovation in these early years in India is dominated by groups of individuals, or startup companies, who have sprung up in the past decade to create novel solutions to a host of MedTech problems specific to India and other developing countries. Another key finding of the Roberts' study, which is evident even today, is that "the degree of clinical contact between … companies and, particularly, teaching hospitals was strongly correlated with the degree of technological innovation embodied in the products that the companies developed." As he aptly puts it, "it is nearly impossible for a biomedical company to be successful if it does not retain close ties to a clinical environment."[8]

It is important for the innovators to look at the technology strategy that would be used to further the technology development through the various iterations of prototypes. Lenk et al. claim that, "without a clear technology strategy, development projects may not align with product strategy, leading to wasted development efforts or unsuccessful technology transfer attempts."[9] Over the course of figuring out the technology strategy for the startup, some important questions to consider would be: What is the potential of this technology? How can the startup develop this or obtain the necessary technologies? The authors add, "The technology strategy should support the product strategy, but may (also) extend beyond it."[9]

Lenk et al. add that the "benefits of managing strong front-end processes in concept and technology development are lost without a good product development process to bring new ideas and technologies to commercialization." They suggest that to develop new concepts and technologies into successful products, the team should focus on, what they describe as, 'product development project excellence.' This consists of four elements:

[8] http://www.ncbi.nlm.nih.gov/books/NBK218293/
[9] http://www.mddionline.com/article/beyond-product-development-creating-process-drives-innovation

1. Core Teams;
2. Structured Development Process;
3. Decision-Making Reviews and Process;
4. Development Tools and Techniques.

A detailed description of these components of project excellence can be found in the Appendix.

"Concept development is the fountain that feeds both technology development and product development."

Taking an idea forward, flushing out its details, creating a workable concept, all require a mechanism that would 'routinely capture, organize, develop and screen ideas.' Concept development can be thought of as routine ideation, which makes attempts to capture spontaneous ideas, and directed ideation, which via established methods enables focused ideation. Routine ideation looks to capture the 'breadth and volume of ideas' from a large number of sources with little effort and time spent on each aspect. Whereas, directed ideation involves spending more time and energy on specific aspects. Both these ideation methods are complementary and used in concept generation and brainstorming. It is the diverging and converging techniques of using these ideation methods that would lead a well thought out innovative concept. More information about Routine Ideation and Directed Ideation can be found in the Appendix.[10]

For an idea to become a successful product is essential that it comprises a clear and consistent focus on delivering differentiated value and performance to the final customers. Michael Raynor and Mumtaz Ahmed, in their 2013 book The Three Rules, describe this phenomenon over time that it makes it more challenging and forces innovators to think and rethink the differentiated value proposition being provided to the end customers.[11] The three rules (Figure 8.2) according to the authors are better before cheaper, revenue before cost, and there are no other rules.

In the words of the authors, Medical Technology innovation is inherently oriented to and does focus on these rules.

"Better before cheaper: Market dynamics encourage MedTech companies to add as much value to their products as possible.

---

[10] http://www.mddionline.com/article/beyond-product-development-creating-process-drives-innovation

[11] http://dupress.com/articles/three-rules-medical-technology/

1. Better before cheaper:

- Rather than competing solely on price, companies achieve sustainable success by focusing on delivering differentiated value.

2. Revenue before cost:

- The advantages of higher revenue are more valuable and durable than the advantages of lower cost.

3. There are no other rules:

- While other pursuits are important and contribute to a company's success, they are ultimately the most successful when they fully align with and reinforce the first two rules.

FIGURE 8.2   The three rules.

Revenue before cost: Companies invest in innovation, incurring higher costs to generate long-term sustainable revenue. These characteristics have positively impacted the industry's overall performance."

This is best exemplified by companies such as Medtronic and Stryker, which according to Raynor and Ahmed are 'exceptional companies' that have adopted these rules, especially the companies' focus on 'better before cheaper.'

The **Deloitte University Press** published an article, written by Snyder et al. (2013) that look at these three rules in MedTech Innovation (Figure 8.3). The article borrows these rules from Raynor and Ahmed and also adds its own 'Pillars' that would lead to the transformation of the industry. The first Pillar, Pillar One, is to have a 'broader view of innovation—one that would offer value beyond product attributes.' This expands on the better before cheaper rule, as it looks to increase the innovation horizon beyond the focus purely on quality of a single product, to a more 'difficult-to-replicate system." The focus shifts from a product, to a pipeline of products. In addition, it includes the service aspect, which was hitherto not in focus, to provide increased 'clinical and economic value.'[12]

The Deloitte University Press outlines three ways a company can drive innovation. These are:

---

[12] http://dupress.com/articles/three-rules-medical-technology/

Develop collateral to support
new stakeholder interactions

Align messages used with all
stakeholders

Focus on value-based models

Align prices globally

Actively manage margin erosion

Track changing customer
behaviors and needs

Monitor segment-specific patterns

Develop and track
predictive measures

Tailored to the customer,
geography, health care model,
and buying process

Mix of new and traditional
channels

Incorporate value-
added solutions

Prioritize high-value
call points

Focus on customer need

Marketing · Sales · Service · Analytics

Graphic: Deloitte University Press | DUPress.com

FIGURE 8.3 Commercial capabilities for today's MedTech market.

1. Innovation can be generated internally through the company's own Research and Development divisions.
2. Companies can buy and integrate innovations via licensing deals and acquisitions.
3. Companies could participate in the external innovation ecosystem with collaborations with academic, venture and startup communities.

Additionally, an innovation consulting firm called *Doblin* that has created its own format builds on these pillars with four key building blocks of innovation capability. These are:

1. New approaches to the processes and methods used to create innovations.
2. New interfaces (and even structures) in the organization to house the capability.
3. New funding mechanisms, employee skills, and other resources and competencies to fuel the work.
4. New metrics and incentives to align action.

These building blocks enable innovators to think about 'carefully designing, orchestrating, and implementing' further aspects in the innovation lifecycle to improve the ability to innovate, not just 'reliably but also routinely.' The second pillar, Pillar Two, looks at 'engaging new influencers and adapting to heterogeneity via new commercial models.' Primarily, this builds on the revenue before cost aspect and seeks to rework existing commercial models in order to better interact with various stakeholders. The third pillar, Pillar Three, relies on 'Effective Value Articulation.' This involves communicating not only the differential value proposition but also the impact on the economics effectively. Lastly, Pillar Four looks at Advanced Pricing, which involves developing better pricing capabilities to compete effectively. Essentially, it suggests that pricing strategies should be crafted that would generate economic value for the healthcare system and returns for the company.

One of the most widely used and well respected processes to develop Medical devices, called **Biodesign,** was created in 2001 at Stanford University. Biodesign is "both a program and a process."[13] It aims to create new and cost-effective medical devices in order to improve patient care via a collaborative multidisciplinary approach. The approach focuses heavily on the 'needs of patients, physicians and the healthcare industry as a whole.' (Biodesign, 2015). The process has been taught to 900+ students, 141 fellows, 100 executives since inception, spurring 37 companies that raised $325 million and have impacted the lives of over 275,000 patients so far.[14]

An interdisciplinary team, comprising engineers, clinicians and product designers, undertakes the Biodesign Program, undergoing a process to identify and characterize unsolved clinical needs before building technology solutions. Each year, a new focus area is selected, in which clinical needs are identified by spending time at clinical settings making 'observations.' The program's mantra is "a well-characterized need is the DNA of a great invention." The textbook 'Biodesign: the Process of Innovating Medical Technologies' has also become a standard and the definitive guide to medical device innovators around the world, with a second edition published in 2014.[15]

One of the authors of Biodesign and Founding Director's of the Biodesign Program at Stanford, Dr. Paul Yock mentions that "in healthcare it is really easy to fall in love with the first need that comes across your

---

[13] http://biodesign.stanford.edu/bdn/about.jsp

[14] http://biodesign.stanford.edu/bdn/news/annualreports/2014AnnualReport.pdf

[15] http://biodesign.stanford.edu/bdn/global/japan.jsp

transom…we teach a process of tough love—making sure that the clinical need is really important before spending the time, energy and money to invent and develop a solution."[16] The process follows three stages—*Identify, Invent, and Implement*. The Identify stage begins with making observations of unsolved clinical needs and documenting it through a 'needs statement.' This needs statement is a one-line description of the need capturing the essential elements of the problem to be solved. Over the clinical immersion, these needs are compiled and then filtered based on parameters set forth by the team. At the end of the immersion, teams usually have around 200 needs statements listed. These parameters typically include epidemiology and market data where available. Using these filters the list is condensed to the top 3 or 5 needs. These needs are researched in more detail, with a detailed document, called the *need specification document* created. This document includes all the information around the need that an innovator would need to come up with solutions in a brainstorming session. The document would include disease state analysis, market analysis and also the competitors already operating in that space. This concludes the identify stage and teams move on to the invent stage.

The invent stage builds on the information learnt through the process of creating the needs specification document. Multiple brainstorming sessions are conducted; with each of the team members moderating the sessions to ensure a conducive brainstorming session. Concepts are bucketed into different approaches for each of the needs and even some early rough prototyping to communicate the concepts is encouraged. Different aspects of the approaches are analyzed, debated and evaluated by the team, till there is consensus on the best approach for each of the needs. At this stage, the team decides which need it wants to work on and begins flushing out the solution in more detail. There are multiple iterations of the prototype and the intellectual property (patent) is also filed at this stage if the team so decides.

The third phase—implement begins with determining the path forward and elements such as the development strategy, regulatory, marketing, etc. are thought through. Following this a product development plan is created all the way to manufacturing. This would also involve understanding and analyzing the stakeholders in the ecosystem and creating a business plan to take the technology developed forward.

---

[16] http://news.stanford.edu/features/2015/biodesign/

Stanford University not only conducts annual Fellowship programs but it also offers its graduate students courses covering different aspects of the Biodesign process. The 'Innovation Course' is a two-quarter sequence course students learn the Biodesign process[17], while the 'Global Biodesign' is a spring quarter course where a global version of the Biodesign process is taught.[18] Other Biodesign courses include a 'Biodesign for Mobile Health, a 'Biodesign Capstone' for undergraduate level students as well as an Executive Education course on Biodesign.[192021] The Biodesign program at Stanford University includes a Biodesign Innovation Fellowship[22] based at Stanford as well as Global Biodesign fellowships (Singapore-Stanford Biodesign Fellowship)[23] and an FDA Fellowship at the Center for Devices and Radiological Health at the FDA.[2425]

One of the offshoots of Stanford Biodesign is the Stanford India Biodesign (SIB), which was established in 2007 in New Delhi, India. The goal was to train 'the next generation of medical technology innovators in India.' The program was administered as collaboration between Stanford University, the Indian Institute of Technology Delhi, and the All India Institute of Medical Sciences (AIIMS) in partnership with the Indo-US Science and Technology Forum (IUSSTF). The program conducted annual yearlong Fellowships, similar to the Biodesign Innovation Fellowships at Stanford comprising a team of a clinician, engineer, product designer, and scientist. This team would spend six months at Stanford University learning the process and identifying needs. The other six months it would identify needs in Indian clinical settings and would then filter these needs, finally working on the top need selected through a similar filtering process. SIB also conducts internship programs, where individuals are taught the process by the Fellows and faculty in New Delhi, following which they are put into teams and follow the process to work on needs already identified

---

[17] http://biodesign.stanford.edu/bdn/courses/bioe374.jsp
[18] http://biodesign.stanford.edu/bdn/courses/bioe371.jsp
[19] http://biodesign.stanford.edu/bdn/courses/
[20] http://biodesign.stanford.edu/bdn/courses/bioe273.jsp
[21] http://biodesign.stanford.edu/bdn/courses/bioe141.jsp
[22] http://biodesign.stanford.edu/bdn/fellowships/bif.jsp
[23] http://biodesign.stanford.edu/bdn/singapore/index.jsp
[24] http://biodesign.stanford.edu/bdn/career/fda.jsp
[25] http://biodesign.stanford.edu/bdn/fellowships/

by the Fellows.[26] Five companies have been formed resulting from this program in India.[27] 2015 onwards, the program operates as the School of International Biodesign.[28]

Singapore-Stanford Biodesign (SSB), based in Singapore, is a collaboration between Singapore's A*STAR (Agency for Science, Technology and Research), the Singapore Economic Development Board (EDB), and Stanford University. SSB states that its goal is to 'nurture and train the next generation of Asian medical device innovators in Singapore for the world.'[29] The teams undergoing the Singapore-Stanford examine needs within clinical settings typical in Singapore and other Asian countries, and then invent the solution, prototyping and developing the technology. The SSB also taps its existing network of experts from medical technology industry, from legal and investment areas around the world to assist these teams.[30]

Stanford Biodesign established a 'Biodesign Global Affiliate' designation for 'Biodesign-like' programs across the world. Stanford describes these as 'independent programs that align with the training' process at Stanford.[31] One of the more famous Biodesign Global Affiliates is the *BioInnovate program based in Ireland.* BioInnovate too provides a Fellowship program and an Industry Training program for its fellows. BioInnovate describes itself as a 'national medical technology innovation training program that aims to act as a neutral territory in which academia, clinicians and industry can collaborate to develop novel medical technologies.' The program is a partnership between the universities of NUI Galway, University of Limerick and University College Cork, with numerous hospitals across the country, and is supported by industry sponsors including Enterprise Ireland and IMDA among others.[32] The Fellowship program focuses on different therapeutic areas each year, with the recent programs conducted in the areas of ENT, Respiratory Medicine

---

[26] http://biodesign.stanford.edu/bdn/india/
[27] http://news.stanford.edu/features/2015/biodesign/
[28] http://sibiodesign.net
[29] http://www.ssbiodesign.com.sg/about/about-ssb
[30] http://biodesign.stanford.edu/bdn/singapore/
[31] http://biodesign.stanford.edu/bdn/global/affiliates.jsp
[32] http://www.bioinnovate.ie

and Gastroenterology.[33] The process followed is similar to the Biodesign process at Stanford, with the process following the 'identify, invent, and implement' stages to develop impactful medical devices. So far, BioInnovate has trained 28 Fellows, 32 graduate students and 40 industry professionals and have collated over 1000 unmet or under-met clinical needs. BioInnovate has also resulted in 8 technologies, with one Startup Company and one technology licensed out.

A recent program launched by Stanford Biodesign is the Japan Biodesign, which has been setup to train people in Japan in the Biodesign process. The program is a collaboration between Osaka University, Tohoku University, the University of Tokyo, the Japan Federation of Medical Devices Associations (JFMDA) and the Stanford Biodesign. Currently the faculty of the program is undergoing training before the first Fellowships begin.[34]

Several Biodesign-like programs are conducted around the world at different universities and institutions, most of which were not setup by Stanford, but by individual entities wishing to adapt and follow the Biodesign process to develop medical devices (Figure 8.4).[35] A detailed list of such programs can be found in the Appendix. For each of these programs—Biodesign, Biodesign affiliated, and Biodesign-like, the key feature is the focus on an interdisciplinary team identifying needs in the clinical area before thinking about the solution. Through the process, an educational goal is to look for 'translational opportunities in areas that are considered basic science domains'—for example, nanotechnology and cellular and molecular biology (Table 8.1).[36]

A comparison of the Stanford Biodesign and IEB process show that, as opposed to the Biodesign program, the IEB, after performing a thorough characterization of the technology seeks to match it with possible unmet clinical needs. This is a technology driven approach as opposed to the need driven approach practiced and preached by the biodesign process.

The focus here in IEB is on the technology application. They make "Calls for Technologies" where they ask for current technologies being

---

[33] http://www.bioinnovate.ie/programmes/fellowship-programme.html
[34] http://biodesign.stanford.edu/bdn/global/japan.jsp
[35] http://biodesign.stanford.edu/bdn/otherprograms.jsp
[36] http://biodesign.stanford.edu/bdn/perspective.jsp

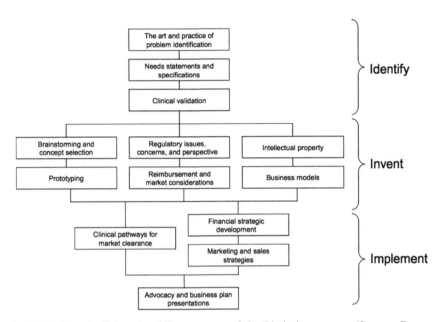

FIGURE 8.4 Outlining the different stages of the Biodesign process (Source: Course Outline—Case Western Reserve University Biodesign course).

TABLE 8.1 Comparison of Inputs, Contents, and Outputs Between Biodesign Innovation and IEB

	BIODESIGN INNOVATION	**IEB**
INITIAL INPUTS	Clinical needs	Technologies under development
CONTENTS	Needs validation	
	Concept development	
	Business model analysis	
	Intellectual property and regulatory issues	
	Prototyping	Implementation planning
OUTPUTS	Business plan/licensing plan	Business plan

worked on/completed at the University (of Porto) to be commercialized. This stems from the program's prior experience (and expertise) in technology commercialization and finding an application, after doing thorough research on the landscape. Similar to the Biodesign process, here too, there is a strong focus on the need statement, the disease state fundamentals, the (present) treatment options, a stakeholder analysis, a market analysis, understanding the patent landscape, and finally deciding on a suitable business model. Concept generation is similar across both. But steps similar to the Biodesign process, originating from different perspectives about the generation of ideas–one originating from a user driven pull factor, the other a market oriented push factor. However, one problem remains true across both the processes–adequate access to clinical sites for each process.[37]

There are numerous processes that can be followed for idea generation, each offering something important in its own way. It is important to follow a process for idea generation however the choice of the process can be made by taking into consideration the geographical location, resources, skills and strengths of the team.

8.3   APPENDICES

APPENDIX 1:

Detailed Description of Project Excellence—Thomas J. Lenk, Aritomo Shinozaki, and Christina Hepner Brodie

1. **Core Teams.** A cross-functional team should be formed to focus on a project and empowered to deliver results. Both the team's authority and the expected results must be clearly defined.
2. **Structured Development Process.** A common framework should be designed to guide repeatable product development activities. Deliverables should be clearly defined, activities should be grouped into distinct phases, and the project should be reviewed at the completion of each phase. By grouping the activities properly, it is also possible to coordinate the phases with the completion of requirements for design control reviews.
3. **Decision-Making Reviews and Process.** A senior management product approval committee should review projects at the completion of each phase of product development. Both project progress and business potential must be evaluated. The project team receives a crisp decision of *go* (continue the project to the end of the next

[37] http://venturewell.org/open2014/wp-content/uploads/2013/10/MAIA.pdf

phase), *no go* (end the project), or *redirect* (change the goals and scope of the project).

4. **Development Tools and Techniques.** Working tools like checklists and templates for standard communications should be provided so that teams can focus their energy on project progress and the content—rather than the format—of reports and presentations. Clear metrics, such as due-date slippage or turnover on core teams, allow the process to be monitored for early detection and correction of problems.

APPENDIX 2:

Case Study: Medtronic (Extracted from Raynor and Ahmed)[38]
Medtronic has created value across multiple markets with a common product platform and by diversifying its portfolio with innovative offerings. It leveraged the electro-mechanical technology of modulating physiology though electrical current to address spinal, gastrointestinal, and neurological disease. Though Medtronic's product portfolio has always been anchored in cardiac rhythm disease management (CRDM), it has diversified into other areas to tap additional growth. In 1975, roughly 80% of Medtronic's $100 million in revenue was generated from CRDM. That same year, Medtronic officially formed its neurological division to begin to differentiate its offerings. Today, CRDM represents 30% of a $16.6 billion revenue base.

APPENDIX 3:

Case Study: Stryker (Extracted from Raynor and Ahmed)[39]
"...One of the driving forces behind Stryker being considered "exceptional" was its eventual move upmarket from medical products (such as stretchers and hospital beds) to implants (such as hip, knee, and spinal implants). Stryker originally concentrated on relatively low-tech products such as mobile hospital beds and cast cutters, where clever design and close attention to the minutiae of daily use made the difference. This led

---

[38] http://dupress.com/articles/three-rules-medical-technology/

to great success for the company and continues to drive substantial value today—but Stryker's exceptional performance over the last decade can be tied to its shift in position from a maker of medical products into a high-tech implantable MedTech player (Figure 8.3). The therapeutic nature of these products, the margins they command, and, until recently, the minimal price pressure of its market have helped Stryker achieve impressive financial results…"

APPENDIX 4:

Case Study 3: Medtronic's acquisition of Cardiocom in 2013 (extracted).

"…Medtronic's 2013 acquisition of Cardiocom showcases the company's ability to innovate in product systems, service, and customer engagement—three types of innovation directed toward one market solution. With the Cardiocom acquisition, Medtronic is seeking to expand into disease management. Cardiocom had a portfolio of tele-health offerings such as home glucose monitors and scales to help doctors remotely monitor indicators of patient health. By integrating diagnostics, therapies, and patient management solutions, Medtronic can offer an innovative disease management service to help reduce readmission rates and save hospitals money.

Medtronic saw in Cardiocom a platform that could be applied to multiple chronic diseases. In fact, Medtronic plans to create a disease management platform around heart failure—a disease Medtronic is familiar with because of its implantable heart rhythm products. The platform also gives Medtronic the ability to complement its own suite of products and offer differentiated economic value to hospitals by helping to reduce readmission rates through chronic disease management…"

APPENDIX 5:

Routine Ideation: Idea Collection and Screening

For medical manufacturers, there is a wealth of potential idea sources that could lead to product improvements or new product concepts. Sales personnel routinely interact with customers; applications specialists, service technicians, and call-center operators continuously interface with customers as part of their jobs; engineers and marketers may find themselves troubleshooting or visiting customers. If these people are trained to identify the problems they see and to listen for opportunities, then useful ideas will be generated. Outside inventors and creative thinkers within the company may also spark ideas that can be added to the pool. To mine this ready source, the firm's system must be designed to facilitate documenting and screening of ideas.

Some of the major requirements for an effective system are that it is easily accessible, that it has a well-defined screening process run by a small cross-functional team, that it provides acknowledgment to all contributors, and that it recognizes and rewards people who submit promising ideas.

Directed Ideation: Voice of the Customer
The concept sounds easy enough. Team members go out and talk to customers, using what the customers say to better understand a new product's requirements. To productively obtain, analyze, and act on the voice of the customer, however, a company must put together the right team and follow the right approach.

A voice-of-the-customer team should consist of a cross section of personnel from the key functions that are responsible for defining, developing, marketing, selling, and servicing a product. Since the members of the project team carry on direct discussions with the customers, it is each team member's frame of reference—built from years of experience in a given company or industry—that allows him or her to listen in a distinctive and penetrating way. It is the combination of what the interviewer and the interviewee bring to the discussion that determines the value of the interview content.

APPENDIX 6:

Intellectual Property Strategy. Extracted from http://www.mddionline.com/article/beyond-product-development-creating-process-drives-innovation.

There are several IP Strategy options for a company, each with its own benefits and constraints, as follows:

Exclusionary Enforcement. Companies maintain competitive advantage by denying access to technology and patents. This is a common mode of operation in the medical device industry, where high development and testing costs require a high return on an investment in new technology.

Return on Investment. Balancing internal-use and licensing agreements can generate additional revenues beyond product sales. Tracking of agreements often results in greater IP management costs, however, and there must be a clear technology strategy to guide which technologies are suitable for licensing and which should be retained exclusively.

Freedom of Action. Broad cross-licensing results in high product design flexibility by providing access to a broad range of technologies, but it comes in exchange for a lower ability to exploit technological superiority. This can be effective in high-volume industries where a firm can exploit manufacturing and design engineering expertise.

Benign Neglect. Benign neglect results when there is no effort toward cross-licensing or patent enforcement. This usually leads to fast time to market and low IP management costs, albeit with higher risk and lost opportunities for maximizing technology benefits. It is most suitable for technologies that are easily innovated around or otherwise difficult to defend.

APPENDIX 7:

S. No.	Name	Location	Programs
1.	Monterrey Institute of Technology and Higher Education (ITESM)	Monterrey, Mexico	Independent Biodesign-like fellowship
2.	University of California—Berkley and University of California—San Francisco	San Francisco	Venture Innovation program
3.	University of Minnesota	Minneapolis, Minnesota	Innovation Fellows Program, Medical Devices Center
4.	University of Missouri—Columbia	Columbia, Missouri	Biodesign and Innovation Fellowship
5.	University of Michigan	Ann Arbor, Michigan	Medical Innovation Center

S. No.	Name	Location	Programs
6.	Karolinska Institute, The Royal Institute of Technology and Karolinska University Hospital	Stockholm, Sweden	Center for Technology in Medicine and Health
7.	North-western University	Evanston, Illinois	NuVention
8.	Washington University	St. Louis, Washington	Biodesign-like program
9.	Johns Hopkins University	Baltimore, Maryland	Masters Program
10.	Aarhus University	Finland	InnoX Healthcare Program
11.	Purdue University		Biomedship Program
12.	University of Toronto	Toronto	Biomedical Device Innovation Fellowship
13.	University of Wisconsin-Madison		Bio Innovations and Opportunities in Medicine and Engineering (BIOME)
14.	University of Cincinnati		Medical Device Innovation Program
15.	Case Western University and Cleveland Clinic		Biodesign Course
16.	University of Chicago	Chicago, Illinois	MedTech Innovation Program
17.	University of Kentucky		Von Allmen Center for Entrepreneurship
18.	MedStar Institute for Innovation	Baltimore, Maryland	Not for profit setup collaborating between academic engineering groups and industry
19.	University of Southern California	Los Angeles, California	Health, Technology, and Engineering (HTE@USC)
20.	BioCat	Catalonia, Span	Design Health (d.health)
21.	UT South-western Medical School	Dallas, Texas	Biodesign like course for medical students
22.	University of California—Los Angeles	Los Angeles, California	Course and fellowship offered jointly by schools of medicine and engineering

S. No.	Name	Location	Programs
23.	Harvard University	Cambridge, Massachussetts	Harvard Biodesign Lab
24.	Cornell University's School of Medicine	Ithaca, New York	Innovation Course
25.	University of California—San Diego	San Diego, California	Fellowship program
26.	NhIce (Nice health Innovation Concept)	Nice, France	Biodesign-like program
27.	University of Pittsburgh	Pittsburgh, Pennsylvania	Graduate level courses offered by Center for Medical Innovation
28.	University of Hawaii		Biodesign Innovation Course
29.	Rowan University	New Jersey	Bioengineering Scholars Program
30.	University of Copenhagen	Copenhagen, Denmark	Health Design Program
31.	McGill University, the Ecole de Technologies Superieure and Concordia University	Montreal, Canada	Surgical Innovation Program
32.	University of British Columbia	Vancouver, Canada	Engineers in Scrubs Program
33.	InnAccel	Bangalore, India	Entrepreneur in Residence Program, Affordable Innovation in MedTech Entrepreneurship Program

Table is recreated based on information from http://biodesign.stanford.edu/bdn/otherprograms.jsp [39]

APPENDIX 8:

IEB Worksheet Example

---

[39] http://biodesign.stanford.edu/bdn/otherprograms.jsp

TABLE 8.2 Worksheets Used in IEB

WORKSHEET NAME	MAIN CONTENTS
PROJECT DESCRIPTION	Technology description, including technology advantage and possible areas of application.
NEED STATEMENT	Problem and need statement, need criteria, need classification.
DISEASE STATE FUNDAMENTALS	Includes, among others, pathophysiology, clinical presentation and outcomes, economic impact.
TREATMENT OPTIONS	Clinical, economic, and utilization profile of current treatments, emerging treatments.
STAKEHOLDER ANALYSIS	Cycle of care, flow of money, stakeholders, and trade-offs.
MARKET ANALYSIS	Market segmentation and quantification (top-down and bottom-up), Porter's Five Forces, and SWOT analysis of competitors.
PRODUCT CONCEPT	Value proposition, requirements, and features (physical, performance, approvals, etc.).
BUSINESS MODEL	Business Model Canvas.
PATENT LANDSCAPE	Main patents in the area of the product concept, and how they affected freedom-to-operate.

KEYWORDS

- **affordable healthcare**
- **biodesign**
- **InnAccel**
- **innovation**
- **medical technology**

REFERENCES

"Beyond Product Development: Creating a Process That Drives Innovation | MDDI Medical Device and Diagnostic Industry News Products and Suppliers." *http://Mddionline.com*. N.p., 2016. Web. 12 Mar. 2016.

"Biomedical Innovation Takes Off in India, With Stanford Roots." *http://News.stanford.edu*. N.p., 2015. Web. 12 Mar. 2016.

"Global Stanford Biodesign Programs." *http://Biodesign.stanford.edu*. N.p., 2016. Web. 12 Mar. 2016.

National Institute (US), and Karen Ekelman. "Technological Innovation And Medical Devices." *National Academies Press (US)* (1988): N.p., 2016. Web. 12 Mar. 2016.

"School of International Biodesign." *http://Sibiodesign.net*. N.p., 2016. Web. 12 Mar. 2016.

"Singapore-Stanford Biodesign." *http://Biodesign.stanford.edu*. N.p., 2016. Web. 12 Mar. 2016.

"Stanford Biodesign—About." *http://Biodesign.stanford.edu.* N.p., 2016. Web. 12 Mar. 2016.

"Stanford Biodesign—Courses." *http://Biodesign.stanford.edu.* N.p., 2016. Web. 12 Mar. 2016.

"Stanford Biodesign—Fellowships." *http://Biodesign.stanford.edu.* N.p., 2016. Web. 12 Mar. 2016.

"Stanford Biodesign—Medical Device Innovation Fellowships." *http://Biodesign.stanford.edu.* N.p., 2016. Web. 12 Mar. 2016.

"Stanford-India Biodesign." *http://Biodesign.stanford.edu.* N.p., 2016. Web. 12 Mar. 2016.

"The Three Rules in Medical Technology: The Transformation of an Industry." Deloitte University Press. N.p., 2016. Web. 12 Mar. 2016.

Training, Fellowship, Industry Training, and Meet Fellows. "Home—Bioinnovate Ireland—Innovative Medical Device Training." *http://Bioinnovate.ie.* N.p., 2016. Web. 12 Mar. 2016.

User, Super. "About SSB | About." *http://Ssbiodesign.com.sg.* N.p., 2016. Web. 12 Mar. 2016.

User, Super. "Fellowship Program—Bioinnovate Ireland—Innovative Medical Device Training." *http://Bioinnovate.ie.* N.p., 2016. Web. 12 Mar. 2016.

CHAPTER 9

LOGIC-BASED MEDICINE VERSUS EVIDENCE-BASED MEDICINE FOR MODELING QUALIFIED-SELF HEALTH KITS

PATRIK EKLUND

Umee University, Department of Computing Science, SE-90187 Umee, Sweden

CONTENTS

9.1 INTRODUCTION

In this chapter we propose to use formal logic in order to bridge the gap between information management in Qualified-Self apps and information classification and structures residing within health and healthcare ontology. *Lative logic*[40] embraces signatures, terms and sentences arising from monads and functors in category theory, and can be arranged in order to enable well-founded logical and ontology representation. modeling uses these theoretical notions in order to extend the logical structure of classifications of health.

---

[40] http://www.glioc.com

Our focus is on Active and Healthy Ageing (AHA) including aspects of assessment (Eklund, 2009) and classification.

Qualified-self aspects within AHA requires having emphasis on *empowerment* and how citizens as individuals and patients can manage their own data, in particular for self-monitoring purposes. For this management to meet reply properly to the societal grand challenge of AHA, there is the need to shift from society owning all individual health data to individuals themselves owning their data. Another aspect is that the Quantified-Self movement is still rooted mostly in wellness and even fitness, and as having various apps at their disposal. Focus is then not always just on health but on performance more in general.

Apple's Health Kit was launched to promote such self-qualification, and is made at least for the purpose of further promoting the use of Apple's mobile phone. Various technology partners have been foreseen to become included, in particular as far as medical record systems and other related registries are concerned. The GoogleFit and Samsung's Sami follow similar ambitions and potential bindings. Google's approach is more device oriented than in Apple's approach, and so is Sami, but Samsung's approach is integrated to their overall scope of medical devices. Samsung has been working on medical devices already for a long time and is in fact in the same league e.g. as Philips, Siemens and GE. Microsoft's HealthVault is closer to HealthKit but the ambition is broader obviously since the Microsoft Health unit has been around for quite a while. Microsoft appears to comprehend health records better than Apple, and Microsoft indeed is operating systems and computer languages more than as compared to Apple, and more than Samsung.

Another aspect here is the emerging mHealth market, where *mobile medical* devices and solutions will eventually need to go down the same path of approvals (FDA) as compared to other medical devices and drugs. The approval procedures are, however, yet to be defined. The distinction between wearable and nonwearable will be important, as compared to being obtrusive or unobtrusive. In situations involving clinical situations all these platforms run into difficulties as the clinical side defends the professional view on managing health and medical data. However, inclusion of healthy lifestyle interlinked with disease management will promote further use of approaches by Apple, Google, Microsoft and Samsung.

The question is obviously how the market responds concerning inter-links and as related to maintaining integrity with the health records. Qualified-Self solutions still overlook and neglect nomenclature and ontology.

Within analytics and computation, evidence-based medicine (EBM) uses the notation and language of probability and statistics in order to analyze observation of outcomes of individuals in need of care, where we expose individuals to certain treatments or contexts. Logic-based medicine[41] (LBM) explains how terminology and nomenclature in medicine can be logically formulated by means of underlying signatures, which in turn leads to the possibility to construct formal terms and sentences, and as they eventually appear within reasoning mechanisms. LBM thereby opens up a logic foundation of probability theory, where notions in probability theory and statistics are enriched with concept used in formal logic.

Logic, as a structure, contains signatures, terms, sentences, theoremata (as structured sets of sentences, or 'structured premises'), entailments, algebras, satisfactions, axioms, theories and proof calculi (Eklund et al., 2014). Lative logic produces a huge potential of applications using termi-nology, nomenclature and ontology in particular in social and healthcare. WHO classifications are logically lative (Eklund, 2016). The reference classifications ICD and ICF then appear in structured relation with each other. Similar transformations can be made for the derived classifications as well as for the related classifications ICPC-2, ICECI, ISO9999, ATC/DDD and ICNP.

Formal mappings, e.g., between ICD and ICF are rare, and this is mostly due to a lack of understanding terminology and nomenclature as terms in a logic. ATC/DDD for drugs embraces 'dose' but not 'interven-tion,' which means that drug-drug interactions are possible to describe whereas drug-condition is more complicated. IHTSDO's SNOMED CT subdivides concepts within its hierarchy consisting e.g. of clinical find-ings disorders, body structure, pharmaceutical/biologic product, social context, staging and scales, and qualifier values, but has been devel-oped only with intuitive connections with WHO classifications. Fur-ther, SNOMED's assumption that "health ontology" needs the same or a

---

[41] http://www.glioc.com/logic/health/lbm/

similar underlying logic as web ontology, is a fatal mistake not promoting the dialog and interrelation of classifications and nomenclature in useful application oriented directions. It is also all too narrow to assume that description logic will suffice as a logic for health ontology even if it is suggested to support web ontology.

All this information management is then not just about data and information but indeed about information and process. Information as structure and logic is nomenclature and ontology based, and processes similarly require language far beyond just drawing circles and arrows. Specifically, encoding processes in a more formal and logical manner will need to make use of modeling standards like UML, SysML and BPMN.

For *prediction* purposes, there is a distinction to be made between a computational algorithm, which includes pattern recognition, neural and Bayesian networks, and similar computational/numerical methods, and logical algorithm, the latter involving inference mechanisms for reasoning is some selected logic, where sentences and statements are based on terms which in turn are founded on nomenclature and ontology. Logical inference manages uncertainty in a different way as compared to computational methods (Eklund et al., 2016). Type theoretical innovations are needed because nomenclature constructions appear in logic as a natural ingredient, but not per se in intelligent computing. A *condition* is also more of a matter of truth than just a matter of value.

KEYWORDS

- **ageing**
- **care process**
- **category theory**
- **health ontology**
- **lative logic**
- **mobile health**

REFERENCES

Eklund, P. *Assessment Scales and Consensus Guidelines Encoded in Formal Logic*, Journal of Nutrition, Health and Aging (19th IAGG World Congress of Gerontology and Geriatrics, Paris, 2009). 13 Suppl 1, S558–S559.

Eklund, P. *Lative Logic Accommodating the WHO Family of International Classifications.*

Eklund, P., Galán, M. A., Helgesson, R., Kortelainen, J. *Fuzzy Terms*, Fuzzy Sets and Systems 2014, 256, 211–235.

Eklund, P., Höhle, U., Kortelainen, J. *Non-Commutative Quantales for Many-Valuedness in Applications*, in preparation.

Encyclopedia of E-Health and Telemedicine (Eds. Maria Manuela Cruz-Cunha, Isabel Miranda), IGI Global, 2016 (in print). URL: http://www.igi-global.com/book/encyclopedia-health-telemedicine/141916.

CHAPTER 10

VIRTUAL MOBILE INTERFACES, BUSINESS INTELLIGENCE, AND ANALYTICS CONTENT PROCESSING

CYRUS F. NOURANI

Research Professor, Simon Fraser University, British Columbia, Canada

CONTENTS

ABSTRACT

Intelligent business interfaces are designed with intelligent multitier, interfaces applying agents, and intelligent business objects with applications to intelligent WWW. Basic intelligent content management with multitier designs for interfaces is presented. The field of automated learning and discovery has obvious financial and organizational memory applications. There are basic applications to data discovery techniques with agent multiplayer game tree planning. The computing techniques, the Morph Gentzen deductive system and its models are applied towards designing an active multimedia intelligence database. The computing model is based on novel competitive learning techniques with model discovery and customizing interface design. Intelligent visual computing paradigms are applied to define the multimedia computing paradigm and active databases. The Intelligent Multimedia paradigms are applicable to databases and query processing, illustrated with applications to stock forecasting analytics. A view-model-controller design prototype for mobile business platforms with content processing specifics are presented.

10.1   INTRODUCTION

The chapter addresses how to questions on intelligent interfaces to mobile business from the design, modeling, and the application perspective? The design tier-layers, intelligent databases, content processing and web-interfaces with new specific logics are presented as bases to paradigms that render realistic rapid response systems. Intelligent business interfaces might apply automated learning and discovery—often called data mining, machine learning, or advanced data analysis—has new w-interface relevance. There are obvious financial and organizational memory applications applied at times in our projects. E-commerce, e-business, trust, trustworthiness, usability, human-computer interaction, cognitive ergonomics, user interface design, ease of use, interaction design, and online marketing are the business user modeling issues addressed in this chapter. Financial companies have begun to analyze their customers' behavior in order to maximize the effectiveness of marketing efforts. There are routine applications to data discovery techniques with intelligence databases. Management process controls at times calls on warehouse data and relies on organizational memory to reach decision. Recent research has led to progress—both in the type methods—that are available and in the understanding of their character-istics. The broad topic of automated learning and discovery are inher-ently cross-disciplinary in nature. As there is increased reliance on visual data and active visual databases on presenting and storing organizational structures, via the internet and the WWW, the role of data discovery and intelligent multimedia active databases become essential. Knowl-edge management (KM) and organizational memory (OM) are the areas where model discovery with active Intelligent Databases applying pre-dictive logic (Nourani, 1995a, 1999a,g, 2000). KM is one of the key progress factors in organizations. In an organization, know-how may relate to problem-solving expertise in functional disciplines, experi-ences of human resources, and project experiences in terms of project management issues, design technical issues and lessons learned. Corpo-rate memory (CM) or OM is regarded as the central prerequisite for IT supports of KM. It is the means for knowledge conservation, distribu-tion, and reuse. Identification and analysis of a company's knowledge-intensive work processes (e.g., product design or strategic planning, using KM and OM are data discovery and data warehousing intensive operations. A new computing area is defined with Intelligent Multime-dia principles with business applications (Nourani, 1999a). The area for which the chapter provides a foundation where multimedia computing is bound to be applied at dimensions and computing phenomena unimag-ined; thus, yet inevitable with the emerging technologies. The principles defined are new practical multimedia artificial intelligence business applications. Multimedia AI systems are proposed with new computing techniques are defined. Multimedia objects and rules, and multimedia programming techniques are presented via a new language (Nourani, 1999c, 2000). The concept of Hybrid Picture is the start to define intel-ligent multimedia objects automatic hybrid picture transformation with a multimedia language in the author's projects. A preliminary mathe-matical basis to the Morph Gentzen computing logic are presented in Nourani (1999a,c,e, 2000). The foundations are a new computing logic with a model theory and formal system. Multimedia objects and rules are presented and shown in programming applications. Intelligent Mul-timedia context defines the applications. Practical Multimedia Design is illustrated by pictorial examples. The project has applications to topics dealing with usability engineering, culture and design, international differences in software user training, and case studies on international user interface design as in Del Galdo and Nielsen (Nourani, 2006). A practitioner for developing usable interfaces can apply intelligent multimedia to the practical designs (Nourani, 2005).

10.2   THE VISUAL DYNAMICS

10.2.1   WHY MULTIMEDIA DATABASES?

Defining compatibility and visual effects relations allows objects to be selected and applied to design and compare customized views. Multimedia programming is combined with visual multiagent objects to define specific visual compatibility for customized active databases. Active databases deploy certain computing which lend themselves naturally to the Intelligent Multimedia principles (Nourani, 1999c). The concept of active intelligent objects and "events" are embedded by computing defined on IM as a basic computing with intelligent trees, intelligent objects, and hybrid pictures. The characteristics of an Active DMBS, or ADMBS (Bailey, 1995) supports definition and management of ECA rules, for example, event, condition, and action. Hence, an ADMBS must have means to define ECA's. An ADBMS must support rule management and rule-base updates. It must carry out actions and evaluate conditions. An ADBMS must represent information in ECA-rules in terms of its data models. The IM computing paradigm provides a basis for designing multimedia ADBMS's. The IM computing paradigm allows the design for multimedia ADBMS (Nourani, 2000) to apply agent computing to ADBMS, to base an ADBMS on multimedia agent computing, and to carryout meta-level reasoning and KB with multimedia intelligent objects.

10.2.2   KR AND DIAGRAMS FOR RELEVANT WORLD MODELS

Let us brief on knowledge representation with G-diagram models (Nourani, 1995a, 1999a) and applications to define computable models and relevant world reasoning. G-diagrams are diagrams defined from a minimal set of function symbols that can inductively define a model. Generic diagrams are applied to relevance reasoning with model-localized representations for a minimal efficient computable way to represent relevant knowledge for localized AI worlds. We show how computable AI world knowledge is representable. G-diagrams are applied towards KR from planning with non-determinism and planning with free proof trees to partial deduction with predictive diagrams applied in Nourani (1999a,c,g). The applications to proof abstraction and explanation-based generalization by abstract functions are alluded in Nourani (1995a). A brief overview to a reasoning grid with diagrams is presented in the above referenced papers. Generalized diagrams are used to build models with a minimal family of generalized Skolem functions. The minimal sets of function symbols are functions with which a model can be built inductively. The functions can correspond to objects defining shapes and depicting pictures. We cannot formalize the real world, however, the relevant descriptions for problem solving can be specified. Knowledge representation has two significant roles: to define a model for the AI world, and to provide a basis for reasoning techniques to get at implicit knowledge. An ordinary diagram is the set of atomic and negated atomic sentences that are true in a model. Generalized diagrams are diagrams definable by a minimal set of functions such that everything else in the model's closure can be inferred, by a minimal set of terms defining the model. Thus providing a minimal characterization of models, and a minimal set of atomic sentences on which all other atomic sentences depend. To prove Gödel's completeness theorem, Henkin defined a model directly from the syntax of the given theory. This structure is obtained by putting terms that are provably equal into equivalence classes, then defining a free structure on the equivalence classes. The computing enterprise requires more general techniques of model construction and extension, since it has to accommodate dynamically changing world descriptions and theories. Let us define a simple language L = <{tweedy}, {a}, {bird}, predicate letters at first order logic- FOL>. A model may consist of {bird(tweedy), penguin(tweedy) (bird(tweedy), bird(tweedy) v (bird(tweedy), …}, others may consist of {p(a), (p(a) (p(a), p(x), p(a) v p(x) v p(y), …}. Because we can apply arbitrary interpretation functions for mapping language constructs into worldviews, the number of models for a language is infinite. Although this makes perfect sense from a theoretical and logical point of view, from a practical point of view, this notion of model is too general for our applications. Since for AI we want models that could be computed effectively and efficiently. Thus, it is useful to restrict the types of models that we define for real world applications. Primarily, we are interested in models with computable properties definable from the theory. The generic diagram, G-diagram for models (Nourani, 1991, 1995a, 1999g) is a diagram in which the elements of the structure are all represented by a minimal family of function symbols and constants. Thus it is sufficient to define the truth of formulas only for the terms generated by the minimal family of functions and constant symbols. Such assignment implicitly defines the diagram. This allows us to define a canonical model of a theory in terms of a minimal function set. The following sections apply KR with visual business objects and Section 10.5 presents the applications to heterogeneous computing and model discovery on business data.

10.3   CONTENT MANAGEMENT AND PROCESSING

Current content processing, e.g., Google and search engines industry relies on processing 'content' based on web address, tags, and indices. Existing web extraction techniques are either tag-based or tree based with heuristics applied to solve the semantics problems. Structure augmented tag techniques with a specific algorithm to accomplish the structuring are presented. Templates are applied to do match web pages. Sequence matching algorithm and a preprocessing grouping algorithm to the tree matching part. On meta-model based approach for extracting ontological relations OWL-encoded ontologies from transformations from UML descriptions. Rules are defined for extracting ontological semantics. The transformation rules are XML-based implemented. OWL encoded ontology id constructed for UML designs.

The content management arena is encompassed as follows:
- Enterprise Content Enterprise Content
- Web Content: Server's side processing and content side processing and content
- Content and Databases

- Multimedia Content Processing
- Content Presentation Languages
- Real Content and MPEGs Res

Content management is a broad term used to describe many different ways of organizing many different types of information. Example areas are: how to identify content that is appropriate for a platform or user group, appropriate for; how to load and modularize a document are important areas to address in a content management system. That increases the use of the information in an enterprise and relieves the IT resources. For example, linking up business partners and employee directly via Internet can optimize available expertise for business processes. Further it facilitates how to administer information and data, independent of format, model enterprise centrally, and to generate synergies. Besides, the system saves costs, since many locations can be standardized with external employees that are systematized. Basic systems can be extended, instead of a complete solution for all conceivable requirements, according to topical and future needs individually that are modular. Thus system can present advantages with lasting positive influence on productiveness at organizations.

10.3.1 ENTERPRISE CONTENT MANAGEMENT

The World Wide Web was originally built for human consumption. Although everything on it is machine readable, this data is not machine understandable. It is very hard to automate everything on the Web, and because of the volume of information the Web contains, it is not possible to manage it manually. The solution proposed is to use metadata to describe the data contained on the Web. Metadata is "data about data" (e.g., a library catalog is metadata, since it describes publications) or specifically in the context of this specification "data describing Web resources." The distinction between "data" and "metadata" is not an absolute. It is a distinction created primarily by a particular application, and many times the same resource will be interpreted in both ways simultaneously. Resource Description Framework (RDF) is a foundation for processing metadata; it provides interoperability between applications that exchange machine understandable information on the Web. RDF emphasizes facilities to enable automated processing of Web resources. RDF can be used in a variety of application areas; for example, in resource discovery to provide better search engine capabilities, in cataloging for describing the content and content relationships available at a particular Web site, page, or digital library, by intelligent software agents to facilitate knowledge sharing and to exchange, in content rating, in describing collections pages that represent a single logical "document," for describing intellectual property rights of Web pages, and for expressing the privacy preferences of a user as well as the privacy policies of a Website RDF with digital signatures will be key to building the "Web of Trust" for electronic commerce, collaboration, and other trust for applications.

10.3.2 WEB CONTENT

Web interfaces and information systems are the decade's newest essential technology to business, engineering, sciences, and all sectors where rapid extrapolation is important. The proceedings preliminaries are three keynotes that address management the web information systems technological state and the technological change implications. The push-pull effect of web environments on the data management requirements and the underlying technological changes drives the next generation search engines, e.g., ambient multimedia content search, onto domain independent platforms. Search methodology and for the most part academic systems, deploy real-time correlations among keywords to generate queries based on specific known relations. Object level vertical searches: there are lacking deep or are incomplete relations to link-up. Innovations include queries composed from schema instances based on page levels, or manifold ranking algorithms on webpage blocks that the initially retrieved pages based on Cosine measures and vision-based page segmentation. Preference-based search techniques based on modeling user preference to find a best match with preference elicitation is a newer area with hill climbing techniques applying Pareto optimality to choose options. Problem solving PMS is represented with OWLs and Horn-like rules are applied. Front-end applications, at times apply web component presentation models like GUI widgets resembling WebXML. Hierarchical image semantics structure captures image semantics from ontology trees with visual features as semantic domains. Sematic domains are wavlet transformations effectively generate representation of visual features. Similarity is computed from image scans. The above areas benefit from the present invention.

Example Web Content Management offered on systems is as follows:
Product | Usage | References | Partner | Services | Home
Product > Web Content Management
Product Web > Web Content
Content Management
SmartEdit
Asset > Asset Manager
Site Manager > Site Manager
Translation > Translation Editor > Editor
Translation > Translation Manager > Manager
Web > Web Compliance > Compliance Manager > Manager
Archive > Archive
Import Manager
CMS > New Features CMS 7.0 > 10 CMS Tips 10 CMS Tips
Enterprise > Enterprise Content > Content Management
Personalization
Download
Product film
Modules > Module
SmartEdit > Technology Actualization
Asset Manager > Corporate Design
Site Manager Site Manager
Help > IT-Experts
Specialization
Websites, Portals, Intranets Portals
Translation Editor
Additional Modules
Web Compliance Manager

10.3.3 XML CONTENT

How can we provide a mechanism that allows additional elements to be added into existing content models?

Problem: At the time of designing the document type, the designer may not be able to foresee all of the uses and situations where document instances will be used. To provide for flexibility, the contents of elements can be made to be definable by the document instance.

Context: This is a very general mechanism that can be used anytime additional flexibility is needed.

Forces: Flexibility is often required for a document type to be able to be used effectively. Flexibility, however often makes processing of the documents more difficult. Customization of software is often needed to deal with the flexibility.

Solution: The designer of the document can add a mechanism to allow the author of a document instance to extend an element definition from the document type.

Example System: Adobe Premiere APIs provide access to all points of the video-editing pipeline: import, video and audio filtering, playback, and output can all be performed.

10.3.4   ADOBE EXAMPLE CONTENT

Adobe Premier Plug-ins
Premiere API Plug-in Types
Media Abstraction Layer
Record Records from an external (usually hardware) source. Import media types into premiere beyond those it supports. Synthetic importers, a subset, dynamically generate media. Synthetic importers, a subset, dynamically generate media.

Playback Accelerate video playback by controlling the timeline. Playback Accelerate video playback associated with a playback module to form an Editing Mode.

Filters: Filters Video Process a series of frames. Parameters are Video Process a series of frames. Parameters are animatable over time.

Audio Process Audio Clips: Parameters are Audio Process audio clips. Parameters are animatable over time.

Transition Blend: Blends one movie clip into another over time.

Edit Decision List Export: Create a text based EDL file to use in Edit Decision List, Device Control and external device (VCR, camera, etc.).

The SDLT: Separate layout and content templates.

Documentation Layout Templates: SDLT produced in set of generic and comprehensive set of Adobe FrameMaker templates, for formatting technical software documentation. Sample material for different types of document is provided separately, as content templates themselves formatted using the SDLT. This separation (of layout and content templates) offers the following advantages: visual consistency across the various documents for a project can be achieved in a manageable way, and requires the maintenance of only one set of layout templates. Simplification on only templates: adding a template for a particular document type requires only the creation of a content template, consisting only of content specific sample material.

Some features of the SDLT are: comprehensive predefined formats for all typical software documentation; predefined formats in the SDLT FrameMaker paragraph catalog for the SDLT chapter template, for the SDLT chapter template, showing paragraph tag names for list items, levels 1, 2 and 3. The showing paragraph tag names SDLT define catalogs of tagged format definitions for paragraph, characters, master pages, reference pages, cross-references, variables and tables contains only the formats required by that template file, for example, the front matter and chapter template each contain a set of predefined formats, but each only contain what is necessary to format the front matter and chapters, respectively.

HTML, SQL, PHP & MySQL are the most widely used open source database and scripting open source technologies on the Web today. A starting point in your journey is to creating dynamic websites and setting up relational databases. Building Your Own Database Driven Website using BPHP & MySQL: there are a practical hands on guide to learning all the tools, principles and techniques needed to build a fully functional database driven Website using PHP & MySQL SQL.

10.3.5 ANALYTICS AND BIG DATA

Big Data is a popular term used to describe the exponential growth and availability of data, both structured and unstructured. And big data may be as important to business—and society—as the Internet has become. Why? More data may lead to more accurate analyzes. More accurate analyzes may lead to more confident decision making. Better decisions can mean greater operational efficiencies, cost reductions and reduced risk. Good data governance only multiplies the value of big data. Big Data has big value, it also takes organization's big effort to manage well and an effective governance discipline can fulfill its purpose, facing big data exponentials, content, and applications: Aps.

Consumers have been pledging their love for data visualizations for a while now, and data mining with multimedia discovery is the area being explored. There is emerging a debate about the relative importance of ever-bigger data versus ever better predictive techniques to avoid bigger data. Not enough people have the necessary skills to make rigorous use of data. It's been more than 70 years since American national technology policy that Vannevar Bush famously declared "there is a new profession of trail blazers that find delight in the task of establishing useful trails through the enormous mass of the common record."

10.4   A VISUAL CONTENT LOGIC

A problem-solving paradigm is presented in the Double Vision Computing paper (Nourani and Grace, 1999). The basic technique to be applied is viewing the televised scene combined with the scripts as many possible worlds. Agents at each world that complement one another to portray a stage by cooperating. The A.I. techniques can be applied to define interactions among personality and view descriptions. Object coobject pairs and agents solve problems on boards by cooperating agents. The Intelligent Multimedia computing paradigm define multiagent computing with multimedia objects and carry on artificial intelligence computing on boards. The IM Hybrid Multimedia Programming techniques have a computing mathematical logic, with a Gentzen (1943) or natural deduction Prawitz (1965) system defined by taking multimedia objects coded by diagram functions. By transforming hybrid picture's corresponding functions a new hybrid picture is deduced. Multimedia objects are viewed as syntactic objects defined by functions, to which the deductive system is applied.

Thus we define a syntactic morphing to be a technique by which multimedia objects and hybrid pictures are homomorphically mapped via their defining functions to a new hybrid picture. The deduction rules are a Gentzen system augmented by Morphing, and Trans-morphing.

The logical language has function names for hybrid pictures. The Morph Rule—An object defined by the functional n-tuple $<f1, ..., fn>$ can be morphed to an object defined by the functional n-tuple $<h(f1), ..., h(fn)>$, provided h is a homomorphism of intelligent objects as abstract algebras, and h(f) is the corresponding structure to what f selects, at the morphed world. The Trans-Morph Rules—A set of rules whereby combining hybrid pictures p1, ..., pn defines an Event {p1, p2, ..., pn} with a consequent hybrid picture p. Thus the combination is a morph sequencing initiating event. The deductive theory is a Gentzen system in which hybrid pictures are named by parameterized functions; augmented by the MIM morph and transmorph rules. The formal AI and mathematics appear in the first author's mathematical logic publications since 1997 and applied to business areas (Nourani, 1999c,g). The intelligent syntax languages are applied with Morph Gentzen (Thrun et al., 1998).

10.4.1 THE MODELS

A computational logic for intelligent languages is presented in brief with a soundness and completeness theorem from Nourani (1994, 1999a) and applied to intelligent business object computing. A brief overview to context abstraction shows how context free and context sensitive properties might be defined with agents. Agents are in the sense defined in Thrun et al. (1998) and the A.I. foundations Genesereth (1987). A set of function symbols in the language, referred to by Agent Function Set, is the set of function symbols that are modeled in the computing world by AI Agents. The idea is to characterize computation with abstract syntax trees without grammar specifics. As an example, suppose you are told there is an academic department with a faculty member which is Superman, and two faculty members which are Swedish speaking, and three which do not talk to anybody not in their expertise area. Without telling you anything else about what they do, abstract syntax properties can be defined.

When the signature's specific agent functions are defined, it implies the signature has defined message paths for them. From the signature Intelligent Models are defined for abstract syntax trees. An abstract language that is capable of specifying modules, agents, and their communications expresses the computation. The implementing agents, their corresponding objects, and their message passing actions can also be presented by the two-level abstract syntax. The agents are represented by function names that appear on the free syntax trees of implementing trees. A signature defines the language tree compositionality degree and defines the abstract syntax.

10.4.2   RELEVANT KR AND VISUAL BUSINESS OBJECTS

Knowledge representation has two significant roles: to define a model for the AI world, and to provide a basis for reasoning techniques to get at implicit knowledge. An ordinary diagram is the set of atomic and negated atomic sentences that are true in a model. Generalized diagrams are diagrams definable by a minimal set of functions such that everything else in the model's closure can be inferred, by a minimal set of terms defining the model. Thus providing a minimal characterization of models, and a minimal set of atomic sentences on which all other atomic sentences depend. We want to solve real world problems in AI. Obviously for automating problem solving, we need to represent the real world. Since we cannot represent all aspects of a real world problem, we need to restrict the representation to only the relevant aspects of the real world we are interested in. Let us call this subset of relevant real world aspects the Relevant World for a problem. AI approaches to problem solving represent the knowledge usually in some kind of first-order language, consisting of at least constants, functions and predicate symbols. Our primary focus will be the relations among KR, AI worlds, and the computability of models. Truth is a notion that can have dynamic properties. To keep the models, which need to be considered small and to keep a problem tractable, we have to get a grip on a minimal set of functions to define computable models with. The selector functions are applied to create compound business objects.

10.4.3   LEARNING FROM MULTIMEDIA DATA

Many datasets contain more than just a single type of data. The existing algorithms can usually only cope with a single type data. How can we design methods that can take on multimedia data from multiple modalities? Are we to apply separate learning algorithms to each data modality, and combine their results, or are there to be algorithms that can handle multimedia multiple modalities on a feature-level. Learning casual relationships among visual stored data is another important area, which can benefit from our project. Most existing learning algorithms detect only correlations, but are unable to model causality and hence fail to predict the effect of external controls. Visualization and interactive discovery data mining is a process, which involves automated data analysis and control decisions by an expert of the domain. For example, patterns in many large-scale business system databases might be discovered interactively, by a human expert looking at the data, as it is done with medical data. Data visualization is specifically difficult when data is high dimensional, specifically when it involves non-numerical data such as text. The projects might be a basis for designing interactive business tools.

10.4.4   COMPUTABLE WORLD MODELS

The technique in Nourani (1991, 1995a, 1999g) for model building as applied to the problem of AI reasoning allows us to build and extend models by diagrams. This requires us to define the notion of generalized or generic diagram. The G-diagrams are used to build models with a minimal family of generalized Skolem functions. The minimal sets of function symbols are those with which a model can be built inductively. We focus our attention on such models, since they are computable (Bailey et al., 1995). The G-diagram methods applied and further developed here, allow us to formulate AI world descriptions, theories, and models in a minimal computable manner. It further allows us to view the world from only the relevant functions. Thus models and proofs for the specified problems can be characterized by models computable by a set of functions. The G-diagram functions can define IM objects and be applied with the Morph Gentzen logic.

10.5   HETEROGENEOUS COMPUTING AND MODELS

10.5.1   HETEROGENEOUS COMPUTING

In Nourani (1998) we present new techniques for design by software agents and new concepts entitled Abstract Intelligent Implementation (AII) of AI systems. Objects, message passing actions, and implementing agents are defined by syntactic constructs, with agents appearing as functions. The techniques have been applied to design intelligent business objects in Nourani (1998). AII techniques have been applied to Heterogeneous KB Design and implementation. The application areas include support for highly responsive planning. AII techniques are due to be an area of crucial importance as they are applied gradually to the real problems. The applied fields are, for example, intelligent business systems, aerospace, AI for robots, and multimedia.

10.5.2   KNOWLEDGE BASES AND VISUAL MODEL DISCOVERY

Model diagrams allow us to characterize incomplete KR. To key into the incomplete knowledge base we apply generalized predictive diagrams, whereby specified diagram functions on a search engine can select onto localized data fields. The predictive model diagrams (Nourani, 1995a, 1999a) could be minimally represented by the set of functions {f1, ..., fn} that inductively define the model. Data discovery from KR on diagrams might be viewed as satisfying a goal by getting at relevant data which instantiates a goal. The goal formula states what relevant data is sought. We propose methods that can be applied to planning (Nourani, 1991) with diagrams to implement discovery planning. In planning with G-diagrams that part of the plan that involves free Skolemized trees is carried along with the proof tree for a plan goal. Computing with diagram functions allows us to key to active visual databases with agents.

10.5.3   PREDICTION AND DISCOVERY

Minimal prediction is an artificial intelligence technique defined since the author's model-theoretic planning project. It is a cumulative non-monotonic approximation attained with completing model diagrams on what might be true in a model or knowledge base. A predictive diagram for a theory T is a diagram D (M), where M is a model for T, and for any formula q in M, either the function f: q{0,1} is defined, or there exists a formula p in D(M), such that T U {p} proves q; or that T proves q by minimal prediction. A generalized predictive diagram, is a predictive diagram with D(M) defined from a minimal set of functions. The predictive diagram could be minimally represented by a set of functions {f1, ..., fn} that inductively define the model. The free trees we had defined by the notion of provability implied by the definition, could consist of some extra Skolem functions {g1, ..., gl} that appear at free trees. The f terms and g terms, tree congruences. Predictive diagrams then characterize partial deduction with free trees. The predictive diagrams are applied to discover models for the intelligent game trees. Prediction is applied to plan goal satisfiability and can be combined with plausibility (Nourani, 1991), probabilities, and fuzzy logic to obtain, for example, confidence intervals. The author has applied minimal prediction to simply encode knowledge with model diagrams to carry on automated deduction as Loveland and Poole's automated deduction system intended. Modeling with virtual tree planning (Nourani, 1999f) is applied where uncertainty, including effector and sensor uncertainty, are relegated to agents, where competitive learning on game trees determines a confidence interval. The incomplete knowledge modeling is treated with KR on predictive model diagrams. Model discovery at KB's are with specific techniques defined for trees. Model diagrams allow us to model-theoretically characterize incomplete KR. To key into the incomplete knowledge base we apply generalized predictive diagrams whereby specified diagram functions a search engine can select onto localized data fields. The predictive model diagrams could be minimally represented by the set of functions {f1, ..., fn} that inductively define the model. Data discovery from KR on diagrams might be viewed as satisfying a goal by getting at relevant data which instantiates a goal. The goal formula states what relevant data is sought. We propose methods that can be applied to planning (Nourani, 1991) with diagrams to implement discovery planning. In planning with G-diagrams that part of the plan that involves free Skolemized trees is carried along with the proof tree for a plan goal. Computing with diagram functions allows us to key to active visual databases.

10.5.4   TAIM* AND DISCOVERY COMPUTATION FROM WAREHOUSED DATA

The morphing Transformer Active Intelligent Database designs outline in the chapter is abbreviated as TAIM henceforth. Data discovery from KR on diagrams might be viewed as satisfying a goal by getting at relevant data which instantiates a goal. The goal formula states what relevant data is sought. We have presented planning techniques, which can be applied to implement discovery planning. In planning with G-diagrams that part of the plan that involves free Skolemized trees is carried along with the proof tree for a plan goal. The idea is that if the free proof tree is constructed then the plan has a model in which the goals are satisfied. The model is the initial model of the AI world for which the free Skolemized trees were constructed. Partial deductions in this approach correspond to proof trees that have free Skolemized trees in their representation. While doing proofs with free Skolemized trees we are facing proofs of the form $p(g(....))$ proves $p(f(g(....))$ and generalizations to $p(f(x))$ proves for all x, $p(f(x))$. Thus the free proofs are in some sense an abstract counterpart of the SLD. Let us see what predictive diagrams do for knowledge discovery knowledge management. Diagrams allow us to model-theoretically characterize incomplete KR. To key into the incomplete knowledge base

Figure 10.1 depicts selector functions Fi from an abstract view grid interfaced via an inference engine to a knowledge base and in turn onto a database.

Generalized predictive diagrams are defined, whereby specified diagram functions and search engine can select onto localized data fields. A Generalized Predictive Diagram is a predictive diagram where D (M) is defined from a minimal set of functions. The predictive diagram could be minimally represented by a set of functions {f1, ..., fn} that inductively define the model. The functions are keyed onto the inference and knowledge base to select via the areas keyed to, designated as Si's in Figure 10.1 and data is retrieved (Nourani, 1999f). Visual object views to active databases might be designed with the above. The trees defined by

---

*TAIM is the trade name for the Active Intelligent Database design and is the technical property of the authors computing business. Applications must be with permission and venture partnerships

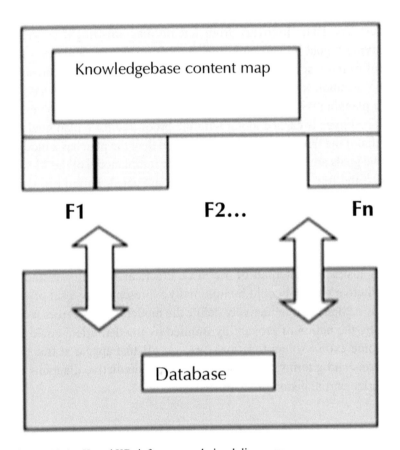

FIGURE 10.1   Keyed KR, inference, and visual discovery.

the notion of provability implied by the definition might consist of some extra Skolem functions {g1, ..., gn}, that appear at free trees. The f terms and g terms, tree congruences, and predictive diagrams then character- ize deduction with virtual trees (Nourani, 1999b) as intelligent predic- tive interfaces. Data discovery from KR on diagrams might be viewed as satisfying a goal by getting at relevant data which instantiates a goal. The goal formula states what relevant data is sought. We have presented planning techniques, which can be applied to implement discovery plan- ning. In planning with G-diagrams that part of the plan that involves free Skolemized trees is carried along with the proof tree for a plan goal. The idea is that if the free proof tree is constructed then the plan has a model in which the goals are satisfied. The model is the initial model of the AI world for which the free Skolemized trees were constructed. Partial deductions in this approach correspond to proof trees that have free Skolemized trees in their representation. While doing proofs with free Skolemized trees we are facing proofs of the form $p(g(...))$ proves $p(f(g(...)))$ and generaliza- tions to $p(f(x))$ proves for all x, $p(f(x))$. Thus the free proofs are in some sense an abstract counterpart of the SLD. Practical AI Goal Satisfaction. The predictive diagram could be minimally represented by a set of func- tions {f1, ..., fan} that inductively define the model. The free trees we had defined by the notion of provability implied by the definition, could con- sist of some extra Skolem functions {g1, ..., gl} that appear at free trees. The f terms and g terms, tree congruences, and predictive diagrams then characterize partial deduction with free trees.

10.5.5   KR AND DATA WAREHOUSING WITH KEYED FUNCTIONS

Let us see what predictive diagrams do for knowledge discovery knowl- edge management. Diagrams allow us to model-theoretically character- ize incomplete KR to incomplete knowledge-base. The following figure depicts selector functions Fi from an abstract view grid interfaced via an inference engine to a knowledge base and in turn onto a database. Practical AI systems are designed by modeling AI with facts, rules, goals, strategies, and knowledge bases. Patterns, schemas, AI frames and viewpoints are the micro to aggregate glimpses onto the database and knowledge bases were masses of data and their relationships-representations, respectively, are stored. Schemas and frames are what might be defined with objects, the object classes, and the object class inheritances user-defined inheritance relations, and specific restrictions on the object, class, or frame slot types and behaviors. From Nourani (2000) scheme might be Intelligent Forecasting.

IS-A Stock Forecasting Technique
Portfolios: Stock, bonds, corporate assets
Member Management Science Techniques

Schemas allow brief descriptions on object surface properties with which high level inference and reasoning with incomplete knowledge can be carried out applying facts and the defined relationships among objects.

Visual objects have mutual agent visual message correspondence.

Visual objects is a way some practical AI is a carried on with to recognize important features, situations, and applicable rules. From the proofs standpoint patterns are analogies to features as being leaves on computing trees. Forward chaining is a goal satisfaction.

Visual objects technique, where inference rules are activated by data patterns, to sequentially get to a goal by apply the inference rules. The current pertinent rules are available at an agenda store. The carried out rules modify the database. Backward chaining is an alternative based on opportunistic response to changing information. It starts with the goal and looks for available premises that might be satisfied to have gotten there. Goals are objects for which there is automatic goal generation of missing data at the goal by recursion backward chaining on the missing objects as subgoals. Data unavailability implies search for new goal discovery. Goal Directed Planning is carried out while planning with diagrams. The part of the plan that involves free Skolemized trees is carried along with the proof tree for a plan goal. If the free proof tree is constructed then the plan has an initial model in which the goals are satisfied. IM's basis for forecasting is put forth at preliminary stages (Nourani, 1999a).

Visual objects logic with predictive model diagrams has been applied as a basis for intelligent forecasting (Nourani, 1999a, 2000). There are graphics sequents for predicting the quarter earnings from the second and third combined with a market condition graph. The way a market condition graph is designed is a propriety issue. It is obtained by Morph Gentzen sequents from known stock market parameters. Data discovery from KR on diagrams might be viewed as satisfying a goal by getting at relevant data which instantiates a goal. The goal formula states what relevant data is sought.

10.5.6   THE STOCK TRADERS INTERFACE MODEL

The basis for forecasting is put forth at preliminary stages in the author's publications since 1998. The idea is to apply Morph-Gentzen logic as a basis for intelligent multimedia forecasting. Figure 10.2 indicates a graphics sequent for predicting the fourth quarter earnings from the second and third combined with a market condition graph. The way a market condition graph is designed is a propriety issue. It is obtained by Morph Gentzen sequents from known stock market parameters. The enclosed are example stock trading and forecasting interfaces.

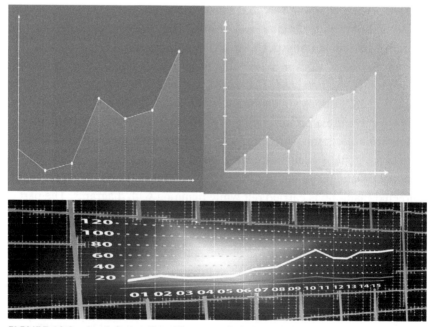

FIGURE 10.2   Stock forecasting. (Courtesy of pixabay.com)

10.5.7   THE VISUAL DB ASSET MANAGEMENT MODEL

The fast track to real media content management is a media asset management environment that allows vendors and customers media applications to interoperate seamlessly within the IBM DB2 Digital Library infrastructure. Asset management is an important area to the efficient intelligent multimedia computing. Cost-effective management of digital content is expected to be another frequent topic. IBM's Grand Central Media "Grand Central Media" provides media asset management that enables a company to manage, secure, share, locate and reuse digital media files. The IBM solution also allows media and entertainment executives to import and index digital content and combine search requests into one results list that can be graphically browsed and shared with others world-wide. IBM Grand Central Media is part of the company's suite of Digital Library applications that are being used by leading film studios, advertising firms, and broadcast and stock footage houses. The Web-based solution supports the synchronization of databases at different physical locations or on wide-area networks.

10.5.8   MULTIMEDIA MIDDLEWARE DATABASES AND WRAPPERS TO USER INTERFACES

Large-scale multimedia information systems today rely on big data stored in systems with differing capabilities. Many of the "mission-critical" tasks these customers do depend on integrating data from several sources. Often the data sources to be integrated include a broad range of sources, such as CAD/CAM systems, text search engines, molecular structure databases, or customer-specific repositories. Garlic (Nourani et al., 2000) offers the ability to interrelate data from multiple sources with a broad range of querying capabilities, in a single, cross-source query. Garlic is an IBM prototype, which allows new sources to be easily added to an existing installation. Garlic offers the ability to interrelate data from multiple sources with a broad range of querying capabilities, in a single, cross-source query. A significant focus of the project is the provision of support for data sources that provide type-specific indexing and query capabilities. Garlic's "wrapper architecture," (Wiederhold, 1992) and the applications at Nourani (1996) encapsulate data sources, allowing new sources to be added quickly, and accommodating a wide variety of sources, with a broad range of traditional and nontraditional query processing capabilities. Wrappers model legacy data as objects, participate in query planning, and provide standard interfaces for method invocation and query execution. The knowledge base is keyed with relevant selector functions. There are worldwide web retrieval designs, which have to apply direct links. The hierarchical abstract structures are being applied to the knowledge base and data structures to accomplish the tasks called for.

10.5.9   CONTENT MANAGEMENT SYSTEM WITH TAIM

To design interfaces with systems we have to provide content management interfaces. The intelligent interface component and the Intelligent Database applying the three-tier model as depicted as the basis (Figure 10.3).

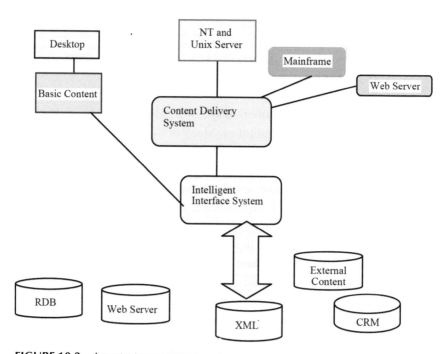

FIGURE 10.3   A content management system.

Tiers and RMI Basics: The remote method invocation based the tiers is depicted in Figure 10.4.

The stub implements an interface with the same business methods as the object itself, but the stubs method does not contain business logic. The data tier consists of one or more databases and may contain data-related logic in the form of stored procedures.

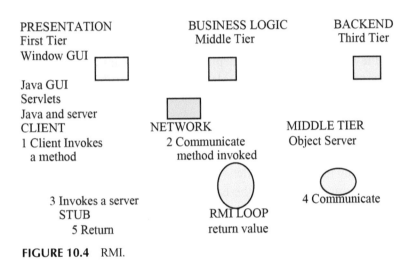

FIGURE 10.4   RMI.

10.6 CONTENT MODELS AND VIEWS—A SPECIFIC DESIGN PROTOTYPE

The model contains the core of the application's functionality. The model encapsulates the state of the application. Sometimes the only functionality it contains is state. It knows nothing about the view or controller. The view provides the presentation of the model. It is the look of the application. We apply predefined user know functions on the view to present the application's look. The view is notified when changes to the model occur. The business logic updates the state of the model and helps control the flow of the application. Action classes as a thin wrapper to the actual business logic accomplish the tasks. The model represents the state of the application. The business objects update the application state. ActionForm bean represents the model state at a session or request level, and not at a persistent level. The JSP file reads information from the ActionForm bean using JSP tags.

Our goal was to develop a minimal prototype that can demonstrate the functionality we are striving towards. Since the XML parser is brought up on the system. Let us start to write tag descriptors for certain generic tags. You can use what tag library or functions there are basic prototype assumption: the layer transparency rule. To each view, there corresponds generic functions that are deployed from the business logic layer to key onto the data layer. Example Tags want to allow the JSP to name the generic functions that the business logic layer deploys, stating certain characteristics and conditions on the functions. Simple example Tag the JSP states I want F1 and F2 and that F1 and F2 are returning values meeting my criteria. We applied Struts MVC model further on. The model contains the core of the application's functionality. The model encapsulates the state of the application. Sometimes the only functionality it contains is state. It knows nothing about the view or controller.

Model: The model contains the core of the application's functionality. The model encapsulates the state of the application. Sometimes the only functionality it contains is state. It knows nothing about the view or controller.

View: The view provides the presentation of the model. It is the look of the application. The view can access the model getters, but it has no knowledge of the setters. In addition, it knows nothing about the controller. The view should be notified when changes to the model occur. Certain functions are provided on the view. Our Morph Programming techniques transmute the functionality to allow the controller to create a model. The model is created with functions that enable the functionality desired from the view, i.e., the presentations layer functions.

Controller: The controller reacts to the user input. It creates and sets the model.

The JSP are not entirely static, since there are tags allowed.

Study tags and customized tags: The design technique flirts with a new programming paradigm that can allow us to deploy tag descriptors to in part code business logic with functions that are transmuted through Struts view onto the content model. Let's call it Morphic programming for the time being. Therefore, the ACID criterion is important, particularly, since Tags communicate with shared objects. MVC helps resolve some of the issues with the single module approach by dividing the problem into three categories:

Struts overview: Client browser

An HTTP request from the client browser creates an event. The Web container will respond with an HTTP response.

Controller: The Controller receives the request from the browser, and makes the decision where to send the request. With Struts, the Controller is a command design pattern implemented as a servlet. The struts-config. xml file configures the Controller.

Business logic: The business logic updates the state of the model and helps control the flow of the application. With Struts this is done with an Action class as a thin wrapper to the actual business logic.

Model state: The model represents the state of the application. The business objects update the application state. ActionForm bean represents the Model state at a session or request level, and not at a persistent level. The JSP file reads information from the ActionForm bean using JSP tags.

View: The view is simply a JSP file. There is no flow logic, no business logic, and no model information—just tags. Tags are one of the things that make Struts unique compared to other frameworks like Velocity (Figure 10.5).

By placing the business logic in a separate package or EJB, we allow flexibility and reuse. Another way of thinking about Action class is as the Adapter design pattern. The purpose of the Action is to "Convert the interface of a class into another interface the clients expect. Adapter lets classes work together that couldn't otherwise because of incompatibility interface" (from Design Patterns—Elements of Reusable OO Software by Gof). The client in this instance is the ActionServlet that knows nothing about our specific business class interface. Therefore, Struts provides a business interface it does understand, Action. By extending the Action, we make our business interface compatible with Struts business interface (An interesting observation is that Action is a class and not an interface. Action started as an interface and changed into a class over time. Nothing's perfect.).

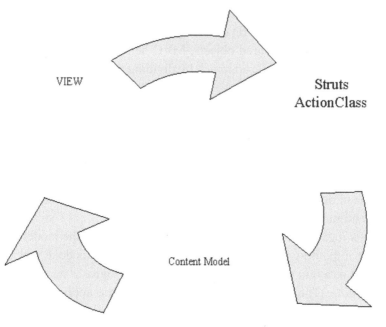

VIEW

Struts
ActionClass

Content Model

FIGURE 10.5   Struts overview.

Our design generates a content model for specific applications with Agent Object Model. The view provides the presentation of the model. It is the look, or the presentation of the model, and the look of the application. We apply predefined user known functions on the view to present the applications look. The view should be notified when changes to the model. The business logic updates the state of the model and helps control the flow of the application. With Struts this is done with an Action class as a thin wrapper to the actual business logic. The model represents the actual business state of the application. The business objects update the application state. The business objects update the ActionForm bean represents the Model state at a session or request level; bean represents the Model state at a session or request level, and not at a persistent level. The JSP file reads information from the ActionForm bean using JSP tags. Our design applies the same functions that are presented on the view for specific application to generate a content model for specific applications.

We can apply Content Model languages such as SGML to carry on the Model languages such as SGML to specifics at the parsing level. The view feels like a flyer with direct throttles onto the content engine. An example prototype was designed with a Humboldt University, Berlin student project some years before.

10.7   BUSINESS INTELLIGENCE AND MOBILE CONTENT

Business Objects XI is the first and only business intelligence (BI) platform that delivers a complete set of BI capabilities: superior reporting, delivers a complete set of BI capabilities: superior reporting, query and analysis, query and analysis, performance management, and data integration, performance management, and data integration. Business Objects XI helps you track performance, understand business drivers, and manage your business performance.

BI content overview is as follows:

Reporting

Reporting allows organizations to access, format, and deliver data as meaningful information to large populations of information consumers both inside and outside the organization.
- Crystal Reports
- Crystal Reports Explorer
- Live Office

Query and Analysis

Query and analysis tools allow end users to interact with business information and answer ad hoc questions themselves, without advanced knowledge of the underlying data sources and structures.
- Web Intelligence
- Desktop Intelligence
- OLAP Intelligence

10.7.1   MULTIDIMENSIONAL CONTENT AND WEB CONTENT

There are important content management intelligent multimedia databases, practical and multimedia databases, practical design areas explored on research projects published on the author's projects from projects from intelligent multimedia content, to databases, and intelligent multimedia content. Interactive visual models allow anyone to quickly turn ordinary Excel spreadsheets into engaging business presentations filled with spreadsheets into engaging business presentations filled with dynamic charts and vibrant graphs. An example is Crystal.

10.7.2   BUSINESS INTELLIGENCE PLATFORMS

The BI platform provides a set of common services to simplify deployment and management of BI tools, reports, and analytics. BI is comprised from data mining, data querying, reporting, and analytics. Business intelligence it is what was commissioned to analytical teams that had the necessary computing resources to manage big data. However, since new platforms have become available now even small businesses are implementing some business intelligence to enhance their successful operations, for example, to improve the decision-making process.

The reports generated from BI are used to make the business operations more effective, or to identify new revenue streams, to identify market trends, or problem areas. Performance management products and services help users align with strategy by tracking and analyzing key business metrics and goals via management dashboards, scorecards, analytics, and alerting. A new Intel-based system through close cooperation with Cyber-Link is illustrating the creative potentials Technology platform, as well as our ready solutions for HD DVD. Retrieval information may also be used to select retrieval and filtering of broadcast "push" material or for personalized advertising. Further descriptions will allow fast and cost effective use of the underlying data, by enabling semiautomatic multimedia presentation and on and editing.

In essence, MPEG I7 is the metadata standard, based on XML Schema, for 7d, based describing features of multimedia content and providing the most features of d providing the comprehensive set of audio-visual description tools available. These visual description tools are based on catalog (title, creator, rights); description tools are based on semantic (the who, what, when and where information about objects and events); and structural (the measurement of the amount of color associated with an image or the timbre of a recorded instrument) features of the audio-visual where they build on the audio ENT. They build on the visual data representation defined by fined by MPEG-1, 2, and 4. A proprietary web technology developed and proprietary web technology developed and provided by Macromedia, Inc. Flash allows creation of animated web content, and can creation of animated web content, and can incorporate text, graphics, animations, video and accessibility, or been unable to address it directly by following the Web Content Accessibility Guidelines following the Web Content.

10.8   CONCLUSIONS

Prespecified views are designed and obtained with intelligent multimedia active databases keyed with functions onto KR with generalized diagrams. As a science IM and Morph Gentzen are developing concepts and vocabulary to help us understand intelligent multimedia. The overview to a multimedia language, a logic—the Morph Gentzen logic and a brief view to its models are presented. The techniques are the basis for encoding intelligent multimedia systems and active databases with morph channels. The knowledge base consists of behavior descriptions, vocabulary definitions, visual objects and relations, decision rules and uncertain facts. Generalized diagrams are shown to be an encoding for a minimal efficient KR technique applied to define relevant world models and KR for data search and discovery. Model checking is simplified to the same degree. A new area where the chapter applies to is heterogeneous computing (Nourani, 1998) and mediation (Wiederhold, 1992). Proof abstraction is yet another area where KR can be keyed to KB and applied to knowledge discovery. Knowledge base data discovery and KB completions can be applied with our techniques developed in Nourani (1999a,g). Multimedia dataware housing and discovery computation techniques with predictive diagrams are briefed. There are management science areas applied on projects with colleagues at the University of Auckland Management Science being reported at conferences (Nourani, 2000). User modeling, mobile interface platforms with content processing are areas that can be cultivated from the basis here.

KEYWORDS

- **Active Databases**
- **Big Data Analytics**
- **Cloud Interfaces**
- **Content Processing**
- **Intelligent Multimedia Database**
- **Mobile Platforms**
- **Multiagent AI Computing**
- **Multitier Designs**
- **Windows Analytics**

REFERENCES

Arion, M., Numan, J. H., Pitariu, H., Jorna, R. 1994. "Placing Trust in Human-Computer Interaction." Proc. of the 7th European Cognitive Ergonomics Conference.

Bailey, J., Georgeff, M., Kemp, D. B., Kinny, D., Ramamohuarao, K. "Active Databases and Agent Systems, A Comparison," Technical Report 95/10. Department of Computer Science, University of Melbourne, Parkville 3052, 1995.

Brajnik, G., Guida, G., Tasso, C. User Modeling in Expert Man-Machine Interfaces: A Case Study in Intelligent Information Retrieval. IEEE Transaction on Systems, Man, and Cybernetics, 1990, 20(1), pp. 166–185.

Cody, W. F., Haas, L. M., Niblack, W., Arya, M., Carey, M. J., Fagin, R., Lee, D., Petkovic, D., Schwarz, P. M., Thomas, J., Roth, M., Williams, J. H., Wimmers, E. L. 1995, "Querying Multimedia Data from Multiple Repositories by Content: The Garlic Project." Proceedings IFIP 2.6 Third Working Conference on Visual Database Systems (VDB-3), Lausanne, Switzerland, Chapman & Hall.

Cyurs F. Nourani, Grace S. L. Intelligent Business Objects and Agent Computing. University of Auckland, April 1998. Parallel and Distributed Computing, Las Vegas, Nevada, June 1999.

Dekker, K., Lesser, V. 1993, "Analyzing the Need for Metalevel Communications," In Proc. of the Twelfth International Workshop on Distributed AI, DAI 93, Hidden Valley, Pennsylvania.

Del Galdo, E. M., Nielsen, J. (Eds.) International User Interfaces. Wiley: New York, NY, 1996.

Genesereth, M., N. J. Nilsson Logical Foundations of Artificial Intelligence, Morgan-Kaufmann, 1987.

Gentzen, G. 1943. Beweisbarkeit und Unbewiesbarket von Anfangsfallen der trasnfininten Induktion in der reinen Zahlentheorie, Math Ann 119, 140–161.

Morph Gentzen, K. R., World Model Diagrams, KR, and World Model Diagrams. April 2, 1998. April 2, 1998. Automated Deductions and Geometry, Zurich, September 2000. Automated Deductions and Geometry, Zurich, September 2000.

Nourani, C. F. "Morph Gentzen Plan Computation with Visual Diagrams Plan Computation with Visual Diagrams ISTA" 2001 the Conference Proceedings published in the GI-Edition. 'Lecture Notes in Informatics,' Austria.

Nourani, C. F. "Versatile Abstract Syntax Meta-Contextual Logic and VR Computing, 36th Lingustische Kolloquium, Austria, Proceedings of the 35th Colloquium of Linguistics.

Nourani, C. F. 1991, "Planning and Plausible Reasoning in AI," Proc. Scandinavian Conference in AI, May 1991, Roskilde, Denmark, 150–157, IOS Press.

Nourani, C. F. 1995a, "Free Pores of Trees and Model-Theoretic Planning, AISB, Sheffield, April 1995.

Nourani, C. F. 1996, "AII and Heterogenous Software Design," May 10, 1995, Eighth European Workshop on Modeling Autonomous Agents in a Multi-Agent World, May 1997, University of Karlskrona/Ronneby, Department of Computer Science and Business Administration, Sweden.

Nourani, C. F. 1997, MIM Logik, December 1997, Summer Logic Colloquium, Prague, July 1998, December 1997, Summer Logic Colloquium, Prague, July 1998. www.math.cas.cz/~lc98/abstracts/Nourani.html.

Nourani, C. F. 1999a, "Agent Computing, KB For Intelligent Forecasting, and Model Discovery for Knowledge Management," June 1998. AAAI Workshop on Agent Based Systems in the Business Context Orlando, Florida, July 18–22, 1999.

Nourani, C. F. 1999b, "AII, Heterogeneous Design, and Retrieval Agents," February 1997. Brief Version at IJCAI-99, IIIS Track, Stokholm, July 1999.

Nourani, C. F. 1999c, "Intelligent Multimedia: New Computing Techniques and Its Applications," February 28, 1997. CSIT'99, Proceedings of 1st International Workshop on Computer Science and Information Technologies, January 18–22, 1999, Moscow, Russia. Ch. Freytag and V. Wolfengagen (Eds.): MEPhI Publishing 1999, ISBN 5-7262-0263-5.

Nourani, C. F. 1999d, Competitive Models and Game Tree Planning, November 1999. Applications to Economic games. A version published at SSGRR, L'Auquila Rome, Italy, September 2001. Invited paper.

Nourani, C. F. 1999e, Intelligent Multimedia: Computing Techniques and Design Paradigms, Preliminary Textbook completed August 1999 published at Treeless Press, Berkeley, California. New edition from Lulu Press, http://www.lulu.com/CrisFN.

Nourani, C. F. 1999f, Virtual Tree Computing-Abstract Posted at the ECCAD, Carolinas, May 1999.

Nourani, C. F. 1999g, "KR and Model Discovery with Predictive Logic," brief abstract publish at the Australian AI Conference, AKA Workshop, Sydney, December.

Nourani, C. F. 2000, "Intelligent Heterogeneous Multimedia and Intelligent Active Visual DB and KB," ICCIT 2000, April 2000, Las Vegas, Nevada.

Nourani, C. F. 2002, Game Trees, Competitive Models, and ERP. New Business Models and Enabling Technologies, Management School, St Petersburg, Russia. http://www.math.spbu.ru/user/krivulin/Work2002/Workshop.htm

Nourani, C. F. 2003, "Versatile Abstract Syntax, MetaContextual 1 Logic and VR Computing," the third international conference on Information in Tokyo, November 29–December 2, 2004. http://www.information-iii.org/conf/info2004.html iii.org/conf/info2004.html

Nourani, C. F. 2004, "Versatile Abstract Syntax, "MetaContextual Logic and VR Computing," The third international conference on Information in Tokyo, November 29–December 2, 2004. http://www.information-iii.org/conf/info2004.html iii.org/conf/info2004.html

Nourani, C. F. 2005, Intelligent Multimedia Computing Science-Business Interfaces, Databases, Data Mines, and Wi-Fi American Scientific Publishers, 2005. http://www.aspbs.com/multimedia.html

Nourani, C. F. 2006, "Intelligent Interface Design Project," Humboldt Universitat, Berlin.

Nourani, C. F. 2013, W-Interfaces, Business Intelligence, and Content Processing, Invented Industry Track Keynote, IAT–Intelligent Agent Technology, Atlanta, November 2013.

Nourani, C. F., "A Multiagent Intelligent Multimedia Visualization Language and Computing Paradigm. February 2000. Visualization 2000, Workshop on WWW Interfaces, Seattle, September 2000.

Nourani, C. F., "Predictive Model Discovery, and Schema Completion, "International Cybernetics and Systems Conference, Florida 2003.

Nourani, C. F., "The TAIM Intelligent Visual Database, "12th International Workshop on Database and Expert Systems Applications, Workshop Records, (DEXA 2001) 3–7 September 2001 in Munich, Germany. IEEE Computer Society Press.

Nourani, C. F., 1999, "Business Modeling and Forecasting AIEC-AAAI99, Orlanda, July 1999, AAAI Press.

Nourani, C. F., Grace S. L. Loo, K. R., Model discovery from active DB with Predictive logic, the University of Auckland, Data Mining 2000 Applications to Business and Finance. Cambridge, UK, August 2000.

Prawitz, D. 1965, "Natural Deduction: A Proof Theoretic Study. Stokhom, Almqvist and Wiksell.

Sebastian Thrun, Faloutsos, C., Mitchell, T., Wasserman, L. Automated Learning and Discovery: State-of-the-Art and Research Topics in a rapidly Growing Field September 1998 CMU-CALD-98–100. Center for Automated Learning and Discovery Carnegie Mellon University, Pittsburgh, PA 15213.

Trenner, L., Bawa, J. (Eds.) The Politics of Usability: A Practical Guide to Designing Usable Systems in Industry. Springer-Verlag: London, UK, 1998.

Widerhold, G. "Mediation in the Architecture of Future Information Systems," IEEE Computer Magazine, 1992, 25(5), 33–49.

CHAPTER 11

A HAPTIC COMPUTING BASIS FOR FACIAL OR VISUAL EMOTION EXPRESSION RECOGNITION

CYRUS F. NOURANI

Research Professor, Simon Fraser University, British Columbia, Canada

CONTENTS

ABSTRACT

The chapter presents novel modeling techniques for facial and visual expression computation and recognition. A haptic control virtual computing logic is applied with Nourani's (1997) Morph Gentzen system to characterize facial and visual expressions. Agent trees computing logic carries visual structures via functions. Designated functions define computing haptic motion and ontology epistemics. Based on the functions on the haptic computing logic we can state expression-spanning schemas, hereon called Eigen Schemas that on tuple characterize morph compose to characterize facial expressions. The Eigen schemas allow us to express or detect human emotions expressed on facials. The haptic logic encompasses a predictive Bayesian confidence on the characterizations. Genetic algorithms and neurocognitive bases for the above are presented in brief. The techniques are not competing cognitive psychology trends, rather new processing capabilities that facilitate for the preceding experimental cognitive psychologist or neurocognitive scientists to examine their methods with precise direct processor for facial expression recognition.

11.1   INTRODUCTION

The author presents novel techniques with a neuro-cognitive inspired modeling basis to facial and pictorial visual emotion recognition based on haptic Morph Gentzen natural like deductive system the author has developed over a decade. An overview to a virtual tree computing haptic logic with applications to the new Expression Schema cognitive computing techniques are presented. The reasoning system that is capable to lift from context is combined with the haptic Morph Gentzen logic, to a pictorial deductive algebra, comparable to natural deduction systems that the author had presented in 1997, to address facial computation and recognition areas. Agent trees on the languages can carry visual structures via functions. Designated functions define agents, as specific function symbols, to represent languages with only abstract definition known at syntax. Computing haptic motion and ontology epistemic are modeled. Starting with basic AI agent computing multimedia AI systems is presented necessitating esthetics with world models. Multimedia context computing and context abstraction are introduced leading into visual object perception dynamics. Linguistics, cognition, and vision was motivated by the urge to bridge the gap from logic, metaphysics, philosophy and linguistics to computational theories of AI and practical AI systems. Practical artificial intelligence, AI, is concerned with concepts and practice of building intelligent systems. Intelligent multimedia techniques and paradigms are being defined whereby AI is applied to all facets of the enterprise starting from the basic multimedia programming stated in Nourani (2000). The techniques are developed here for facial expression computing models and facial recognition. To put the thought on a chronological track, apart form the artistic 17th century, onto to the 19th century, facial expression analysis has a direct relationship to the modern day science of automatic facial expression recognition by Charles Darwin. Darwin grouped various kinds of expressions into similar categories, for example: low spirits, anxiety, grief, despair joy, high spirits, love, tender feelings, devotion, surprise, astonishment, fear, hatred, anger, self-attention, shame, shyness, modesty. This chapter addresses more contemporary areas on facial expressions based on the Eckman (1971) and Russell's (1994) critique that questions the claims of universal recognition of emotions.

The section outlines are as follows: Section 11.1 is all about introduction and outline of this chapter. Section 11.2 is a brief on haptic agent computing and affective models, merging to a "new" Kant illusion logic (author since 1995's) with applications to the neurocognitive psychology are on dreams, AI, and intelligent multimedia to set the stage for haptic motion logic. Section 11.2 further presents a haptic immersion based on Morph Gentzen computing logic. The mathematical basis is presented in brief with a haptic control logic with examples. The neurocognitive nature is examined based on a decade ago briefs since that area has since become a very important research direction. Section 11.3 begins to state haptic motion and expression Eigen schemas. That is where IM_BID agent model (Nourani 2005), DESIRE Haptic epistemic, is applied towards android logic learning. The visual field is represented by visual objects connected with agents that carry information among objects about the field. That information is mapped onto the intelligent trees for computation. Intelligent trees compute the spatial field information with the diagram functions. The trees defined have function names corresponding to computing agents. The computing agent functions have a specified module defining their functionality. Facial expression morph tupling on expression Eigen schema are presented. Section 11.3 concludes onto a versatile syntax and Meta-contextual Logic for VR-virtual reality computing supporting the expression computations on processors. The basis for facial recognition is different from the contemporary research on the references in that we do not have an experimental simulative approach, rather an essentially mathematical basis with a haptic algebraic logic to characterize or recognize facial expressions and emotions. This not the same as what is known Schmidt's Schema theory or any polyschematics architecture. The author has newer application published with coauthors where it is delineated how usual cognitive architectures are designed, e.g. spanning an attention space. This author's presentation here is not about cognitive architectures, rather specific cognitive systematics for facial recognition and motion epistemics, on a bio-anthropomorphic basis. Rather, basic mathematical artificial intelligence Schemas augmented with a haptic morph Gentzen natural deduction system. For example, in Haptic visual ontology, the author published at Nourani (2006).

11.2   HAPTIC IMMERSION

In the author's Haptic logic beginnings publications, this author examines how intelligent decisions might be based on emotions, alluding to Picard's questions. Other related issues that influence creativity, planning, perception, mood-congruent memory retrieval, with precise computing and cognitive models. Essentially a neuro-cognitive grid system with agents and objects is presented to examine the issues. The author presented an asymmetric view of the application of this computing paradigm and the basic techniques were proposed for various AI systems (Nourani, 1991; Nourani, 1995). Picard's assertions indicate that not all modules of an AI system might pay attention to emotions, or have to have emotional components. Some modules are useful rigid tools, and it is fine to keep them that way. However, there are situations where the human-machine interaction could be improved by having machines naturally adapt to their users. Affective computing expands human-computer interaction by including emotional communication together with appropriate means of handling affective information. Since neurological studies indicate that the role of emotion in human cognition is essential; emotions are not a luxury. Instead, emotions play a critical role in rational decision making, in perception, in human interaction, and in human intelligence. Therefore, agent attention span (Nourani et al., 2013) has to take into considerations the above factors. These facts, combined with abilities computers are acquiring in expressing and recognizing affect, are also important in crystallizing attention spans. Attention relations to changes in facial expression, e.g., (Eimer-Holmes, 2003), has been studied in neuropsychology focusing on change detection of emotion expression by electroencephalography. The peripheral faces remains or randomly changed to joy, anger or disgust. Affective computing can deliberately have an influence on people' emotions. New models are suggested for computer recognition of human emotion, and both theoretical and practical applications are described for learning, human-computer interaction, perceptual information retrieval, creative arts and entertainment, human health, and machine intelligence. Picard suggests that affective intelligence, the communication and management of affective information in human/computer interaction, is a key link that is missing in tele-presence environments and other technologies that mediate human-human communication.

The IM Morphed Computing Logic for computing for multimedia is the new projects with important applications since Nourani (1997, 2009b). Liquid morphic specific realization can be designed for arbitrary immersion with haptic agents applying Morph Gentzen IM. Arbitrary immersion is when virtual tree images are immersed in arbitrary visual and spatial arenas. Morph Gentzen allows for example a morph sequent recording as if virtual images were rippling onto a liquid mirror (Fleischman and Strauss, 1996). The morphing has fluidity with mathematical precision determined with computing agents on specific visual pictures. The basic principles are a mathematical logic where a Gentzen or natural deduction a system is defined by taking arbitrary structures coded by diagram functions. The techniques can be applied to arbitrary topological structures. Thus, we define a syntactic morphing to be a technique by which infinitary definable structures are anthropomorphically mapped via their defining functions to new structures. The deduction rules are a Gentzen system augmented by two rules Morphing, and Trans-morphing. The Morph Rule—A structure defined by the functional n-tuple $<f1, ..., fn>$ can be morphed to a structures definable by the functional n-tuple $<h(f1), ..., h(fn)>$, provided h is a homomorphism of abstract signature structures (Nourani, 1996). The TransMorph Rules—A set of rules whereby combining structures A1, ..., An defines an Event {A1, A2, ..., An} with a consequent structure B. Thus, the combination is an impetus event. The deductive theory is a Gentzen system in which structures named by parameterized functions;

augmented by the morph and transmorph rules. The structures we apply the Morph logic to are definable by positive diagrams. The idea is to do it at abstract models syntax trees without specifics for the shapes and topologies applied (Nourani, 2009b).

According to Kant human knowledge is limited to appearances, whereas things in themselves are "noumena" are thinkable but not actually knowable. Kant termed the doctrine Transcendental Idealism. Given the idealism is the possibility of synthesizing a priori knowledge to possible description and experience is easily explainable, since each object must necessarily conform to the conditions under which they can become objects for us. It assumes the human mind possesses such condition and demonstrating it is Transcendental Aesthetics. The computing import is since explored by the author's projects. To carry on with intelligent multimedia we have to be conscious as to what are the basic knowledge representation techniques necessary to describe knowledge and its significance for perception. Generic model diagrams (Nourani, 1991, 1998) and applications define computable models and relevant world reasoning. Generic diagram are defined from a minimal set of function symbols that can inductively define a model. Basic application areas to start with as examples are designing predefined visual scenes with diagram composition and combination for scene dynamics.

11.2.1 AGENT COGNITION PROCESSES

Let us start with the popular agent-computing model the Beliefs, Desire, and Intentions, henceforth abbreviated as the BID model (Brazier-Truer et al., 1995). BID is a generic agent-computing model specified within the declarative compositional modeling framework for multiagent systems, DESIRE. The model, a refinement of a generic agent model, explicitly specifies motivational attitudes and the static and dynamic relations between motivational attitudes. Desires, goals, intentions, commitments, plans, and their relations are modeled. Different notions of strong and weak agency are presented at (Wooldridge and Jennings, 1995). To apply agent computing with intelligent multimedia some specific roles and models have to be presented for agents. The BID model has emerged for a "rational agent": a rational agent described using cognitive notions such as beliefs, desires and intentions. Beliefs, intentions, and commitments play a crucial role in determining how rational agents will act. Beliefs, capabilities, choices, and commitments are the parameters making component agents specific. A generic BID agent model in the multiagent framework DESIRE is presented towards a specific agent model. The main emphasis is on static and dynamic relations between mental attitudes, which are of importance for cooperative agents. DESIRE is the framework for design, and the specification of interacting reasoning components is a framework for modeling, specifying and implementing multiagent systems (Brazier, Dunin-Keplicz, Jennings, and Treur, 1995, 1996; Dunin-Keplicz and Treur, 1995). Within the framework, complex processes are designed as compositional architectures consisting of interacting task- based hierarchically structured components. The interaction between components, and between components and the external world is explicitly specified. Components can be primitive reasoning components using a knowledge base, but may also be subsystems that are capable of performing tasks using methods as diverse as decision theory, neural networks, and genetic algorithms. As the framework inherently supports interaction between components, multiagent systems are naturally specified in DESIRE by modeling agents as components. The specification is sufficient to generate an implementation. Specific techniques for such claims might be further supported at (Nourani 1993a, 1999a). A generic classification of mental attitudes is presented and a more precise characterization of a few selected motivational attitudes is given. The specification framework DESIRE for multiagent systems is characterized. A general agent model is described. The framework of modeling motivational attitudes in DESIRE is discussed.

Agents are assumed to have the four properties required for the weak notion of agency described in Wooldridge and Jennings (1995). Thus, agents must maintain interaction with their environment, for example observing and performing actions in the world: reactivity; be able to take the initiative: proactiveness; be able to perform social actions like communication, social ability; operate without the direct intervention of other (possibly human) agents: autonomy. Four main categories of mental attitudes are studied in the AI literature: informational, motivational, social and emotional attitudes. Examining the distinction between human

Cognition and machine-generated or also lower-level (human) cognition at Nourani et al. (2013), considering cognition, as being the "higher level capacity of discursive thought" in the sense of Kant "I think so I am," these processes include thinking, knowing, remembering, deciding, and problem-solving. Cognition or cognitive processes, therefore, in general, can be natural or artificial, conscious or unconscious. Human Cognition is affected by mental, attitudes, as well as social and environmental conditions involving the person. Cognition design is essential to solving design problems in cognitive agent systems.

It is obvious that human Cognition is significantly different from any virtual or cyber-physical agent system that has to act in a prescribed environment as they are having inherent "machine" cognition capabilities. Cognitive intelligence uses a human mental introspective experience for the modeling of intelligent system thinking. Cognitive intelligence may use brain models to extract brain's intelligence properties (or functions). On the other side modeling or designing the computational cognitive intelligence is still a very hard task to be solved, even if the progress in this area has been amazing. Cognitive intelligence in cyber-physical worlds takes a totally new dimension in terms of complexity and dynamicity of the emergent and interaction complex multiagent systems that include humans as well as objects, devices and complex applications or environments.

11.2.2   EXPRESSIONS, AND CONSCIOUSNESS STAGES

In order to present our techniques for visual expression recognition and facials it might be important to consider the process in reverse cognition the causes the expressions. That is further explored on the neurocognitive models in the author's publications past decade and the newer schools, e.g. Swiss neuro- haptic research.

A Multiagent Cognitive theory had been put forth by Nourani (1997) defines a Cognitive syntax and might provide a paradigm for Language Visualization. Intelligent syntax carries most cognitive computing aspects. The Double Vision Computing artificial intelligence paradigm (Nourani 1995) is a problem-solving paradigm with pairs and agents defined on the pair. The agents from the object and coobjects cooperate for problem

solving on boards. The paradigm has further visual linguistics components. The world is viewed by dual pairs of possible worlds, with agents
cooperating on boards. Intelligent tree computing and linguistic theories
from our recent research are applied to put forth a basis for formalizing
the computing paradigm.

The multiagent cognition project had started in 1993 with the Double Vision Computing, IAS 1995, Karlsruhe its initial publication. Since
there has been the 1994–95 Abstract Linguistic and Meta-Contextual Reasoning, Intelligent Multimedia, MIM logic, and its consequent paper on
Consciousness Science, abstract enclosed. The context abstraction and
met-contextual reasoning abstract is also enclosed. In the papers diagrams for Cognitive modeling is applied and scientific techniques applied
towards a Conscience Science.

11.2.3   NEUROCOGNITIVE MODELS

The spotlight of attention shines on the stage where Conscience Experience is on stage and there are Fringes. There is a memory system, ways to
interpret conscience context, autonomolism, and it all rides on a motivational system. There are theater diagrams for, for example, context behind
a scene. The fundamental mind and Kant's Dialectics can be examined
towards an agent computational perception, e.g., (Nourani, 2003, 2009).
The spandrels of sleep: How can we be sure that we are not always dream-
ing. For Kant conscience operates in the dichotomy between thinking
objects and the thought object. There are two components of knowledge:
spontaneity and receptivity. In cognition Kant's spontaneity is not in the
void. If acts of thought have objective bearing it is because they are filled
with intuition of something that is given to the person, towards which the
person is receptive. Whenever we know something through intuition something is given us. Kant calls it "sensibility." Intuition is never anything but
sensuous (Kant, 1990, 1993). Cognitive modeling issues can be applied.
The Consciousness science formalized by the author's project since 1993
have applied positivist thoughts. However, we have a logical route to
Kant's sensibility with mathematical precision upto infinitary models and
logics, diagrammatic techniques, a multiagent cognitive theory, dynamic

epistemics, and the IM MIM logic towards such science (Nourani, 1987, 1998) papers.

A computing conscience science can only be defined by combining AI, IM, Diagrammatic and analogical reasoning, and computational epistemics. The knowledge base consists of behavior descriptions, vocabulary definitions, objects and relations, decision rules and uncertain facts. A basic route to neurocognitive computing modeling biological systems consists of modeling certain aspects of a biological system, modeling general principles of intelligence, and using these principles in the design of functioning robots or androids. A multi agent cognitive theory was presented by the author at Nourani (1996). The premise is that cognition is at particle neurons resembling micro-computer processors. Though that specific detail is not applied here, the genetic computing role is a motivation for biologically inspired modeling. Thus a neuron is itself capable of a form of computation. Specialized neurons might compute certain functions in the most efficient manner. Our minds carry a very complex multiagent computing cognitive system not easily explained on a high-level "cognitive architecture." Therefore, we attempt no such characterizations for cognition in general. Genetic secretion algorithms are based on hypotheses that indicate the present theories might be genetic secretions computations. Recent biological scientific discoveries are presented to further support the cognitive intelligence theory proposed. More recent publications are on neurocognitive models (Borscht and Snader, 2003) or psychology are (Sun, 2002) on cognition and multiagent systems. These authors, for example, indicate that processes contribute to successful recognition memory, some of which can be associated with spatiotemporally distinct event-relate. Neurophysiological-based models of recognition memory retrieval allow examination of the time course of the processes that contribute to illusory memories. Neurocognitive models are further explored at Max Planck Institute, Liepzig (Mecklinger) and at Tubingen University (Germany). The former study is a neurocognitive model of recognition memory based on event related memory retrieval. The event-based computations are areas where the techniques in the present chapter are applicable. The latter is exploring techniques that might have applications with the present modeling cognitive designs on a vector machine, e.g., ambient cognitive tracks (Nourani et al., 2013).

11.2.4   MACRODOT MORPHING

Macrodot morphing is a specific technique to detail agent Morph Gentzen computation on interest point-focal bases (Nourani, 2004). Intelligent Multimedia is applied with multimedia interfaces to areas ranging from virtual reality tangible media and multimedia learning with interactive media, to television programming, telecommunications media, business and financial computing to multimedia commerce. Multimedia AI systems are designed according to the new computing techniques defined. The concept of a Hybrid Picture is the start to define intelligent multimedia objects. Visual dynamics based on general principles can be projected and the effects of scenes projected on viewers can be predicated. On the virtual reality logic (Nourani, 1993) agents at each world compliment one another to portray a computing visual stage by cooperating. The IM agent computing techniques can be applied to define interactions among personality and view descriptions. The basis to a Haptic computing logic that was developed preceding this exposition and briefed on the following section are applied with microdot morphing for applications to facial expression modeling. Facial expressions are defined by morph tupling on basic facial expression schemas. Macrodots (c.f. Figure 11.1), on pictures correspond to agents that can vary and characterize the facial structures based on the morph Gentzen h: whereby a functional n-tuple $<f1, \ldots, fn>$ can be morphed to a structure definable by the functional n-tuple $<h(f1), \ldots, h(fn)>$. The techniques were applied to plan computation for applications to spatial computing in (Nourani, CFRM, 2001).

11.2.5   A HAPTIC CONTROL LOGIC

Affective computing expands human-computer interaction by including emotional communications together with appropriate means for handling affective information. New models can be presented for computing recognition of human emotions- both practical and theoretical applications can be and are described for learning, human computer interactions, and perceptual information retrieval, creative arts and entertainment, and machine intelligence. Scientists have discovered many surprising roles

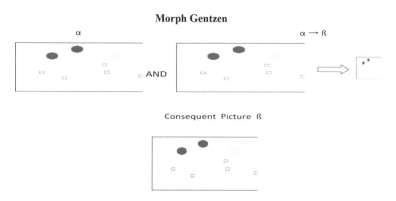

FIGURE 11.1   Morph Gentzen Glimpse (Nourani, 1977).

played by human emotion- especially in cognitive processes, such as perception, decision making, memory and more. Human intelligence includes emotional intelligence, especially the ability to accurately recognize and express affective emotions. The techniques briefed here are the bases to a haptic logic with multiagent cognition, where central affective computing questions might be addressed. Emotions might signal cognitive changes. These are the premises for briefing on a haptic logic in this and the following section towards applications to facial recognition systems.

Agent computing is introduced to interactive intelligent multimedia. An overview to a practical agent-computing model based on beliefs, intentions, and desire is presented and possible augmentation to intelligent multimedia is explored. (Nilsson-Genesereth, 1987) introduces agent architectures. A specific agent might have internal state set I, which the agent can distinguish its membership. The agent can transit from each internal state to another in a single step. With our multiboard model agent actions are based on I and board observations. There is an external state set S, modulated to a set T of distinguishable subsets from the observation viewpoint. A sensory function: S → T maps each state to the partition it belongs. Let A be a set of actions that can be performed by agents. A function action can be defined to characterize an agent activity action: T→A. There is also a memory update function mem: I x T → I.

Worlds, epistemics, and cognition for androids are introduced with precise statements in the author's preceding publications on computational epistemology onto a haptic logic. The foundations are applied to present a brief on Computational Illusion, affective computing, and Virtual Reality. KR for AI Worlds, and Computable Worlds are presented with diagrams. Are intelligent decisions based on emotions? If there is a Gestalt model decided on, the answer might be affirmative. Furthermore, emotions might be independent of consciousness modes (Nourani, 1998, 1999). Deduction models and perceptual computing is presented with a new perspective. Intelligent multimedia interfaces are an important component to the practical computational aspects. Visual context and objects are presented with multiagent intelligent multimedia. Context abstraction allows us to reason above context, denoted met-contextual reasoning, and published as a new direction in logic and computational linguistics fields. Multiagent visual multiboard planning is introduced as a basis to cognitive planning intelligent multimedia with applications to spatial computing.

Desire, and Intentions, henceforth abbreviated as the BID model (Brazier-Truer et al., 1997). BID is a generic agent-computing model specified within the declarative compositional modeling framework for multiagent systems, DESIRE. The model, a refinement of a generic agent model, explicitly specifies motivational attitudes and the static and dynamic relations between motivational attitudes. Desires, goals, intentions, commitments, plans, and their relations are modeled. The BID model has emerged for a "rational agent": a rational agent described using cognitive notions such as beliefs, desires and intentions. Beliefs, intentions, and commitments play a crucial role in determining how rational agents will act. Beliefs, capabilities, choices, and commitments are the parameters making component agents specific. A generic BID agent model in the multiagent framework DESIRE is presented towards a specific agent model. The main emphasis is on static and dynamic relations between mental attitudes, which are of importance for cooperative agents. DESIRE is the framework for design, and the specification of interacting reasoning components is a framework for modeling, specifying and implementing multiagent systems (Brazier et al., 1995, 1996; Dunin-Keplicz and Treur, 1995). Within the framework, complex processes are designed as compositional architectures consisting of interacting task-based hierarchically structured components.

A specifying BID agents, specifics a mathematical basis to such models with agent signatures might be obtained from Nourani (1996a), whereas the author had introduced that since 1994. The generic model and specifications of agent computing described above, can be refined to a generic model of a rational BID agent capable of explicit reasoning about its beliefs, desires, goals and commitments. closure can be inferred, by a minimal set of terms defining the model. Thus providing a minimal characterization of Android Haptic Epistemics. Since planning with IM_BID is at times with the pictorial window agent computing groups, communicating, as two androids might, with facial gestures, for example (Picard, 1998). In virtual or the "real-world" AI epistemic, we have to note what the positivists had told us some years ago: the apparent necessary facts might be only tautologies and might not amount to anything to the point at the specifics. Philosophers have been faced with challenges on the nature of absolute and the Kantian epistemic (Kant, 1990; Nourani, 1999a) for years. It might all come to terms with empirical facts and possible worlds when it comes to real applications. Most reasoning about beliefs, desires, and intentions can be modeled as an essential part of the reasoning an agent needs to perform to control its own processes. The preliminaries to VR computing logic are presented since Summer Logic Colloquium 1997, Prague. These techniques are applicable with description logics (Badder et al., 2003), Nourani (2003, 2009) cognitive modeling in view of the preceding paragraphs, to have basic modeling preprocessor inputs to a Morph Gentzen deductive system for facial recognition. Following the preceding publications on a computational epistemology on perception and cognition (Nourani, 1994), the author begins to apply description logic to cognition paradigms encoding FACS. AU's described with agent description logics to present inputs to the Morph Gentzen processor depicted as in Figure 11.2.

11.3 LEARNING AND EXPRESSION COMPUTATIONS

11.3.1 EMOTIONS AND EXPRESSIONS

Emotions are visually expressed through changes in facial expressions. Whether or not facial expressions are the same in all cultures we can define

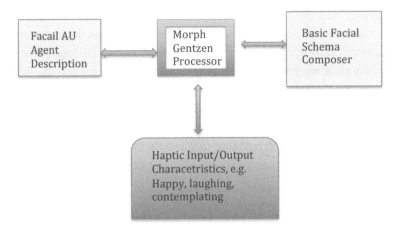

FIGURE 11.2   The Facial Deductive System.

this author's stance is that we can define invariants that can be applied as morph tuples on Eigen expression schemas. Based on his theory of evolution, Darwin suggested that the expressions are universal. However, there was no general consensus. In 1971, Ekman and Friesen conducted studies on subjects from western and eastern cultures and reported that the facial expressions of emotions are "constant" across cultures (Ekman, 1971). However, in 1994, Russell wrote a critique questioning the claims of universal recognition of emotion from facial expressions. This author does not see a need to adhere to such general universality, but maintains that there are universal invariants defined based on Eigen tupling morph schemas. That Russell was refuted by Ekman and Izard, or however, is not all on common accepted strong "scientific" bases, and might not be consequential. One reason for not engaging in such disagreements on our part is that there is not a universal cognitive basis that can be interpreted across all cultures. All we need is invariants on what the six emotional states are.

Newer expression recognition systems, e.g., Tian et al.'s (2000) AFA systems have developed methods that attempt to recognize the basic expressions and some attempts at recognizing nonbasic expressions. There have been very few attempts at recognizing the temporal dynamics of the face. The agent computing Morph Gentzen models here sequent with, for example, Sandewall Features are capable to further address that area's specifics. Pantic and Patras have reported successful recognition of facials and their temporal segments. Psychologists have proved that posed expressions are different from spontaneous expressions, in terms of their appearance, timing and temporal characteristics. Facial features can be classified as being basic or transient. Permanent features are the features like eyes, lips, brows and cheeks that remain permanently. Transient features include facial lines, brow wrinkles and deepened furrows that appear with changes in expression and disappear on a neutral face. Understanding the emulating human emotion might help in out efforts to understand intelligence.

11.3.2 *EXPRESSION AND HAPTIC COMPUTING*

Considering the six emotional states that are primary according to the preceding sections, namely happiness, sadness, anger, surprise, disgust and fear, based on the agent haptic computing logic we can state expression spanning schemas: let us call that expression Eigen schemas.

Let us state the above with schemas as above to span with six Eigen schemas. The Eigen schemas allow us to detect human emotions expressed on facials. There are new computing techniques, languages, and a new deductive system with models. A new computing area is defined by artificial intelligence principles for multimedia. It is not a reinvention of AI, however, an exponential degree of computational complexity on a deductive system is reduced on a new pictorial system that is carried onto a haptic computing logic. Such computability is possible with the MIM and Morph Gentzen logic the first author had introduced around 1997.

Example Morph Schema:
Schema {Face Has 2 Eyes Has 1 Nose Has 1 Mouth Has 2 cheeks}
Motion agent
Morph Rule {
That is turn agent signals a morph 90 degrees to the feature agents.}

Comparing to Eckman et al.'s FACS system experiments the premise is that Ekman and Friesen d to code facial expressions. FACS coders decompose facial expressions in terms of the apparent intensity of 46 component movements, which are to correspond to individual facial muscles. What such authors consider elementary movements are called action units (AU) to be regarded as the "phonemes" of facial expressions. Examples are:

Inner brow raiser, Outer brow raiser, Upper eye-lid raiser Nose wrinkle, Upper lip raiser Lip corner puller, Dimpler Lip corner depressor, Chin raiser, Lip stretcher, Blink. However, there is no mathematical system that characterizes such AU's and expressions. In the present exposition, e.g., Section 10.4.1 on this author presents a mathematical basis for facial and visual expression epistemics that can characterize systems similar to FACS with more flexibility yet mathematical precision. This is because morph Gentzen epistemics is a direct mathematical codding for visual haptic encoding logics with cognitive agents.

11.3.3 FACS MORPH TUPLING

Basic Facial Morph Schema is composed with Eigen schema tuplings to present an expression. Since we have Macrodot agent models, the facial variations can be haptic logic computed and be assigned temporal sequencing (Figure 11.3).

Schema {Face Has 2 Eyes Has 1 Nose Has 1 Mouth Has 2 Cheeks)

Motion agent

Morph Rule {That is turn agent signals a morph 90 degree to the feature agents.}

Features {shape, eye agent: a}

Features {shape, size, nose agent: n}

Features {size, mouth agent: m}

Features {shape, cheek agent: ck}

Features {turns function agent, degree) Turn Agent (a, n, m, ck, degree)

Now we define the Facial Eigen Schemas composing the base facial schema, abbreviated BFS with transform function tuples, to a tuple morphing Eigen schemas on the six Facial expression states.

Happy State: mouth agent: open: Cheek (turns function agent: 10–20 degrees)

FIGURE 11.3   Free to display basic Facial Morph, Germany.

Eye agent (turns dimmer 10 degrees)

Eigen Happiness function is: <mouth feature, eye feature> composed with Happy State Features

Sad State mouth agent closed: cheek (turns function agent −5 degrees) Eye agent (turns −2 to −5 degrees).

Eigen Sad <mouth agent closed, eye agent dimmed low>

Eigen Anger: <mount agent pressed tight, eye agent clamped close>

Eigen Surprise <mouth agent opening, eye agent dilating>

Let us leave the latter two not so specific now and open to imagination.

Eigen Disgust

Eigen Fear

The techniques here with agent computing allow a free to culture characterization cognition, c.f. (Franova, 2005), or facial expressions that are robust enough to tune to the variations, from Darwin to now. We do not have the time and space in this publication to detail all the "action units" since we can vary that to whatever action units on facials, including a mime face expressions, MIM-Logic 1997.

11.3.4 LEARNING AND ONTOLOGY TRANSFER

Our transfer-learning model applies the BID model to specify learning arenas M1 and M2. Each arenas BID is presented with intelligent signatures Σ1 and Σ2. Predictive game models are presented with agent signature game trees where the above formalism can is applied to realize competitive learning models. The predictive modeling techniques are applicable with Bayesian confidence measures (Nourani, 2003; Schulte, 2011). The following process is applied to transfer game tree and completive model learning across domains since modeling and realizability are based on morphism preserved formulas. The term ATL here refers to the process of abstract transfer learning from an abstract characterization of a world, or learning domain to a second arena or world (e.g., Nourani et al., 2013). Thus, ATL express the relationship between two forms of representations. The notion of abstract transfer learning is either algebraic or model-theoretic (algebraic logic definitions) (Nourani, 2005; Nourani et al., 2013). Predictive learning is explored in the author's publications past several years. Minimal prediction is an artificial intelligence technique defined since the author's model-theoretic planning project (1991). It is a cumulative approximation attained with completing model diagrams on what might be true in a model or knowledge base, based on a Bayesian confidence measure for example. A predictive diagram for a theory T is a diagram D (M), where M is a model for T, and for any formula q in M, either the function f: $q \rightarrow \{0,1\}$ is defined, or there exists a formula p in D(M), such that T U {p} proves q; or that T proves q by minimal prediction. The predictive model diagram could be minimally represented by a set of functions {f1, …, fn}. The predictive diagrams are applied to model discovery. Prediction is applied to plan goal satisfiability and can be combined with plausibility (Nourani, 1991), probabilities, or fuzzy logic to obtain, for example Bayesian confidence intervals.

11.3.5   *VIRTUAL REALITY LOGIC AND FACIAL EXPRESSIONS*

A logical paradigm that can be applied to facial sequencing details might be further explored from the author's newer publications on VR (Nourani, 2002), and meta-contextual logic (Nourani, 1998, 2012). The preliminaries to VR computing logic are presented since Summer Logic Colloquium 1997, Prague. The basic mathematics emerging was that Morph Gentzen is a sound and complete logic to characterize visual reasoning with objects and agents, e.g., on a Macrodot morph computation, hence is a sound basis for logic on virtual reality computations, abbreviated VR.

Linguistics knowledge representation and its relation to context abstraction are defined in Nourani (1999a), where the author has put forth new visual computing techniques for intelligent multimedia context abstraction with linguistics components. Model-based computing (Nourani, 1998) can be applied to automated data and knowledge engineering with keyed diagrams. Specific computations can be carried out with predictive diagrams (Nourani, 1995a). For cognition, planning, and learning the robot's mind, a diagram grid can define state. The designs in the author's papers are ways for a robot to update its mind state based on what it encountered on its path. That which the robot believes can be defined on a diagram grid. The array grid entries are pointing to things to remember and the degree the cognitive agent believes them.

The grid model is a way to encode the world with the model diagram functions. Designated functions define agents, as in artificial intelligence agents, or represent languages with only abstract definition known at syntax. For example, a function Fi can be agent corresponding to a language Li. Li can in turn involve agent functions among its vocabulary. Thus context might be defined at Li. An agent Fi might be as abstract as functionals defining functions and context with respect to a set and a linguistics model. Generic diagrams for models are defined as yet a second order lift from context. The techniques to be presented have allowed us to define a computational linguistics and model theory for intelligent languages. Models for the languages are defined by the author's techniques. Meta-contextual logic is combined with Morph Gentzen, a new computing logic the author presented in 1997, towards a Virtual Reality design languages and their computing logic.

Features and Fluents, e.g. (Sandewall 1995) complements this author's newer visual logic with more basic techniques for reasoning about actions a change in the physical world being one of the classical research topics in artificial intelligence. It is motivated by the needs of autonomous robots that must be able to anticipate their immediate future, to plan their future actions. Newer cognitive applications are presented in Nourani et al. (2013) on current cognitive agent systems and points to the design of intelligent system interfaces using higher-level cognitive capabilities.

11.4 CONCLUDING COMMENTS

The chapter presented a novel deductive system for graphical and visual computing with multiagent cognition for facial and visual recognition schemes based on novel mathematical techniques. What might come closest to how the mathematical formalisms are applied to visual data is in the proceedings on Diagrammatic reasoning (Glasgow et al., 1995). However, the techniques here have to specific relations to what had transpired there. Furthermore, that specific area was not agent computing or intelligent multimedia at all. Rather a static characterization on visual data. Meta-contextual logic is combined with Morph Gentzen, a new computing logic the author presented in 1997, towards a Virtual Reality design languages and their computing logic and Haptic computing (Picard, 1999; Nourani, 2005, 2006).

Facial or visual expression models recognition techniques can be a promising area to explore with the Morph Gentzen deductive system as a scientific basis and a sound and complete deductive system. The Haptic logics developed are natural systems for characterizing and studying facial expressions with the new agent cognitive paradigms. The challenge remains to determine precisely how the any regulatory signaling cognitive functions and affective systems work their influences in characterizing expression to facilitate a recognition processing system encoding.

Practical areas to be treated are to detail all morph compositions on all FACS AU's as examples. Next stage is to essentially motion track facial movements and mimic emotional cognitions projected on a real Android epistemics. We can apply predictive diagram knowledge representation to compute to discover facial similarities from observed data and visual object images keyed with diagram functions.

ACKNOWLEDGMENTS

The author wishes to thank his newer colleagues on cognitive computing groups, Anna, Codrina, and Rasmus for comments. The author further thanks his colleague Oliver Schulte, SFU Computation logic lab for comments on Bayesian inference.

KEYWORDS

- **agent cognitive computing models**
- **facial Eigen schemas**
- **Haptic computing logic**
- **model-based reasoning**
- **neurocognition**
- **virtual trees**
- **VR computing**

REFERENCES

Anderson, K., McOwan, P. W. "A Real-Time Automated System for Recognition of Human Facial Expressions," IEEE Trans. Systems, Man, and Cybernetics, Part B, 2006, 36(1), 96–105.

Barbara Khittl, Herbert Bauer, Peter Walla, "Change Detection Related To Peripheral Facial Expression: An Electroencephalography Study." Springer-Verlag 2008. J Neural Trans, 2009, 116, 67–70; doi: 10.1007/s00702-008-0125-5.

Bettadapura, Vinay. Face Expression Recognition and Analysis: The State of the Art 25 291, Cambridge, UK, Aug. 23–26, 2004.

Biederman, I., "Recognition-By-Components: A Theory of Human Image Understanding," Psychological Review, 1987, 94(2), 115–147.

Brazier, F. M. T., Dunin-Keplicz, B. M., Jennings, N. R., Treur, J. DESIRE: Modeling Multi-Agent Systems in a Compositional Formal Framework. International Journal of Cooperative Information Systems, 1997, 6(1), 67–94.

Brazier, F. M. T., Jonker, C. M., Treur, J., Formalization of a cooperation model based on joint intentions. In: Lecture Notes in Computer Science, 1997, 1193, 141–155

Brazier, F. M. T., Treur, J., Wijngaards, N. J. E., Willems, M. Temporal semantics of complex reasoning tasks. In: B. R. Gaines, M. A. Musen (Eds.), Proc. of the 10th Banff Knowledge Acquisition for Knowledge-Based Systems Workshop, KAW'95, 1995.

Brosch, T., Sander, D. The appraising brain: Towards a neuro-cognitive model of appraisal processes in emotion. Emotion Review 2013, 5, 163–168.

Chalmers, D. J. The Conscience Mind. In: Search of a Fundamental Theory, Oxford University Press.

Codrina Lauth, Cyrus F. Nourani, Rasmus Uslev Pedersen, Anna Blume, Cognitive Agent Systems and the Design of Intelligent Interfaces using Human Cognition, Special Issue on Multidisciplinary Perspectives of Agent-based Systems, Sept. 2013.

Cooper et al. A Systematic Methodology for Cognitive Modeling, In: AI'85, 1996, pp. 3–44.

Donato, G., Bartlett, M. S., Hagner, J. C., Ekman, P., Sejnowski, T. J. "Classifying facial actions," IEEE. Trans. Pattern Analysis and Machine Intelligence, vol. 21, no. 10, pp. 974–989, Oct. 1999.

Dunin-Kęplicz, B., Nguyen, L. A., Szałas, A. Tractable Approximate Knowledge Fusion Using the Horn Fragment of Serial Propositional Dynamic Logic. Int. Journal of Approximate Reasoning, 2010, 51(3), pp. 346–362.

Dunin-Kęplicz, B., Szałas, A., Agents in Approximate Environments. In: Games, Actions and Social Software, College Publications, 2010.

Dunin-Kęplicz, B., Treur, J. Compositional formal specification of multi agent systems. In: M. Wooldridge and N. R. Jennings, Intelligent Agents, Lecture Notes in Artificial Intelligence, Springer Verlag, Berlin, 1995, Vol. 890, pp. 102–117.

Dunin-Kęplicz, B., Verbrugge, R., M. Slizak. TeamLog in Action: a Case Study in Teamwork. In: Computer Science and Information Systems 8, 2010.

Eimer, M., Holmes, A. The role of spatial attention in the processing of facial expression: an ERP study of rapid brain responses to six basic emotions. Cogn Affect Behav Neurosci 2003, 3(2), 97–110.

Ekman, P. "Strong evidence for universals in facial expressions: A reply to Russell's mistaken critique," Psychological Bulletin, Mar. 1994, 115(2), 268–287.

Ekman, P., Friesen, W. V. "Constants across cultures in the face and emotions," J. Personality Social Psychology, 1971, 17(2), 124–129.

Ekman, P., Friesen, W. V. "Manual for the Facial Action Coding System," Consulting Psychologists Press, 1977.

Ekman, P., Rosenberg, E. L. "What the Face Reveals: Basic and Applied Studies of Spontaneous Expression using the Facial Action Coding System (FACS)," Illustrated Edition, Oxford University Press, 1997.

Farah, M. J., Wilson, K. D., Drain, M., Tanaka, J. N. "What is 'special' about facial perception?" Psychological Review, 1998, 105(3), 482–498.

Fleischmann, M., Strauss, W. "Digitale Körperbilder oder Inter-Faces als Schlüssel zur Imagination," in Kunstforum, 1996, Vol. 132, Die Zukunft des Körpers.

Ford, K. M., Glymour, C., Hayes, P. J. Android Epistemmology, AAA/MIT Press, 1995.

Genesereth, M., Nilsson, N. J. Logical Foundations of Artificial Intelligence, Morgan-Kaufmann, 1987.

Gentzen, G, Beweisbarkeit und Unbewiesbarket von Anfangsfallen der trasnfininten Induktion in der reinen Zahlentheorie, Math Ann, 1943, 119, 140–161.

Glasgow, J. L., Narayanan, N. H., Chandrasekaran, B. (Eds.), Diagrammatic Reasoning: Cognitive and Computational Perspectives, Boston, MA: MIT Press and Menlo Park, CA: AAAI Press, 1995

Graf, S. Adaptively in Learning Management Systems Focusing on Learning Styles, Ph.D. Thesis, Vienna University of Technology, 2007.

Hameroff, S. R., Kasznaic, A. W., Scott, A. C. (eds.) Towards a Science of Consciousness. The First Tucson Discussion and Debates, MIT Press 1996.

Holyoak, K. J., Thagard, P. Mental Leaps, Analogy in Creative Thought. Cambridge, MIT Press.

Hoshiyama, M., Kakigi, R., Watanabe, S., Miki, K., Takeshima, Y. Brain responses for the subconscious recognition of faces. Neurosci Res 2003, 46, 435–442.

Hummel, J. E., Holyoak, K. J. "LISA: A Computational Model of Analogical Inference and Schema Induction," Proc. 18th Ann. Conf. Cognitive Science, La Jolla, July 1996.

Izard, C. E. "Innate and universal facial expressions: Evidence from developmental and cross-cultural research," Psychological Bulletin, Mar 1994, 115(2), 288–299.

Jennings, Intelligent Agents, Lecture Notes in Artificial Intelligence, Vol. 890, Springer, Berlin, pp. 102–117.

Jerome R. Busemeyer, Adele Diederich, Cognitive Modeling April 2, 2009, ISBN-10: 0761924507; ISBN-13: 978-0761924500; 1st Edition.

Kanade, T., Cohn, J., Tian, Y. "Comprehensive Database for Facial Expression Analysis," Proc. IEEE Int'l Conf. Face and Gesture Recognition (AFGR'00), pp. 46–53, 2000.

Kant, I., 1990, Critique of Pure Reason, Translated by J. M. D. Meiklejohn and D. Kinny.

Kant, I., 1993, Opus Postumum, Cambridge University Press.

Kotsia, I. Pitas, "Facial Expression Recognition in Image Sequences Using Geometric Deformation Features and Support Vector Machines," IEEE Trans. Image Processing, 2007, 16(1), 172–187.

Lucas, B. D., Kanade, T. "An Iterative Image Registration Technique with an Application to Stereo Vision," Proc. 7th Int. Joint Conf. on Artificial Intelligence (IJCAI), 1981, pp. 674–679.

Marta Franová, 2005, "Symbiosis descarto-ackermanno-filkornised: Why and How?" Laboratoire de Recherche en Informatique Bât. 490, Université Paris-Sud, 91405 Orsay.

Mecklinger , A. 2000, "Interfacing mind and brain: A neurocognitive model of recognition memory" Max Planck Institute of Cognitive Neuroscience, Leipzig, Germany.

Michel, P., Kaliouby, R. "Real Time Facial Expression Recognition in Video Using Support Vector Machines," Proc. 5th Int. Conf. Multimodal Interfaces, Vancouver, BC, Canada, 2003, pp. 258–264.

MIT Encyclopedia of Cognitive Sciences—MIT Cognetcognet.mit.edu/MITECS/Edited by Robert A. Wilson and Frank C. Keil. 2010 The MIT Press.

Nina Gaissert, Steffen Waterkamp, Roland, W., Fleming, Isabelle Buelthoff, 2012, Haptic categorical perception of shape. Published: April 12, 2012. doi: 10.1371/journal. pcbi.1002453 Tubingen Neuroscience, BCCN publications.

Nourani, C. F. "A Descriptive Computing," Information Sciences Forume, Leipzig, March 2009a.

Nourani, C. F. "A Multiagent Cognitive Theory," Revised January 1995, International Conference Cognitive Science, La Jolla, July 1996.

Nourani, C. F. "A Multiagent Intelligent Multimedia Visualization Language and Computing Paradigm, February, VL2000-WWW Interface Track, Seattle, September 2000.

Nourani, C. F. "Aesthetics, CL, and Models. Friedrich-Schiller-Universität Jena Institut für Germanistische Sprachwissenschaft, Institut für Anglistik/Amerikanistik Fürstengraben 30, Ernst-Abbe-Platz 8 the 37th Linguistic Colloquium Germany, September 25th to 27th 2002. Motto "Language and the modern media." "http://www.uni-jena.de/fsu/anglistik/Lingcoll/"

Nourani, C. F. "Agent Languages, Visual Virtual Trees, and Models," IJPAM 2012–19–175. International Journal of Pure and Applied Mathematics, 2012.

Nourani, C. F. "Agent Planning, Models, Virtual Haptic Computing, and Visual Ontology "International Federation for Information Processing ("IFIP") for presentation at its conference on August 2006 (name of conference) held on August 2006 at Santiago, Chile. Springer-Verlag, 2006.

Nourani, C. F. "Intelligent Languages—A Preliminary Syntactic Theory," 1995, Mathematical Foundations of Computer Science 1998, 23rd International Symposium, MFCS'98, Brno, Czech Republic, August 1998, Jozef Gruska, and Jiri Zlatuska (Eds.): Lecture Notes in Computer Science; 1450, Springer, 1998, ISBN 3-540-64827-5, 846 pp.

Nourani, C. F. "Intelligent Trees, Genetic Algorithms, and Thought Processes 6th World Multiconference on Systemics, Cybernetics and Informatics (SCI 2002) to be Orlando, USA, in July 14, 2002.

Nourani, C. F. "Intelligent Trees, Thought Models, and Intelligent Discovery," Model-Based Reasoning in Scientific Discovery (MBR'98) Pavia, Italy, December 17–19, 1998b.

Nourani, C. F. "KR, Data Modeling, DB and KB Predictive Scheme Completion," A version published at International Systems and Cybernetics, Florida, July 2003.

Nourani, C. F. "MIMLogik," Summer Logic Colloquium, August 1997.

Nourani, C. F. "Planning and Plausible Reasoning in AI," Proc. Scandinavian Conference in AI, May 1991, Roskilde, Denmark, 1991, 150–157, IOS Press.

Nourani, C. F. "Towards Computational Epistemology—A Forward," Proc. Summer Logic Colloquium, Clermont-Ferrand, France, July 1994.

Nourani, C. F. "Virtual Tree Computing, Meta-Contextual Logic, and VR," February 12, 2001 ASL Spring 2002, Seattle WA, March, BSL Vol. 8. No. 3, ISSN 1079–8986.

Nourani, C. F. 2005, "A Haptic Computing Logic," in The Future of Learning, Volume 1, 2006. Affective and Emotional Aspects of Human-Computer Interaction. In: Game-Based and Innovative Learning Approaches, Edited by Maja Pivec, ISBN 978-1-58603-572-3.

Nourani, C. F. A Descriptive Computing, Information Forum, Liepzig, Germany, March 2009. SIWN2009 Program, 2009. The Foresight Academy of Technology Press International Transactions on Systems Science and Applications, Vol. 5, No. 1, June 2009, pp. 60–69.

Nourani, C. F. A Haptic Computing Logic—Agent Planning, Models, and Virtual Trees. In: Pivec, M. (Ed.) Affective and Emotional Aspects of HCI: Game-Based and Innovative Learning Approaches, IOS Press, 2006, p.317.

Nourani, C. F. A Multi Agent Cognitive Theory. Proceedings of the Eighteenth Annual Conference of the Cognitive Science, UCSD, La Jolla, Garrison W. Cottrell—editor, 1996.

Nourani, C. F. Abstract Linguistics—A Brief Overview, ICML, Mathematical Linguistics, Tarragona, Catalunia, Spain. May 1995.

Nourani, C. F. Intelligent Multimedia Computing Science- Business Interfaces, Databases, Data Mines, and WiFi American Scientific Publishers, 2005. http://www.aspcs.com/multimedia.htm. Intelligent Multimedia: New Computing Techniques and Its Applications, February 28, 1997.

Nourani, C. F. Intelligent Trees and Consciousness Science, Consciousness in Science and Philosophy '98, Illinois, November 1998.

Nourani, C. F. Morph Gentzen, K. R., World Model Diagrams April 2, 1998. Automated Deductions and Geometry, The Third International Workshop on Automated Deduction in Geometry Zurich, Switzerland, September 25–27, 2000.

Nourani, C. F. Proceedings of 1st International Workshop on Computer Science and Information Technologies, January 18–22, 1999, Moscow, Russia. Ch. Freytag and V. Wolfengagen (Eds.): MEPhI Publishing 1999, ISBN 5-7262-0263-5, Vorotnikovskiy per., 7, bld.4 Moscow 103006, Russia JurInfoR-MSU Institute for Contemporary Education (JMSUICE).

Nourani, C. F. Slalom Tree Computing: A Computing Theory For Artificial Intelligence, June 1994 (Revised December 1994), A. I. Communication December 1996a, 9(4).

Nourani, C. F. Versatile Abstract Syntax Meta-Contextual Logic and VR Computing 36th Lingustische Kolloquium, Austria Proceedings 36th Lingustische Kolloquium, Austria Proceedings of the 35th Colloquium of Linguistics, Innsbrucke. Europa Der Sprachen: Sprachkopetenz-Mehrsprachigeit-Translation, TIEL II: Sprache und Kognition, Sonderdruc 2003, Lew N. Zybatow (HRSG). 1998.

Nourani, C. F. Virtual World Models, Illusion Logic, and Morphs, In Information Sciences Forum, Leipzig, March 2009.

Nourani, C. F. Virtuelle Macrodot Morph Kino Und Das FERNSEHN, IMK- Netzspannung.org, Sank Augustine, Germany, 2004.

Nourani, C. F., "Morph Gentzen Plan Computation with Visual Diagrams, "ISTA" 2001 the Conference Proceedings published in the GI- Edition 'Lecture Notes in Informatics,' Austria. Kharkiv, Ukraine Proceedings of the 2001 international conference on Information systems technology and its applications—vol. P-2 Kharkiv, Ukraine, 2002, 215–228. ISSN: 1617-5468, 3-88579-331-8.

Nourani, C. F., "Visual Computational Linguistics," July 29, 1997. Brief at the 34th Linguistics Colloquium, September 1999, Mainz, Germany.

Nourani, C. F., Codrina Lauth, and Rasmus Pedersen, WI-IAT 2013 IOT special session. Cognitive Agent Planning with Attention Spanning–A Preliminary. IAT Special Session on IOT, Atlanta, November 2013.

Nourani, C. F., Intelligent Trees, Genetic Algorithms, and Thought Complexity Abstract June 18, 1997 Accepted to the BioComplexity Conference, Stanford.

Nourani, C. F., Worlds, Models, and KM Workshop on Philosophy and Knowledge Management, 2–4. April 2003, at the WM 2003, Luzern, Switzerland. http://www.dfki.uni- kl.de/~klein/wm2003-preproceedings/htmls/index.htm

Oliver Schulte, "A tractable pseudo likelihood function for Bayes Nets applied to relational data." Proceedings of the SIAM SDM Conference on Data Mining, 2011, pp. 462–473.

Pantic, A., Patras, I. "Dynamics of Facial Expression: Recognition of Facial Actions and Their Temporal Segments Form Face Profile Image Sequences, "IEEE Trans. Systems, Man, and Cybernetics Part B, 2006, 36(2), 433–449.

Pantic, M., Patras, I. "Detecting facial actions and their temporal segments in nearly frontal-view face image sequences," Proc. IEEE conf. Systems, Man and Cybernetics, Oct. 2005, 4, 3358–3363.

Pantic, M., Rothkrantz, J. M. "Facial Action Recognition for Facial Expression Analysis from Static Face Images," IEEE Trans. Systems, Man arid Cybernetics Part B, 2004, 34(3), 1449–1461.

Pantic, M., Rothkrantz, L. J. M. "Automatic analysis of facial expressions: the state-of-the-art," IEEE Trans. Pattern Analysis and Machine Intelligence, 2000, 22(12), 1424–1445.

Parrott, W. G., "Emotions in Social Psychology," Psychology Press, Philadelphia, October 2000.

Pedersen, R. U. Micro Information Systems and Ubiquitous Knowledge Discovery In: Lecture Notes in Computer Science, No. 6202, 2010, 216–234.

Picard, R. T. Affective Computing, TR#321, MIT Media Lab. 1998.

Picard, R. W. "Affective Computing for HCI," In: Proceedings of HCI, Munich, Germany, August 1999.

Picard, R. W., Papert, S., Bender, W., Blumberg, B., Breazeal, C., Cavallo, D., Machover, Strohecker, C.: Affective Learning–A Manifesto, BT Technical Journal, 2004, 22(4), 253–269.

Prawitz, D., "Natural Deduction: A Proof Theoretic Study, Stokhom, Almqvist and Wiksell, 1965.

Putzeys, T., Matthias. Bethge, Felix Wichmann, Johan Wagemans, Robbe Goris. BCCN and Max Planck Institute for Intelligent Systems, Abteilung Empirische Inferenz, Tübingen, Germany ax Planck Institute, 2012.

Rao, A. S., Georgeff, M. P. "Modeling rational agents within a BID-architecture," In: R. Fikes, E. Sandewall (eds.), Proceedings of the Second Conference on Knowledge Representation and Reasoning, Morgan Kaufman, 473–484.

Rao, A. S., Georgeff, M. P. Modeling rational agents within a BID-architecture. In: R. Fikes, E. Sandewall (eds.), Proceedings of the Second Conference on Knowledge Representation and Reasoning, Morgan Kaufman, 1991, pp. 473–484.

Russell, J. A., "Is there universal recognition of emotion from facial expressions? A review of the cross-cultural studies," Psychological Bulletin, vol. 115, no. 1, pp. 102–141, Jan. 1994.

Sandewall, Erik: Features and Fluents, The Representation of Knowledge about Dynamical Systems, Volume 1, Clarendon Press: Oxford Logic Guides 1995, 30, pp. 346, 978-0-19-853845-5, Hardback.

Shoham, Y., Cousins, S. B. Logics of mental attitudes in AI: a very preliminary survey. In: G. Lakemeyer, B. Nebel (eds.) Foundations of Knowledge Representation and Reasoning, Springer Verlag, 1994, 296–309.

Sternberg, R. J. (Ed.), Cognitive Psychology, Wadsworth, Australia, 2012.

Sternberg, R. J. (Ed.), The Nature of Cognition. Cambridge, MIT Press, MA, 1999.

Sun, R. Cognitive science meets multiagent systems: Aprolegomenon, Philosophical Psychology, Volume 14, Issue 1, 2001. (Sun 2002).

Thagard, P. (1996). Mind: An introduction to cognitive science. Cambridge, MA: MIT Press.

Tomasi, C., Kanade, T. "Detection and Tracking of Point Features," Carnegie Mellon University Technical Report CMU-CS-91-132, April 1991.

Verbrugge, R., Dunin-Kęplicz, B. Formal approaches to multiagent systems. Introduction in: Journal of Autonomous Agents and Multi-Agent Systems, 2009, 19(1), 1–3.

Zeng, Z., Pantic, M., Roisman, G. I., Huang, T. S. "A Survey of Affect Recognition Methods: Audio, Visual, and Spontaneous Expressions," IEEE Trans. Pattern Analysis and Machine Intelligence, 2009, 31(1), 39–58.

INDEX

T - #0834 - 101024 - C282 - 229/152/13 - PB - 9781774636817 - Gloss Lamination